InDesign CC
Creative Classroom

InDesign CC Creative Classroom
By Peter Bone
Published by Designtuitive
www.designtuitive.com
©2015 Peter Bone. All rights reserved.
ISBN: 978-1-908510-98-3
Version 1.0 March 2015

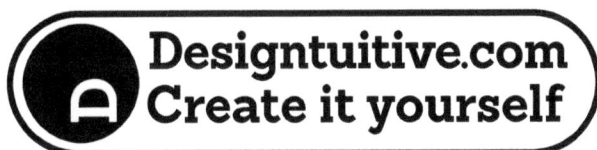

Designtuitive.com
Create it yourself

InDesign CC Creative Classroom

CONTENTS

INTRODUCTION

WORKING FROM AN INDESIGN TEMPLATE

CREATING FLYERS, POSTERS & POSTCARDS

CREATING ADVERTS

CREATING LEAFLETS

DESIGN THEORY IN BRIEF FOR BEGINNERS

PREPARING INDESIGN FILES FOR PRINTING

BRIEF NOTES

From Aruba to Zanzibar
Plan your dream escape
Visit www.ocean-hotels.com for inspiration

From Aruba to Zanzibar
Plan your dream escape
Visit www.ocean-hotels.com for inspiration

From the Turquoise coast of Turkey to the Caribbean coast of Cuba, we know we've got somewhere in the world that's just right for you.
Find your perfect escape with us.
Visit www.ocean-hotels.com for inspiration.

Discover Japan with us

Discover Japan with us

DISCOVER Cultural Tours

Discover Angkor with us

Pacific Coast, Mexico. Wish you were here?

Discover Europe with us
DISCOVER Cultural Tours

Vinales, Cuba
Visit Cuba

"THE MORE WE ADAPTED TO THE CUBAN PACE OF LIFE, THE MORE RELAXED WE BECAME"
Visit Cuba

GO!

BOLIVIA
Salar de Uyuni Tour
GO!

PERU
GO!

Vinales, Cuba
Visit Cuba

Discover Europe
Discover Europe with us
DISCOVER Cultural Tours

Baracoa: Essential Info
Visit Cuba

CUBA: ESSENTIAL INFO
Visit Cuba

HAVANA
Visit Cuba

TRINIDAD
SANTIAGO

Tour Information

Tour Information

Discover Asia with us
Laos   Cambodia
DISCOVER Cultural Tours
Vietnam   Ladakh   Japan   Thailand

INTRODUCTION

About this book

I could describe my history of teaching InDesign over the past ten years in three acts. The first broad group of people I taught were a handful of cutting edge design agencies who could see InDesign's potential over its slightly aging rival QuarkXpress. The second group was a huge wave of migrants from QuarkXpress led by magazine publishers and followed slowly but surely by virtually everyone else already in the world of design, print and publishing. And thirdly, for the past five years or so, the broad group of people to whom I teach InDesign is, er, everybody else. Now, that's a really broad group. Whether that's due to the economic climate or because of broader changes in the culture of work, the past few years have seen InDesign change from a program just used by professional designers to one used by a much wider group of people. This, I am assuming, includes you. And you're who I've written this book for.

I wrote InDesign Creative Classroom because I know that learning to use InDesign requires much more than just knowing which buttons to press or which menu items to use. Because, at the risk of stating the obvious, InDesign is used to *design* things. But it's difficult to know where to start if you don't come from the design world – if you don't know what to design, or indeed very much about design, let alone about how the program works. InDesign Creative Classroom will teach you about the program *and* the context *and* way that it's used all at the same time. Each chapter in the book takes one example of the range of things that are typically created by designers – for example, adverts, flyers or leaflets – and shows you in simple steps how to create a range of them, each one slightly more complex than the last. By the time you've worked through one of the chapters you'll have gained a considerable insight into how InDesign is really used to create that type of work. If you go on to read other chapters your understanding will become broader still, because even though some of the techniques are the same, the way they are employed will differ according to the context in which they are used. I very much hope that InDesign Creative Classroom gives you the skills, knowledge and confidence to get creative with InDesign. Good luck!

Peter Bone

How to use this book

1. This book is designed to read one chapter at a time, but you can read them in any order. Whichever chapter you choose to start with, you'll learn the most by sticking with it before you move onto another, as I'm assuming that you're already familiar with subjects covered earlier in the chapter. The Leaflets and Adverts chapters are more advanced, so unless you need to read about them immediately I'd advise reading other chapters first.

2. I've made two assumptions about you: firstly that your main interest is in creating things *with* InDesign rather than merely acquiring knowledge *about* it. And secondly that you'll want to get to work immediately. If that's the case, simply continue to the next chapter where the exercises begin. I have, however, included some brief notes giving overviews of InDesign and what to do with your documents once you've designed them. These can be found in the *Brief Notes* section at the end of the book, and can be read before or after you've finished the exercises, or not at all.

3. The steps for you to follow are listed in numbered paragraphs like this one.

4. When you need to select a tool or choose a menu command or press a button – in other words *do something* – it's written in **Bold.** It'll be written in ***Bold Italic*** if it's a feature you've not used before.

5. When you need to type in values, measurements or choose something from a pop-up menu, the value will be written in *Italic* as well as the area where you'll need to type it into. Some terms are also *emphasised* using italics.

6. The vast majority of everything shown here can be created with any version of InDesign. Where a feature is used that requires a specific version of InDesign, it will be mentioned.

7. The screenshots are taken from the Mac version of InDesign CC (the version that followed CS6).

8. The only difference PC users need to be aware of is the use of the Mac's Command key (also known as the Apple key), which on the PC is replaced with the Ctrl key. So for example, instead of the **Command+D** shortcut, type **Ctrl+D** instead.

9. If you want to follow along and create the exercises with your own version of InDesign (which is highly recommended) then you'll need to use the templates, images and text used in the originals. You'll need to download the files from us, which you can do by placing an order *on our website* at www.designtuitive.com/collections/downloads (you'll have to go through a checkout process, but it's absolutely free). You will need InDesign CS4 or later to open the templates*.

* *If you need a more modern version of InDesign to work through the book you can download a 30 day trial of the latest version of InDesign at www.adobe.com/downloads.html*

10. In writing this series my aim is to enable you to design work that you'll like. One of the things you'll need to be able to do that is to be able to find, choose, install and use a variety of fonts. So whilst within the brand guidelines I've created for these organisations I've used fonts that come installed with InDesign, I've also used some that you'll need to download and install (as we're not allowed to distribute fonts). I've used fonts that anyone can obtain (because the font designers have generously either made them available for free, or at a *choose your price* rate). If you'd rather not install fonts at this stage, feel free to use ones already installed on your computer, but bear in mind that the text settings you'll use will differ from the ones I specify below (and your documents will look different, too). The fonts used in the book and links to them are listed below.

11. The *Myriad Pro* and *Poplar Std* fonts should already on your computer because they come installed with InDesign, but if you want to follow all the exercises exactly you'll need to download and install* the following fonts: *Amatic, Edmondsans, Lobster Two, Permanent Marker, Signika* and *Ubuntu.* You can easily download them all for free by visiting *www.fontsquirrel.com* with the exception of *Edmondsans,* which you can download at a choose your price rate (please be generous) from *www.losttype.com*

* *Instructions on how to install them can be found at www.fontsquirrel.com/help*

Discover
Japan
with us

To receive our Japan brochure
Call 023445 3456123 or visit
www.discover-tours.com

DISCOVER
Cultural Tours

Vinales,
Cuba

Visit Cuba

Pacific coast, Mexico.
Wish you were here?

Ocean Hotels

Discover Europe

Discover Europe with us

From deserted Greek islands to street markets in Turkey, we'll show you
the very best that Europe can offer even the most seasoned traveller.
Leave it all to us, and discover it with us.

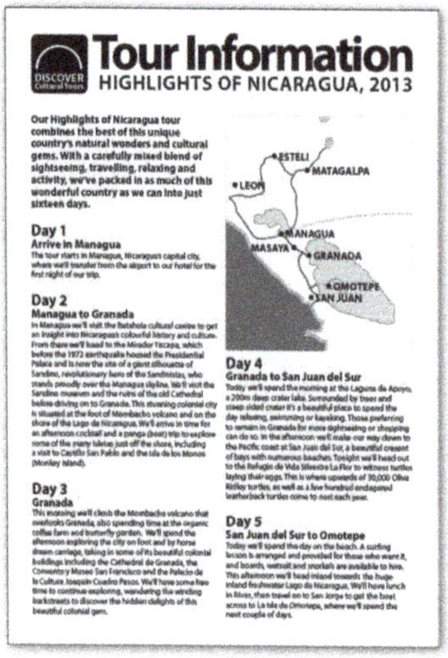

To receive our Europe brochure call 02344 3456123
or visit www.discover-tours.com

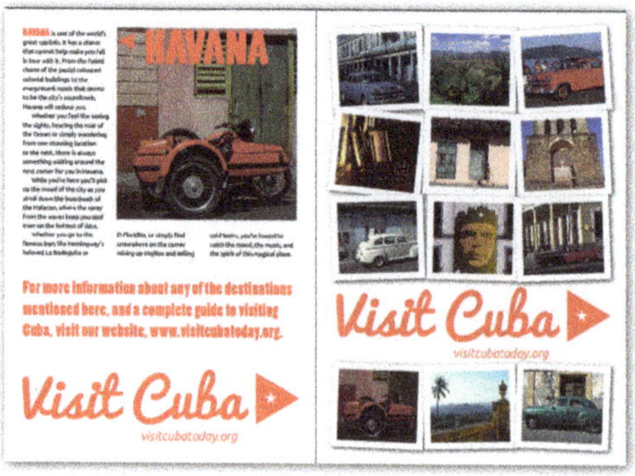

DISCOVER
Cultural Tours

DISCOVER
Cultural Tours

Tour Information
HIGHLIGHTS OF NICARAGUA, 2013

WORKING FROM AN INDESIGN TEMPLATE

This chapter is about creating a variety of InDesign documents from an existing template (as you might have been given by a design agency or a colleague). There are six documents in total including adverts, flyers and leaflets, each one a little more complex than the last. The adverts are created for three fictitious organisations, Discover Cultural Tours, Visit Cuba and Ocean Hotels. As with any real company, they have had logos designed, and they use particular typefaces and colours in their branding.

1) An advert for Discover Cultural Tours

This first exercise will introduce you to an InDesign template and show you some essential aspects of InDesign, including the Selection and Type tools. You'll also learn how to import images and amend basic text.

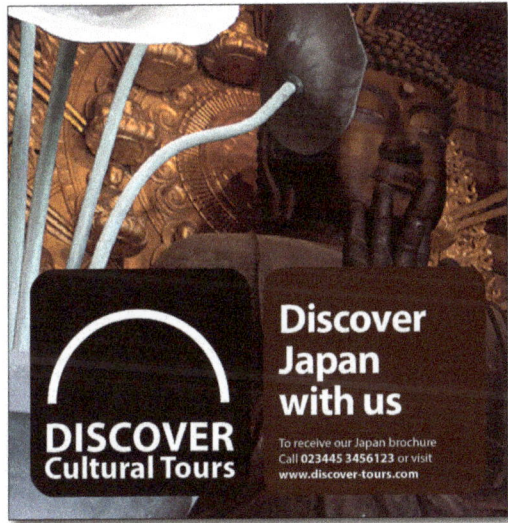

1.   You can see from the screenshot above that you're going to create an advert (for a tour of Japan) with *Discover Cultural Tours*. This is one of many similar adverts from the same company; the only way they differ is in the background image, the place name and possibly the background colour beneath the text.

2.   From the **File menu** choose **Open** to open the InDesign template you're going to use. From the dialogue box that appears, find the *Creative Classroom Templates* folder and from within that select the *1-discover-square-advert.idml* file, then press the **Open** button. If you look at the name of the document you might notice that instead of opening the actual template, InDesign has created a new document based on that template. This is to prevent you accidentally saving over the template.

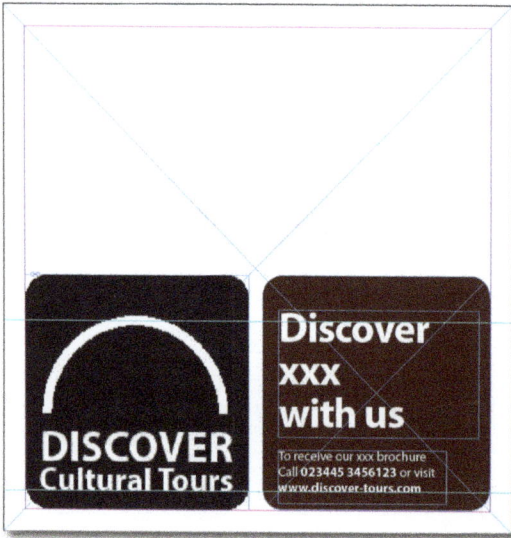

3.   You can probably see that the template you've just opened provides much of what you need to create the final advert. As you probably realise from your own work, this is what an InDesign template is for. It is a file that provides the essential ingredients to create and recreate similar work. Looking at your document (or the image above) you can see that the main thing missing for the advert is the image that will fill the whole page. Notice the large, faint *X* behind the other elements on the page. The X is a visual clue for you that there is something on the page, and that thing is an empty *Frame.* Images and text are placed inside frames within InDesign. For example, the logo on the bottom left of the page is in a frame, and if you look closely at the other elements on the bottom right of the page you might see three frames: an empty frame and two separate frames with text in them.

4. To bring the background image into the document you first need to select the frame that it will go into. To do this, firstly choose the **Selection Tool** by clicking on it at the top of the **Tools Panel** on the left of your screen.

5. Click on the large empty frame with the **Selection Tool** and notice that it changes appearance slightly: a small blue square has appeared on each of its corners. These squares are known as *handles,* and as well as being used to resize frames (which you'll do later) they also indicate that a frame is selected, which means that InDesign knows that you want to work with it.

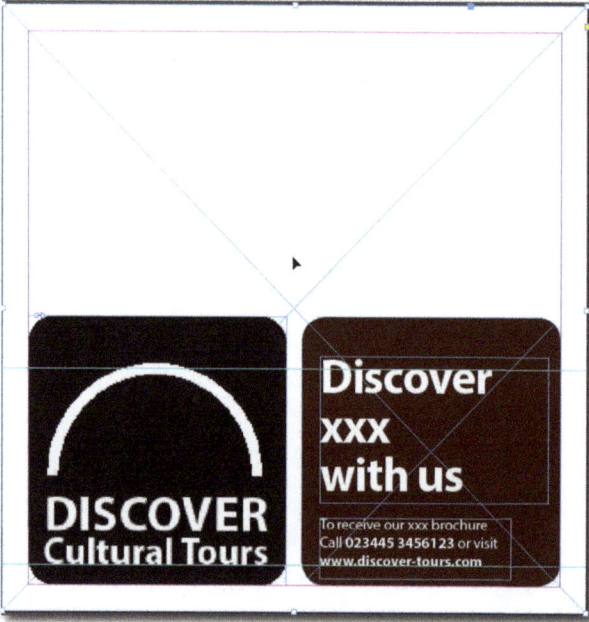

6. With the large frame selected, choose *Place* from the *File menu.*

7. From the dialogue box that appears, find the *Creative Classroom Templates* folder and from within that select the *Discover_japan_nara. jpg* file, then press the **Open** button to place the image in the frame.

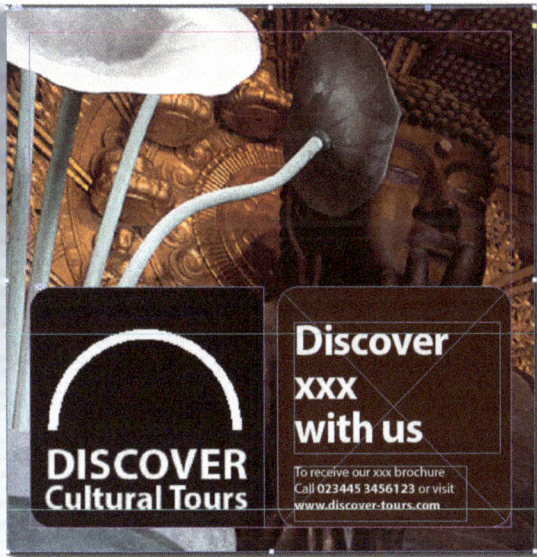

8. When producing a template where only a small amount of text will change, it is common practice to make that text very obvious. On this template the only words that will change are the place name after the words *Discover* and before the word *brochure* in the small text underneath. As you can see, they have been replaced with the letters *xxx* to make them easy to spot. To start working with the text, select the ***Type Tool*** from the **Tools Panel.**

9. Click once on the large *xxx* text with the **Type Tool.** You should see a flashing cursor, indicating that InDesign knows you want to work with the text. Now that you're using the type tool you can work with the text in the same way you can in any text editing program. In this case, drag over the *xxx* text to highlight it and simply replace it by typing *Japan.*

10. Using the same technique, use the **Type Tool** to replace the smaller *xxx* text with the word *Japan* in the lower frame.

11. As you look at your finished advert you might be disappointed by the quality of the logo. That's because when you bring in a logo or similar *vector* graphic (see *Images from Photoshop and Illustrator* in the *Brief Notes* section) by default you'll not see it at full quality. So to get a better idea how your finished advert will appear when it's printed, change to *Presentation Mode** by choosing ***View>Screen Mode>Presentation.***

* *If you're using InDesign CS4 or earlier you won't have Presentation Mode. Instead, you can see the graphics in full quality by choosing **View>Display Performance>High Quality Display**. You can use Preview mode **(View>Screen Mode>Preview)** to hide elements that won't print, returning to Normal Mode using **View>Screen Mode>Normal.***

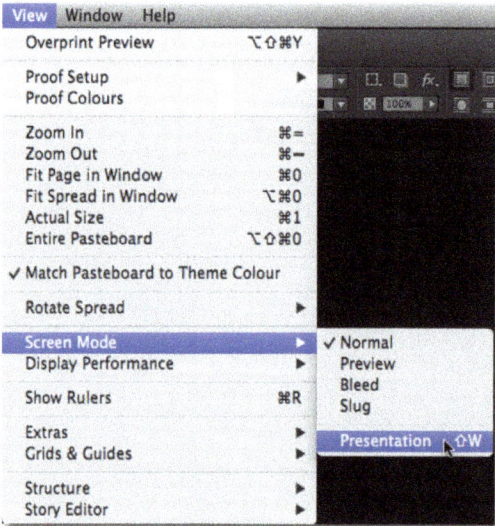

12. Presentation Mode changes InDesign to a full screen mode, hides everything that won't print and shows graphics at their full resolution. To leave Presentation Mode, press the *Esc key* at the top left of your keyboard.

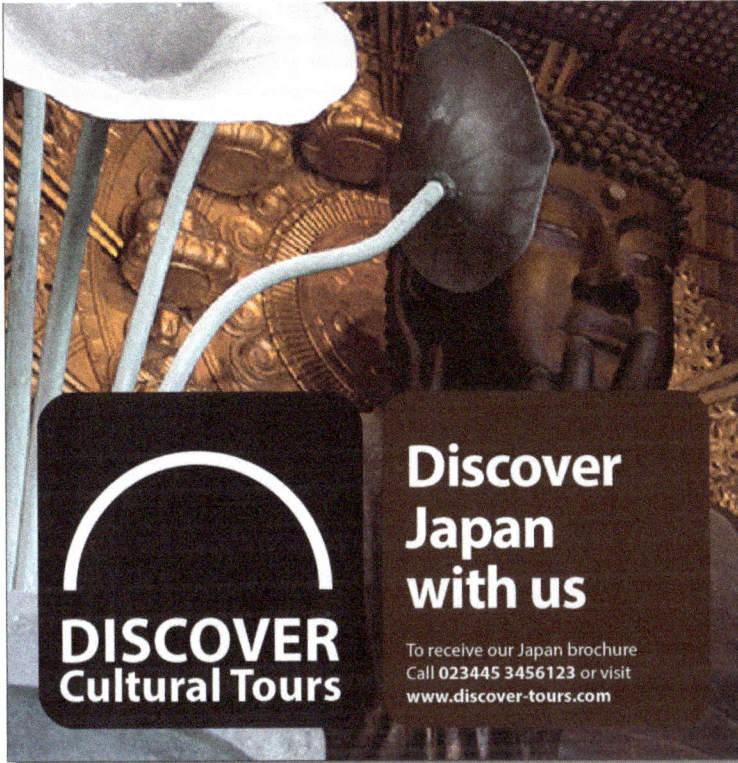

13. Save the completed advert by choosing *Save* from the **File menu,** choosing an appropriate file name and location for your work.

Summary of new menu commands

File>Open *[Command+O]*
File>Place *[Command+D]*
View>Screen Mode>Presentation

Summary of Tools used

Selection Tool
Type Tool

Summary of shortcuts used

Esc: leave Presentation Mode

2) An A5 Flyer for Visit Cuba

Building on what you already know, this second exercise will show you how to change the colour and size of text, and how to replace one logo with another.

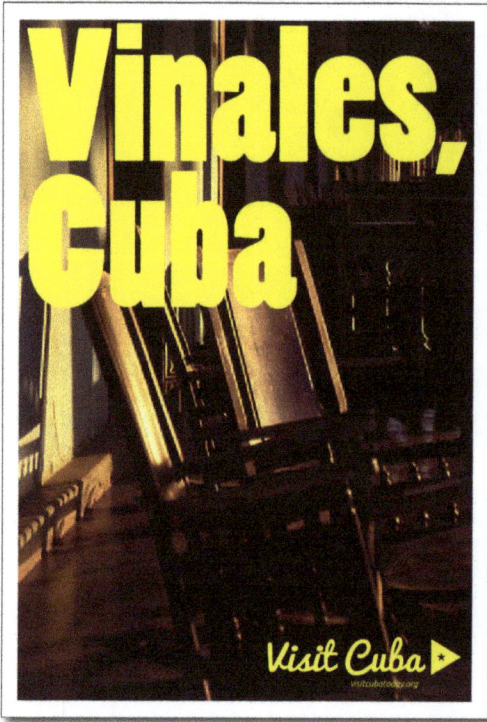

1. As you can see above, the next thing that you're going to create is a basic flyer (that's designed to encourage people to visit Cuba). As with the advert you created previously, it's one of a series, each with an image of a different part of the country. In this case, as well as the text changing, the colour of the text and the logo may change, depending on the colours in the background image.

2. From the **File menu** choose **Open** to open the InDesign template you're going to use. From the dialogue box that appears, find the *Creative Classroom Templates* folder and from within that select the *2-visit-cuba-a5-flyer.idml* file, then press the **Open** button. As before, InDesign has created a new document for you to prevent you accidentally saving over the template. As you can see, on the template the colour of both the text and the logo are red, but for this flyer you will need to change them to yellow.

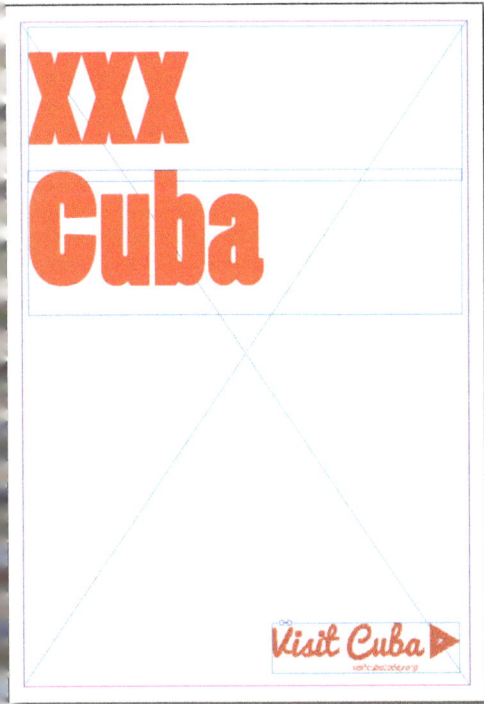

3. Making sure you're using the **Selection Tool,** click on the large empty frame to select it (you can tell it's selected if you can see square *handles* around its edge). Choose **File>Place** and import the *visit-cuba-vinales-a5. jpg* (from the *Creative Classroom Templates* folder) into the frame.

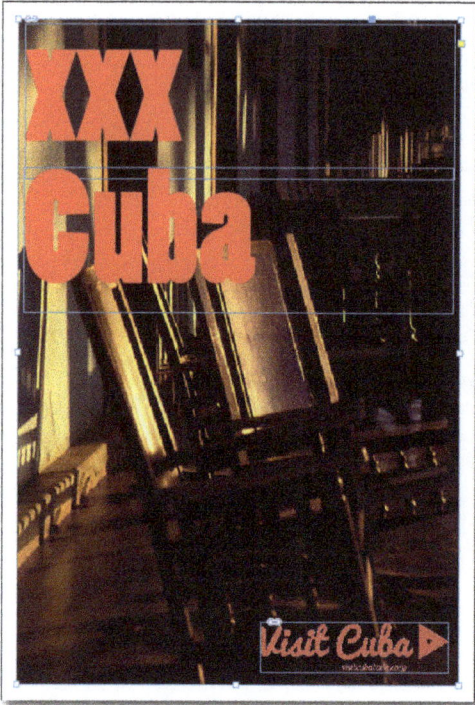

4. Next, choose the **Type Tool** from the **Tools Panel,** select the large *xxx* text and replace it with the word *Vinales,* (including the comma).

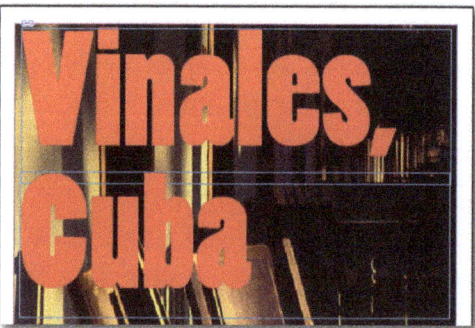

5. Notice that the ***Control Panel*** at the top of the screen is now showing information about the type. If you look at the left edge of the Panel, there are two buttons. Ensure that the ***Character Formatting Controls*** button is selected (if it's darker than the other one, it is).

6. Select all the text you've just typed either by dragging
over it with your mouse, or by choosing **Edit>Select All.**
Notice that the size of the type is currently *130pt.*

7. These flyers have been designed for the text to run all the way
across the top of the page, but you'll notice that this particular
word could be a little larger. To increase the size of the text,
press the ***up arrow*** in the **Control Panel** to the left of the font
size area until the word fits the full width of the frame.

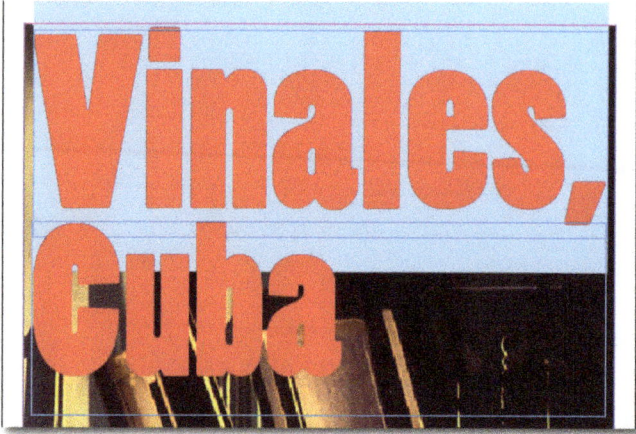

8. If you make the text too large to fit the frame, you'll see that some of your text disappears, and that an *Overset Mark* (a small red +) appears at the bottom right of the text frame.

9. To fix it, make the type size smaller by pressing the **down arrow** in the **Control Panel** to the left of the font size. Similarly, if you want the text to be larger, increase the font size by using the **up arrow** in the same place.

10. The *Cuba* text in the frame underneath should be the same size as the text above. Make a note of the size of the *Vinales* text, then select the *Cuba* text with the **Type Tool** and adjust its size to match.

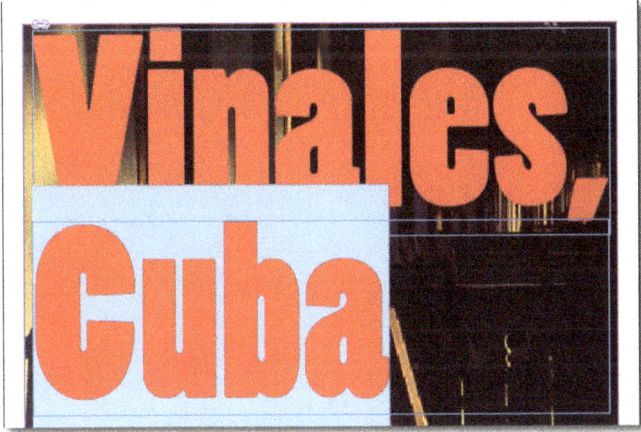

11. Many of the features found within InDesign use *panels* that are docked to the side of the screen. Your first look at one of these is the **Swatches Panel,** which you'll use to change the colour of the text. To see what's inside of the panel, click once on the name of the panel (in this case, click on where it says *Swatches*).

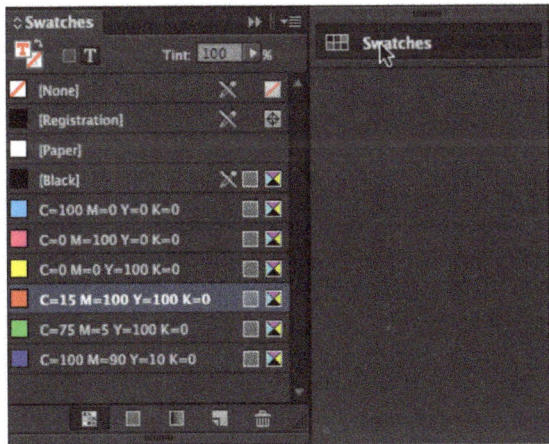

12. If the *Cuba* text is not already selected, drag over it with the **Type Tool.** Notice that at the top left of the panel there is a small red "T". This tells you that some text is selected, it is red, and that any changes in colour will affect the text and not the frame.

13. Notice also that the red swatch has a faint highlight on it to indicate it's being used. Click on the *Yellow* swatch to change the text to that colour instead, then select the *Vinales* text with the **Type Tool** and change that too.

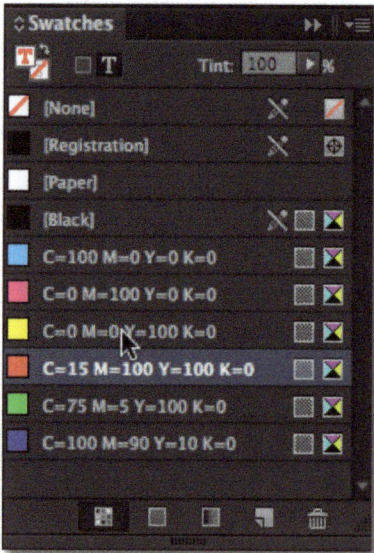

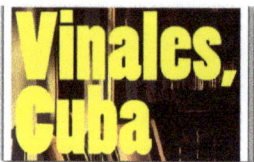

14. Whilst you can change the colour of text in InDesign, the same does not apply to logos. As with photographic images, these are created outside of InDesign (in this case using Adobe Illustrator*) and imported. As is the case with many organisations, Visit Cuba's logo has been created in several different colours. Your task is to swap the red version for the yellow one. To do this, change to the **Selection Tool** and click on the red Visit Cuba logo to select it.

* *For more information on how Illustrator and Photoshop work with InDesign, see the Brief Notes section that follows the final exercise.*

15. InDesign uses the word *link* to describe an image that has been placed into a document, and provides a *Links Panel* for working with those them. As you did with the **Swatches Panel,** open the **Links Panel** by clicking on its name (you'll find it towards the top right of your screen).

16. The *visit_cuba_indesign_red.eps* link should be highlighted, as that is what you've just selected. You're going to tell InDesign to replace it with a different image. To do this, firstly press on the *dropdown menu* at the very top right of the Links Panel.

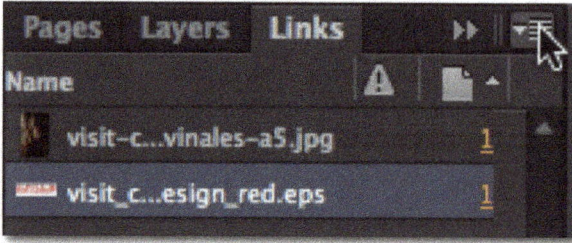

17. From the menu of options that appears, choose *Relink.*

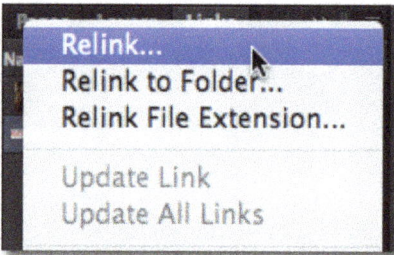

18. From the dialogue box that appears, find the *Creative Classroom Templates* folder and from within that select the *visit_cuba_100yellow.eps* file, then press the **Open** button to replace the red logo with the yellow one.

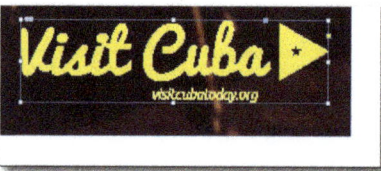

19. As with the previous document, use **Presentation Mode** to view the final flyer in high quality, then press the **Esc key** (at the top left of your keyboard) to return to *Normal Mode.* As you did before, save the document in case you wish to return to it later.

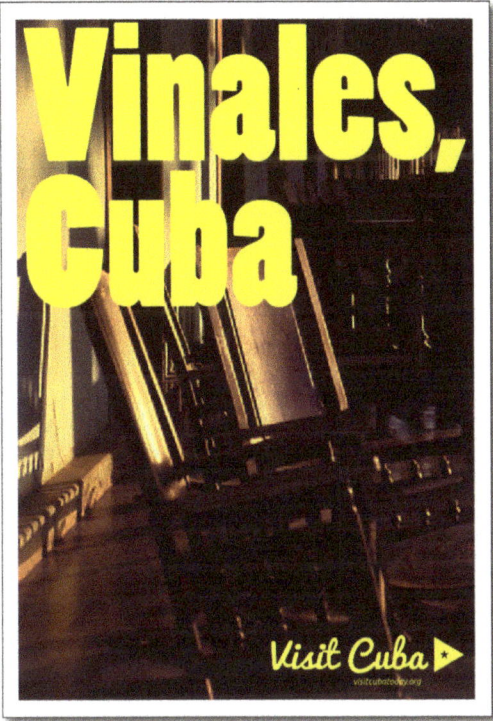

Summary of new menu commands

Edit>Select All *[Command+A]*

Summary of new Panels used

Swatches (to apply a colour to the text)

Control Panel (to change the size of the text)

Links Panel>Relink (to swap one image with another)

3) An Advert for Ocean Hotels

Building on what you already know, this third exercise will teach
you how to deal with missing fonts, how to resize and crop an
image, and how to apply a different colour to a frame.

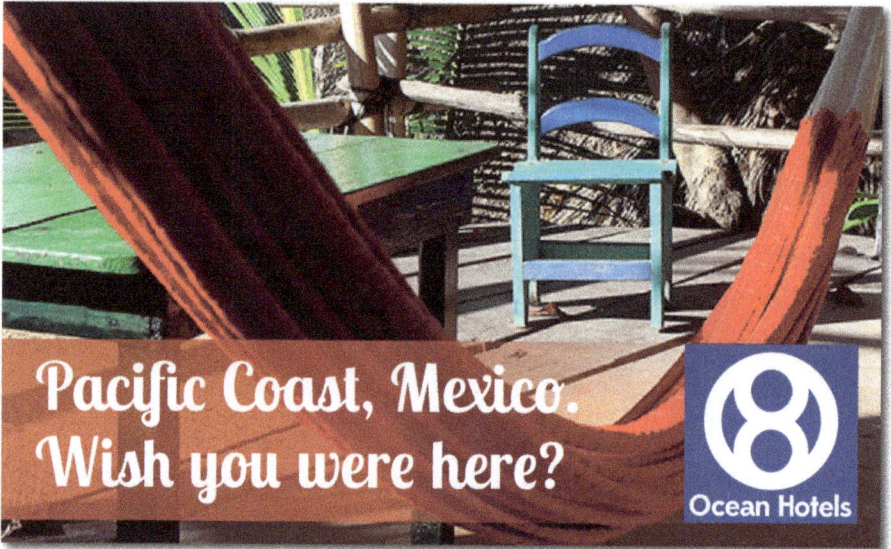

1.   As shown above, your next task is to create an advert for *Ocean
     Hotels*. As with the advert you created previously, it's one of a
     series, each with a different background image. In this case, as
     well as the text changing, the colour of the text's background may
     change, depending on the colours in the image beneath it.

2.   From the **File menu** choose **Open** to open the InDesign template
     you're going to use. From the dialogue box that appears, find the
     Creative Classroom Templates folder and from within that select
     the *3-ocean-hotels-ad.idml* file, then press the **Open** button. The
     screenshot below shows what the template *should* look like, but it's
     likely that what you can see looks like the screenshot underneath it.

3. The reason that your template is likely to look like the second screenshot is that this template was designed using a font called *Lobster Two Bold** that you may not have. If you receive an InDesign document (whether a template or regular document) that was designed using fonts you don't have on your computer, the text will appear highlighted in pale pink. To fix it you're either going to have to install the missing font on your own computer or change the design to use a font that you do have. If you want to install the font, follow the instructions in the footnote below.

* *One of the reasons I've used this font is because it's freely available for anyone to use. If you want to download the font, go to www.fontsquirrel.com and follow their instructions at www.fontsquirrel.com/help for help on how to download and install it.*

4. If you've installed the *Lobster Two Bold* font then the pale pink highlighting should disappear, and instead the text will appear as in the screenshot below.

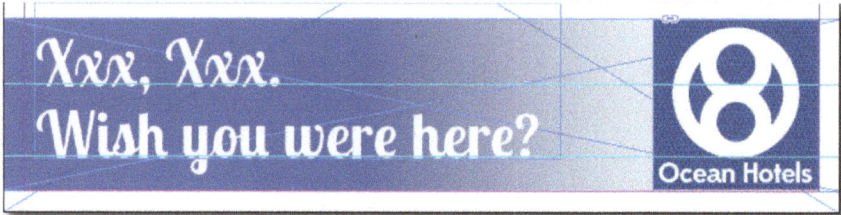

5. If you'd rather not install this font, select the text with the **Type Tool** and select a different *font* from the **Control Panel** at the top left of your screen.

6. Once you've either installed the *Lobster* font or changed the text to a different one, change the *xxx* text so that it reads *Pacific Coast, Mexico*.

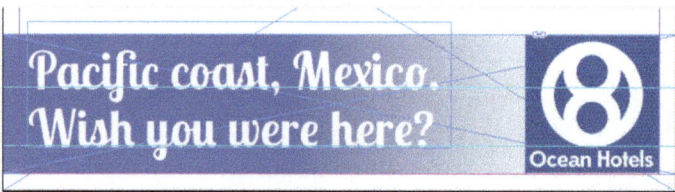

7. Change to the **Selection Tool,** select the empty background frame and use **File>Place** to import the *OH_mexico2.jpg* image.

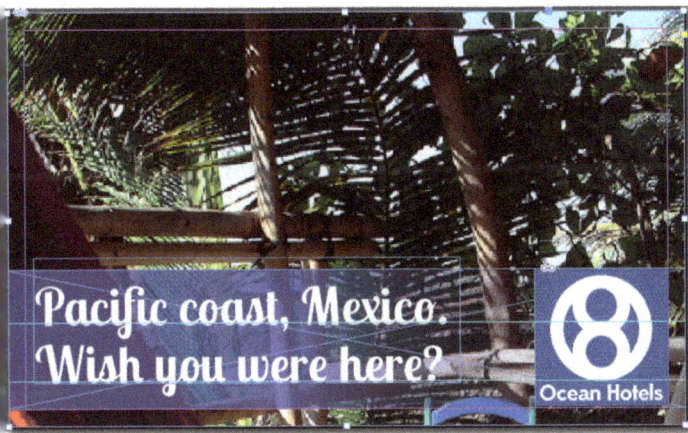

8. So far the images you've placed into InDesign have been carefully cropped so that you haven't had to learn about repositioning or resizing them. But this image is more realistic in that it will need to be adjusted to fit properly. From the **Object menu** choose **Fitting>Fill Frame Proportionally.** This resizes the image so that it fits the frame as best it can without changing the proportion of the image nor leaving any white space in the frame.

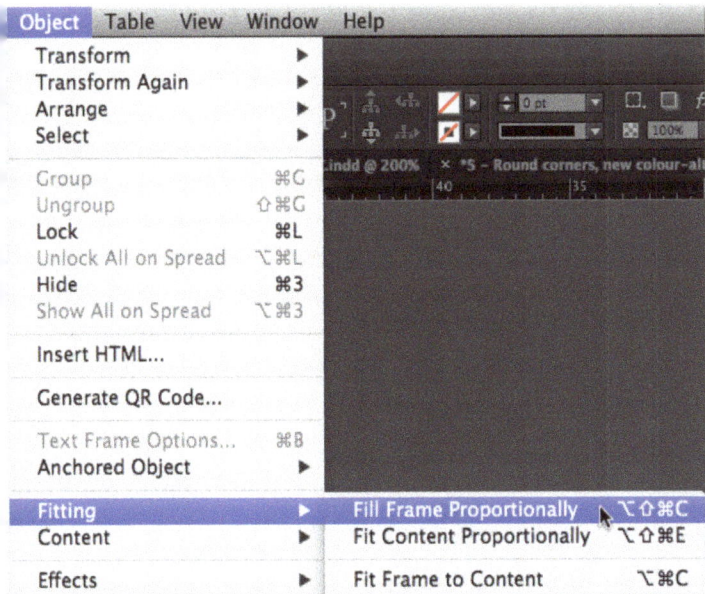

9.   Notice that at the moment the edge of the frame containing the image is *blue.* This indicates that the *frame itself* is selected. However, if you double-click on the image with the **Selection Tool** you will now see a *brown* frame instead*. This indicates that the *picture itself* is selected. This is why the brown frame is not exactly the same shape and size as the blue frame. As the page is probably filling your screen you may need to zoom out a little in order to see the brown frame. To do this, hold down the **Command key** and press the *minus key* a couple of times (when you want to zoom back out, hold down the **Command key** and press the *Zero key* to make the page fill the screen again).

*   *For users of InDesign prior to CS5, change to the **Direct Selection Tool** (the white arrow) instead to adjust the picture as described above, then revert back to the **Selection Tool** (the black arrow) when you've finished.*

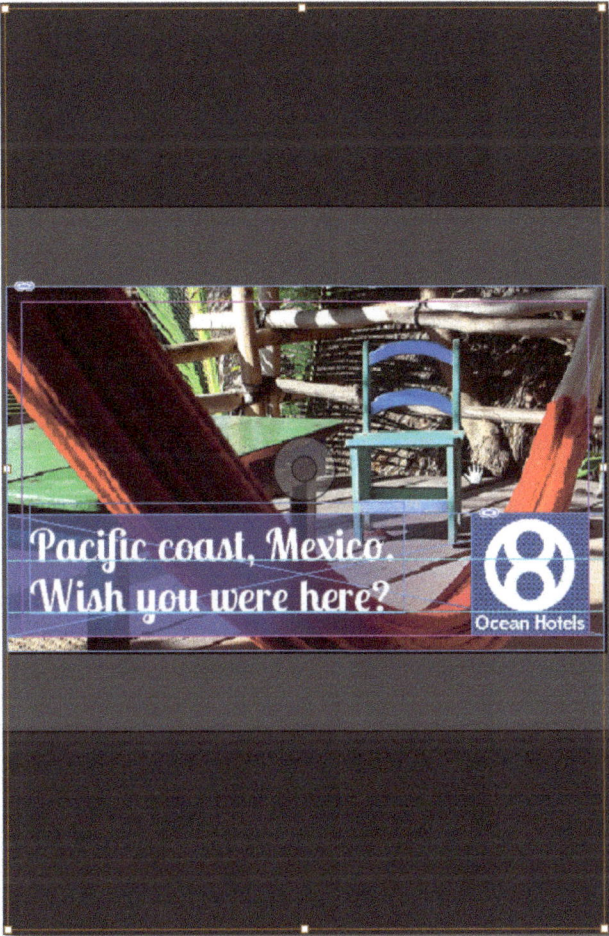

10. With the brown frame selected, if you press and hold down your mouse button, any area of the picture that's outside the blue frame will be seen, but will be ghosted out. If you want to show a different part of the picture, drag your mouse up or down to reposition it.

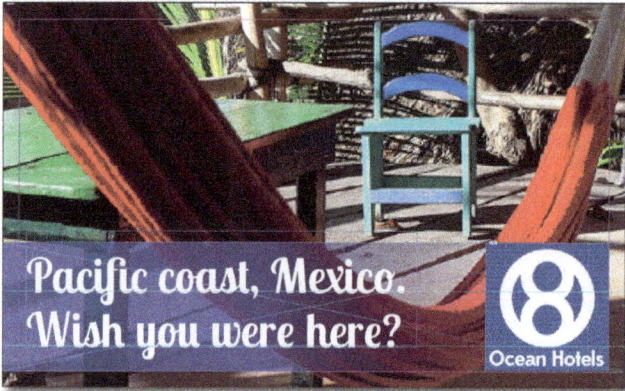

11. To finish you'll change the colour of the frame that stretches across the bottom of the advert. Select it with the **Selection Tool** and then open the **Swatches Panel.** Notice that the icon at the top left corner of the Swatches Panel indicates that the highlighted swatch has been applied to the frame (instead of the text, as you saw before).

12. You can see in the panel that as well as InDesign's default swatches it is possible to add others, as the *Oceans Hotel blue* has been here. Apply the *red* swatch to the frame to finish the advert.

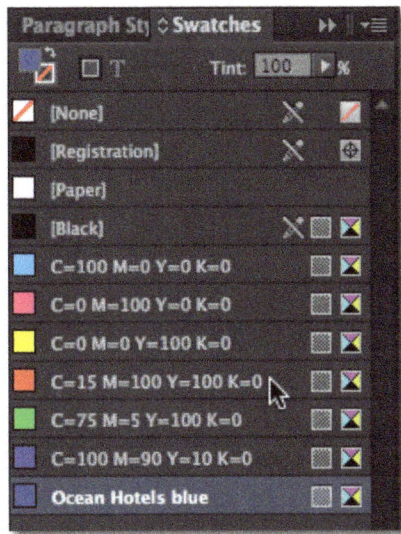

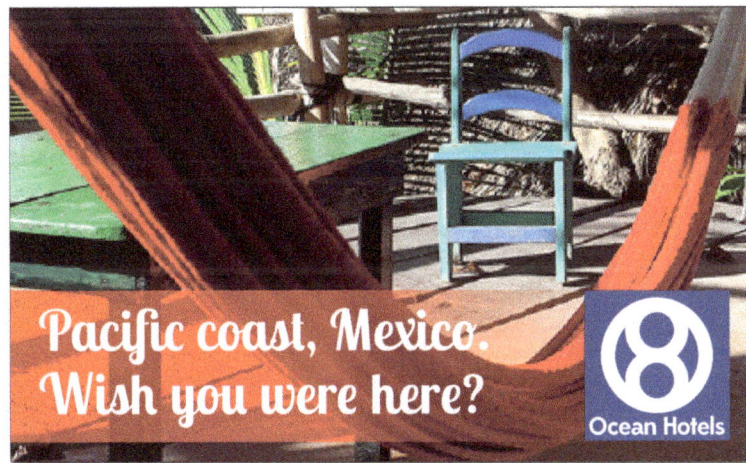

13. As with the previous documents, use **Presentation Mode** to view the final advert in high quality, then press the **Esc key** (at the top left of your keyboard) to return to *Normal Mode*. As you did previously, save the document in case you wish to return to it later.

Summary of new commands used

Object>Fitting>Fill Frame Proportionally

Summary of new shortcuts used

Command – (minus)   Zoom out
Command 0 (zero)   Fit Page in Window

4) A poster for Discover Cultural Tours

Building on what you already know, this fourth exercise will teach you how to import and work with more complex text and how to quickly import and crop multiple images at the same time.

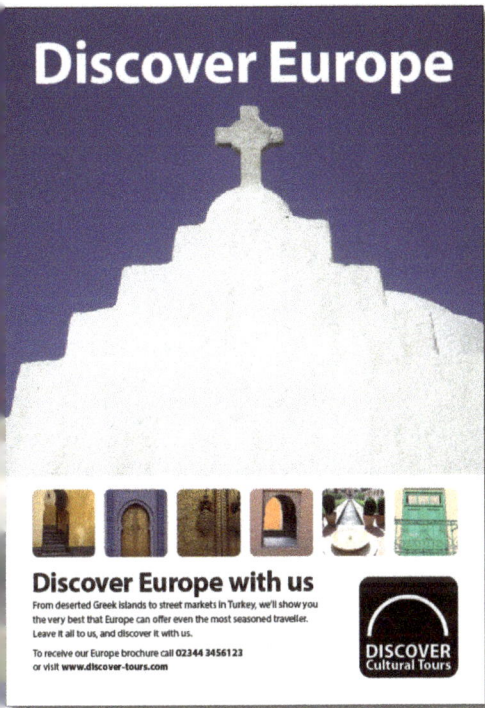

1. You can see from the screenshot above that you're going to create a poster for *Discover Cultural Tours.* As with the other exercises you've worked through, this is one of many similar posters from the same company.

2. Choose **File>Open** to create a new document based on the *4-discover-poster.idml* template. The main difference with this template is in the amount of text it will hold and number of images you'll import into it.

3. Select the background frame and import the *Discover_greece_mykonos. jpg* image. As in the previous exercise you'll want to this image to be resized and cropped (use **Object>Fitting>Fill Frame Proportionally** and then double-click to access the brown frame to adjust it further).

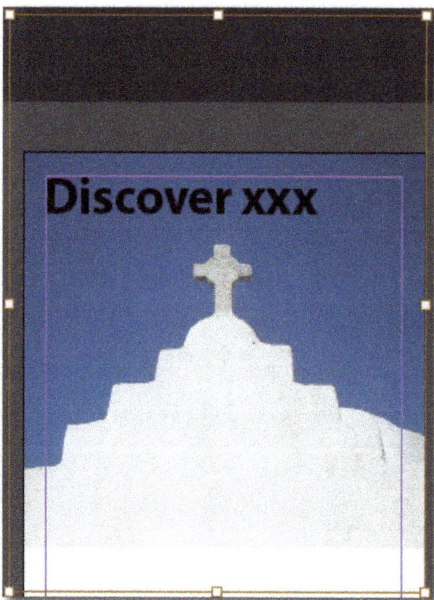

4. Use the **Type Tool** to change the title to *Discover Europe,* using the **Control Panel** to adjust the size of the text if need be, and the **Swatches Panel** to change the colour of the text to *White.*

5. Select one of the text frames at the bottom of the poster with the **Selection Tool** and then press **Command +** several times to zoom in closer (press ***Command –*** several times when you want to zoom back out again). Insert the word *Europe* in the appropriate place in both text frames.

* *Ctrl + on PC.*

6. Before you import the rest of the text into the frame at the bottom of the poster you're going to look more closely at the template for some visual clues as to how the final text should look. Notice firstly the thin blue line that the website address is sitting on – this is a guide, and it's used to help align things. Once the rest of the text is in the frame, the website address should still sit on this line.

7.   You'll only see the next visual clues if you use one of InDesign's most useful (if subtle) features. At the bottom of the *Type menu* choose *Show Hidden Characters.*

8.   You'll then see characters that, whilst they will not print, are nevertheless an essential component of text. Look carefully at the ends of the three lines of *xxx* text. The first two have a ¬ character after them, whereas the final one has a ¶ character. The ¶ character denotes the end of a paragraph, whereas the ¬ character denotes the end of a line within a paragraph. So the person who's created the template is attempting to convey that there needs to be one paragraph of three lines of text to fill the space.

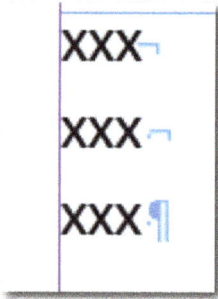

9.   Carefully select all three lines of text with the **Type Tool.**

Discover Europe with us

xxx
xxx
xxx

To receive our Europe brochure call **02344 3456123**
or visit **www.discover-tours.com**

10. Choose **File>Place** and import the *discover-europe-poster.txt* file. This is a plain text document, so the text should come in completely unformatted, as you should see from the screenshot below.

Discover Europe with us

From deserted Greek islands to street markets in Turkey, we'll show you the very best that Europe can offer even the most seasoned traveller. Leave it all to us, and discover it with us.

To receive our Europe brochure call **02344 3456123**
or visit **www.discover-tours.com**

11. If you click on some of the formatted text underneath and look in the **Control Panel** you'll see that it has been formatted using *Myriad Pro Regular* at *12pt* size. Select the newly imported text and change it to match.

Discover Europe with us

From deserted Greek islands to street markets in Turkey, we'll show you the very best that Europe can offer even the most seasoned traveller. Leave it all to us, and discover it with us.

To receive our Europe brochure call **02344 3456123**
or visit **www.discover-tours.com**

12. As you can see, the text fills three lines, so the website address at the bottom still lines up with the guide. However if you look closer at the text you might notice that it looks quite ragged. To improve it you'll specify exactly where you want the lines of text to finish. Place your cursor near the end of the first line, just before the word *the*. On your keyboard hold down the **Shift key** as you press the **Return key.** This inserts a *forced line break* character (as known as a soft return), which is one of these characters you saw earlier: ¬.

13. Insert another soft return just before the word *Leave*. The text remains on three lines, but you've decided how to split them to make the text look as good as possible.

14. You already know how to import a picture into a frame, but now you'll learn how to import several pictures into several frames at once. Firstly choose the **Selection Tool** from the **Tools Panel** and ensure that no frames are selected by clicking somewhere off the edge of the page. Then choose **File>Place** and choose all six pictures in the *Discover_poster_images* folder*. All of the images become attached to your cursor – note the number next to it, telling you how many you have. Press the **up** or **down arrow key** to cycle through the images to find the one you want, and when you want to place it into an empty frame, simply click on it.

* *Once in the dialogue box, the easiest way to do this is to click on the first image, then hold down the **Shift key** and click on the last image before pressing the **Open** button.*

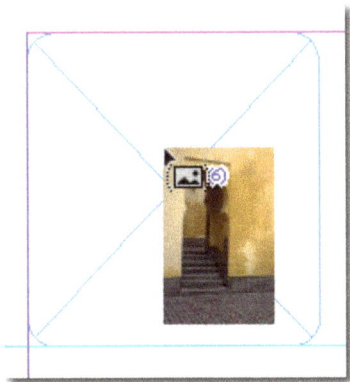

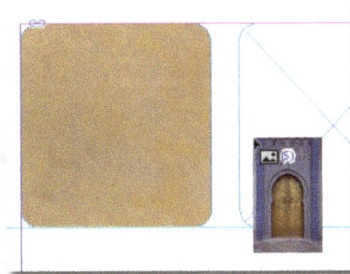

15. Once you've filled all of the frames with images, if you have any images still attached to your cursor, press the **Esc** key repeatedly to remove any leftover images.

Discover Europe with us#

16. Using your **Selection Tool,** click and drag through all six of the frames at once to select them all, and choose **Object>Fitting>Fill Frame proportionally.** As before, this resizes each image so that it fits the frame as best it can without changing the proportion of the image nor leaving any white space around the edge.

17. It may be that some of the images would look better with further adjustment. To do this, double-click with the **Selection Tool** to adjust any of them in the usual way.

Discover Europe with us

From deserted Greek islands to street markets in Turkey, we'll show you the very best that Europe can offer even the most seasoned traveller. Leave it all to us, and discover it with us.

To receive our Europe brochure call **02344 3456123** or visit **www.discover-tours.com**

DISCOVER
Cultural Tours

18. As previously, view the final document in *Presentation Mode,* then having returned to *Normal Mode,* save the document in case you wish to return to it later.

Summary of new commands used

Type>Show Hidden Characters

Summary of new shortcuts used

Shift+Return   Forced Line Break (or Soft Return)

Up or Down arrow   Scroll through images attached to cursor

Esc   Remove any images attached to cursor

5) A double-sided leaflet for Discover Cultural Tours

This document will be the first one you've looked at to use more than one page. It will also be where you learn to use Paragraph Styles, which is a much more reliable way of working with text than you've used before.

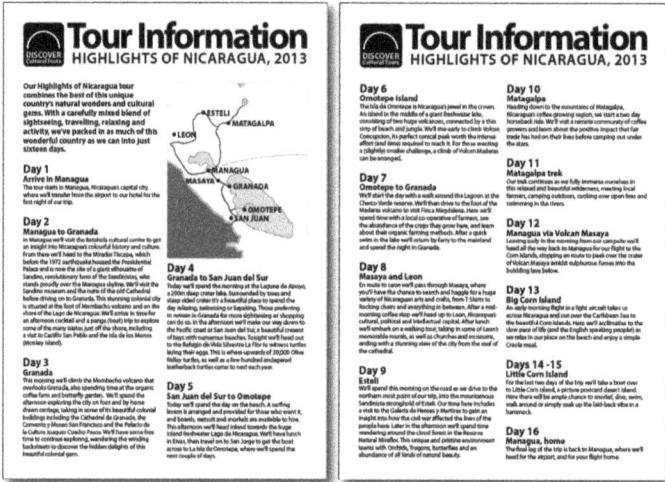

1. From the screenshot above you can see that you're going to create an information sheet for *Discover Cultural Tours.*

2. Choose **File>Open** to create a new document based on the *5-discover-tour-sheet.idml* template. The main difference with this template compared to what you've seen before is primarily in the way the text has been formatted, and also that the text will continue from one column to another, then from one page to another.

3. With your **Type Tool** click once on the text at the top of the left column. Press *Command + 2* to zoom in to 200% to see the text more clearly.

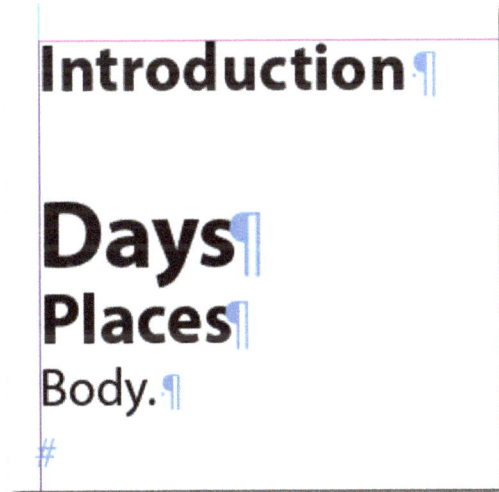

4. Make sure you can see the hidden characters on your screen – if not, choose **Show Hidden Characters** from the **Type menu.** From the previous exercise you know that the hidden ¶ character denotes the end of a paragraph, so here you can see four paragraphs. The word in each paragraph tells you the name of the *Paragraph Style* that has been used, and the order the paragraphs appear in give you some guidance as to how the text will work in the document. To start to understand this you'll need

to look at the *Paragraph Styles Panel,* which may not be showing on your screen. If you can't see it amongst the panels on the right hand side of your screen, from the **Window Menu** choose **Styles>Paragraph Styles.**

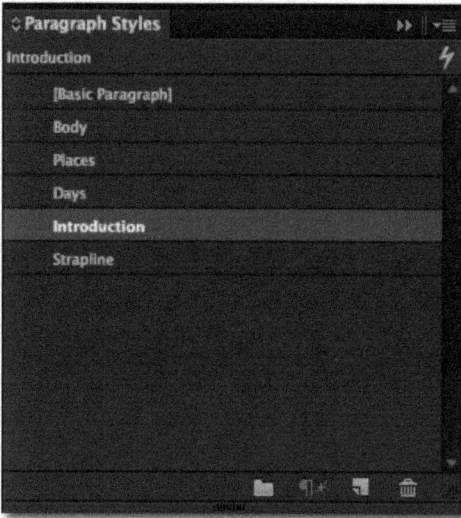

5. Look carefully at the text. Place your cursor in any of the paragraphs, look at your **Paragraph Styles Panel,** and notice that each paragraph uses one of the (highlighted) styles, which are used to apply the correct formatting to the text. The template has been designed in a way to show you how to use the paragraph styles once you've imported the text. Now you've seen this, select all of this text and delete it by pressing the **Delete** or **Backspace** key. Shortly you'll import the text for this document, but before you do, click on the *[Basic Paragraph]* style*.

* *This paragraph style is in every document, and by clicking it now it ensures that the text will come in the way it normally would, without any style automatically being applied to it.*

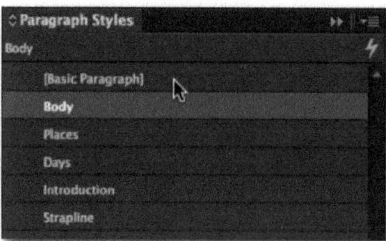

6. Now choose **Place** from the **File menu** and import
    the *discover-nicaragua-highlights.txt* file

> Our Highlights of Nicaragua tour combines the best of
> this unique country's natural wonders and cultural gems.
> With a carefully mixed blend of sightseeing, travelling,
> relaxing and activity, we've packed in as much of this
> wonderful country as we can into just sixteen days. ¶
> Day 1¶
> Arrive in Managua¶
> The tour starts in Managua, Nicaragua's capital city, where

7. From what you saw when you first opened the template, the
    Introduction style was going to be used at the start of the text. So
    click with your **Type Tool** in the first paragraph, then click on the
    Introduction style in the **Paragraph Styles Panel** to apply it.

> **Our Highlights of Nicaragua tour
> combines the best of this unique
> country's natural wonders and cultural
> gems. With a carefully mixed blend of
> sightseeing, travelling, relaxing and
> activity, we've packed in as much of this
> wonderful country as we can into just
> sixteen days.** ¶

8. If you need to, either scroll your page down using the scroll bars
    at the side of the page, or press **Command –** to zoom out so you
    can see the next few paragraphs. Again, using the guidance from
    the original template, apply the *Days* paragraph style to the *Day
    1* paragraph, the *Places* paragraph style to the *Arrive in Managua*
    paragraph and the *Body** paragraph style to the next paragraph.

* *The term body is often used by designers to describe the main
  body of the text, as opposed to headings, subheads etc.*

> # Day 1¶
> ## Arrive in Managua¶
> The tour starts in Managua, Nicaragua's capital city,
> where we'll transfer from the airport to our hotel for the
> first night of our trip. ¶

9. Continue through the document applying the same sequence of styles (Days, Places, Body) until all the text is correctly formatted. As you do, you'll notice that the text flows from the left column to the right, and then across from page one to page two.

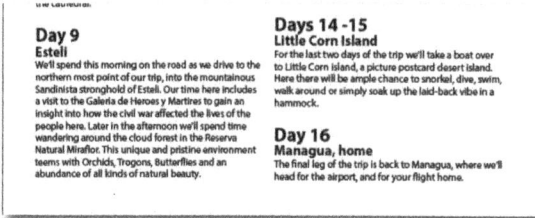

the cathedral.

Day 9
Esteli
We'll spend this morning on the road as we drive to the northern most point of our trip, into the mountainous Sandinista stronghold of Esteli. Our time here includes a visit to the Galería de Heroes y Martires to gain an insight here. Later in the afternoon we'll spend time wandering around the cloud forest in the Reserva Natural Miraflor. This unique and pristine environment teems with Orchids, Trogons, Butterflies and an abundance of all kinds of natural beauty.

Days 14-15
Little Corn Island
For the last two days of the trip we'll take a boat over to Little Corn Island, a picture postcard desert island. Here there will be ample chance to snorkel, dive, swim, walk around or simply soak up the laid-back vibe in a hammock.

Day 16
Managua, home
The final leg of the trip is back to Managua, where we'll head for the airport, and for your flight home.

10. Click on the empty frame on page *one* with your **Selection Tool** and import the *discover-nicaragua-map-bw.ai* file. Finish the document by typing *Highlights of Nicaragua, 2013* into the frame at the top of both pages of the document.

11. As previously, view the final document in *Presentation Mode*, then having returned to *Normal Mode*, save the document in case you wish to return to it later.

How realistic are these exercises?

You might be wondering at this stage if it's always as straightforward as this to create documents from templates, and of course the answer is that very often it's not. These exercises have been designed to give you a realistic understanding of how to use templates, but they've also been designed so that they *work*. As you get to working on your own documents you are likely to find that text that you have to use is either too long or too short. For those that want to explore in more detail what you might do in such circumstances, I've created an alternative exercise that you can find once you've finished the next and final exercise.

Summary of new commands used

Window>Styles>Paragraph Styles

Summary of new shortcuts used

Command+2   Zoom in to 200% size
Delete / Backspace keys

6) A four page leaflet for Visit Cuba

This final document will be the first one you've looked at to use more than two pages. You'll discover different types of pages, gain more experience using Paragraph Styles, and also have a brief look at Character Styles and InDesign's hugely useful Text Wrap feature.

1. The screenshots above show you both sides of the leaflet that you're going to create. It's one of several leaflets that highlights different locations for *Visit Cuba.*

2. Choose **File>Open** to create a new document based on the *6-visit-cuba-4pp-a5-leaflet.idml* template.

3. When you open the template you'll see the first page, but to have an overview of the whole document, click on the *Pages Panel icon** near the top right of your screen to open the **Pages Panel.**

* *If you can't see it, choose **Window>Pages** to open the panel instead.*

4. Your panel may not look exactly like the screenshot below, but you should nevertheless see that page *1* of this document will be the front, page *4* will be the back, and pages *2-3* will be the inside of the leaflet, with a fold in between them. The screenshots at the start of this exercise showed you how the leaflet will look like when it's printed (with pages *1* and *4* also next to each other with a fold in between them).

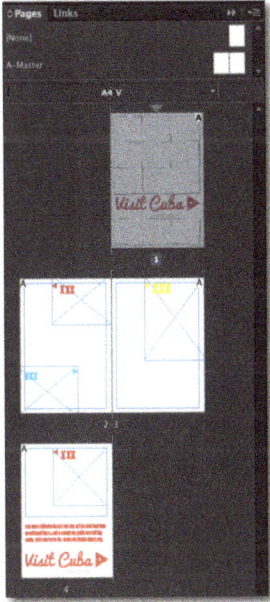

5. The main difference with this document compared to what you've seen in the previous one is that the text will flow all the way from page *two* to page *four,* creating one long *story.* If you want to have an idea of how this will work, firstly double click on the *Page 2 icon* in the Pages Panel to view page 2. Then from the **View menu** choose **Extras>Show Text Threads*.** With your **Selection Tool** click on the large text frame on page two and notice the thick blue line that links the bottom right of the text frame on page 2 to the top left of the frame on page three, and also the line that disappears from the bottom right of the text frame on page three.

* *If you can't see the Extras sub-menu, it's likely that you're using a much older version of InDesign, in which case you'll simply find Show Text Threads inside the View menu.*

6. Select the **Type Tool** and place your cursor into the text frame on page two. Click on the *[Basic Paragraph]* style in the **Paragraph Styles Panel,** then choose **File>Place** to import the *visit-cuba-highlights.txt* file.

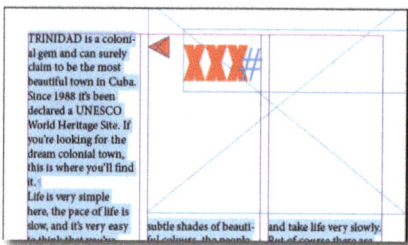

7. Look at the text to check whether all of it is selected (as it is in the screenshot above). If it isn't, choose **Edit>Select All** to select all of the text in the story.* Then, as the vast majority of the text will be styled using the *Body+Indent* paragraph style, click on that style in the **Paragraph Styles Panel.**

* The InDesign term *story* describes all of the text either within or one text frame, or within a series of linked text frames, such as these.

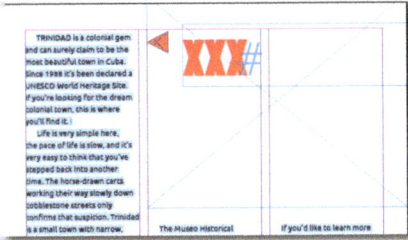

8. It's likely that your text has now acquired a pink highlight, like you saw when you created the *Ocean Hotels* advert. It's another example of InDesign alerting you that you do not have a font that you need. In this case the *Body+Indent* paragraph style that was created as part of the template uses the *Ubuntu* font, so you'll see the pink highlight if you don't have that font installed on your computer. As before, you're either going to have to install the font on your own computer or change the design to use a font that you do have. If you want to install the font, follow the instructions in the footnote below. If you'd rather not install the font, ensure all the text is selected and choose a different *font* from the **Control Panel** at the top left of your screen.

* *One of the reasons I've used this font is because it's freely available for anyone to use. If you want to download the font, go to www.fontsquirrel.com and follow their instructions at www.fontsquirrel.com/help for help on how to download and install it. If you need further guidance there are some other resources listen in the Images, text and fonts section near the start of this book.*

9. Zoom in so you can see the first paragraph of text closely and apply the *Body* paragraph style to it. This style is only for the paragraphs at the start of each different location, as in this *Trinidad* example.

TRINIDAD is a colonial gem and can surely claim to be the most beautiful town in Cuba. Since 1988 it's been declared a UNESCO World Heritage Site. If you're looking for the dream colonial town, this is where you'll find it. ¶

10. From the **Window menu** choose *Styles>Character Styles.* Like paragraph styles these are used to style text, only in this case the styling only affects individual *characters* (or letters).

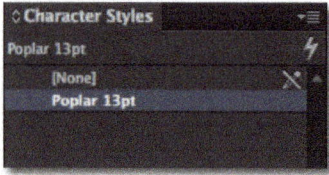

11. Select the word *Trinidad* and apply the *Poplar 13pt* character style. Make the text *Red* to match the heading to the right of it.

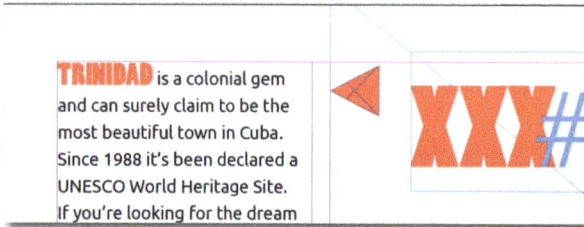

12. Go through the rest of the text and apply the *Body* paragraph style to the three other paragraphs that start with uppercase locations. Apply the *Poplar 13pt* character style to the initial word, and change the colour to match the nearby headings.

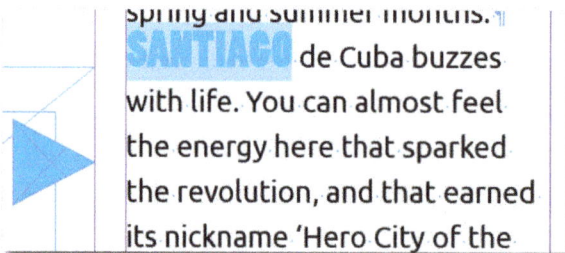

13. This leaflet has been designed to showcase different locations in Cuba, and it's partly doing that by linking the body text with the accompanying images. To make this work well, the start of each section needs to line up with the images. Look at the screenshot above and notice that the *Santiago* text does not line up with the blue arrow that should point to it. To change this, place your cursor just in front of the *S* of *Santiago* and press the **Return key** twice to move it down. This change should also make the rest of the text fall into place.

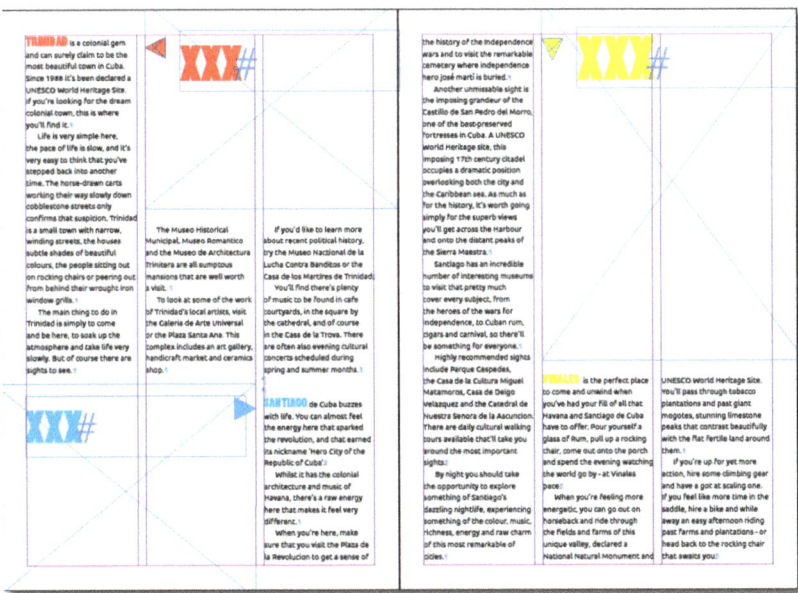

14. Type the place names of the headings into their respective text frames, then using the **Selection Tool** bring the appropriate images (from the same folder you've been using) into the empty frames underneath them.

15. To finish the leaflet, go back to the first page, and make sure you're using the **Selection Tool** with no frames are selected. Using the technique you employed when creating the poster for *Discover Cultural Tours,* bring in all of the images from the *visit_cuba_leaflet_cover_images* folder at once. When all of the images are attached to your cursor, place each one in turn into the frames provided to create the montage for the front cover.

16. View the final document in *Presentation Mode,* then having returned to *Normal Mode,* save the document in case you wish to return to it later.

Summary of new commands used

Window>Pages
Window>Styles>Character Styles
View>Extras>Show Text Threads

Summary of new keys used

Return key

A more realistic version of Exercise 5

As I mentioned previously, I've designed these exercises to give you a realistic understanding of how templates work, and to do that I wanted the exercises to not be too challenging. But I include now a slightly more realistic version of Exercise 5 to give you an idea of what to do if the text is too long to fit in the document.

1. Open the *Templates5-final-long.idml* document. This is based on the same template as you previously used, the only difference being that the imported text is a little bit longer.

2. At first glance it may not appear that anything is wrong and that the text fits, but if you scroll to the end of page 2 you'll see a red plus, called an *overset mark* at the bottom right of the text frame.

3. The overset mark tells you there is more text in the story that can't be displayed in the frame because there is no room for it. To find out how much extra text there is choose *Edit>Edit in Story Editor.*

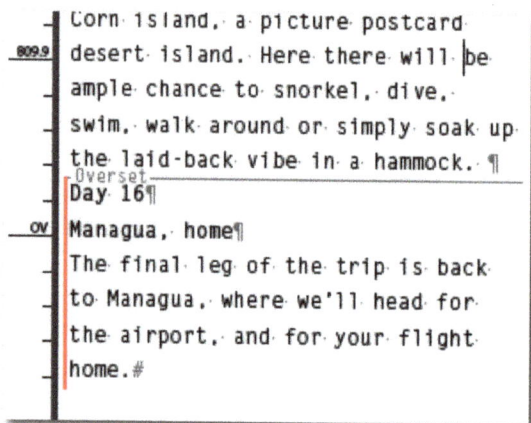

```
      ┐ Corn·Island,·a·picture·postcard·
 809.9 │ desert·island.·Here·there·will·be·
      ┐ ample·chance·to·snorkel,·dive,·
      ┐ swim,·walk·around·or·simply·soak·up·
      ┐ the·laid-back·vibe·in·a·hammock.·¶
        ┌Overset──────────────────────────
      ┐ │Day·16¶
   OV │ │Managua,·home¶
      ┐ │The·final·leg·of·the·trip·is·back·
        │to·Managua,·where·we'll·head·for·
      ┐ │the·airport,·and·for·your·flight·
      ┐ │home.#
```

4. The *Story Editor* gives you an alternative view of the story and is an alternative place to edit your text. But it's especially useful in that it shows you any text that isn't able to fit, which is known as *overmatter.* In this case you can see that the whole of the last day of the tour has been missed off. To see how that's happened, go back to page one. The screenshot below shows you that the body text underneath *Day 3* was a little too long to remain in the left hand column, and it's gone across to the right hand column, pushing everything down in turn.

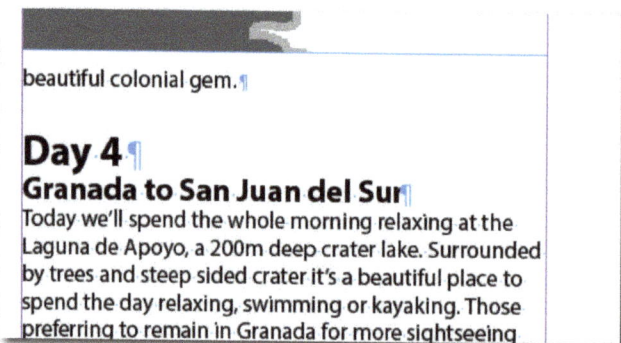

beautiful colonial gem.¶

Day 4 ¶
Granada to San Juan del Sur¶
Today we'll spend the whole morning relaxing at the Laguna de Apoyo, a 200m deep crater lake. Surrounded by trees and steep sided crater it's a beautiful place to spend the day relaxing, swimming or kayaking. Those preferring to remain in Granada for more sightseeing

5. Whilst we'll shortly go through some options that you have to fix the problem, how you would deal with this with your own work would largely depend on your role and responsibility*. What we'll go through now are the two most likely changes you'd look to make to a document like this, given the assumption that it's not your role to edit the text nor adjust the design. To look at the first option, adjust your view so that you can see the whole of the body paragraph under day 3. Using your **Type Tool,** click four times in quick succession to select the whole paragraph.

* *Because it could be that it's within your remit to edit the text, in which case that's the most straightforward thing to do. Or it may be that it's not within your remit to change the text at all, but that you'd be allowed to change the design in some way.*

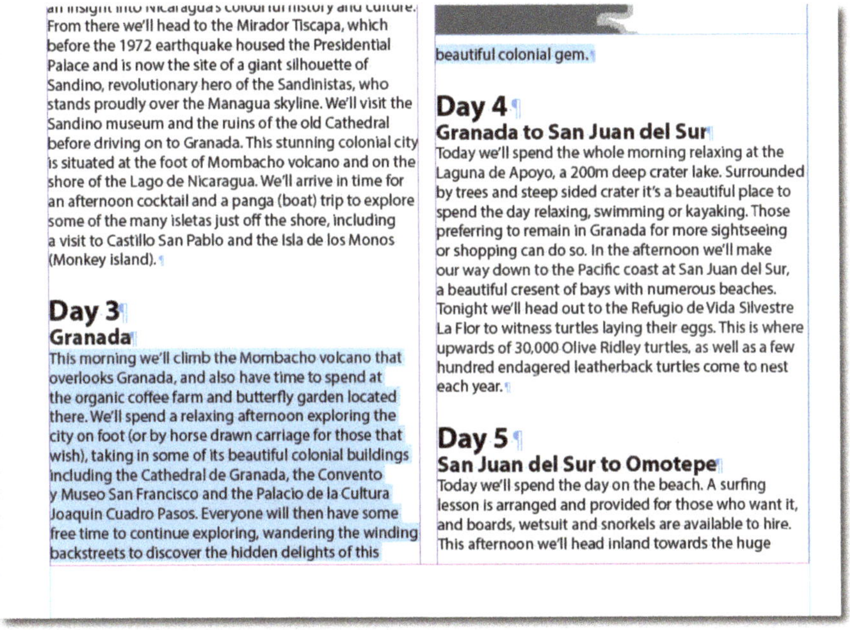

an insight into Nicaragua's colourful history and culture. From there we'll head to the Mirador Tiscapa, which before the 1972 earthquake housed the Presidential Palace and is now the site of a giant silhouette of Sandino, revolutionary hero of the Sandinistas, who stands proudly over the Managua skyline. We'll visit the Sandino museum and the ruins of the old Cathedral before driving on to Granada. This stunning colonial city is situated at the foot of Mombacho volcano and on the shore of the Lago de Nicaragua. We'll arrive in time for an afternoon cocktail and a panga (boat) trip to explore some of the many isletas just off the shore, including a visit to Castillo San Pablo and the Isla de los Monos (Monkey Island).

Day 3
Granada
This morning we'll climb the Mombacho volcano that overlooks Granada, and also have time to spend at the organic coffee farm and butterfly garden located there. We'll spend a relaxing afternoon exploring the city on foot (or by horse drawn carriage for those that wish), taking in some of its beautiful colonial buildings including the Cathedral de Granada, the Convento y Museo San Francisco and the Palacio de la Cultura Joaquin Cuadro Pasos. Everyone will then have some free time to continue exploring, wandering the winding backstreets to discover the hidden delights of this

beautiful colonial gem.

Day 4
Granada to San Juan del Sur
Today we'll spend the whole morning relaxing at the Laguna de Apoyo, a 200m deep crater lake. Surrounded by trees and steep sided crater it's a beautiful place to spend the day relaxing, swimming or kayaking. Those preferring to remain in Granada for more sightseeing or shopping can do so. In the afternoon we'll make our way down to the Pacific coast at San Juan del Sur, a beautiful cresent of bays with numerous beaches. Tonight we'll head out to the Refugio de Vida Silvestre La Flor to witness turtles laying their eggs. This is where upwards of 30,000 Olive Ridley turtles, as well as a few hundred endagered leatherback turtles come to nest each year.

Day 5
San Juan del Sur to Omotepe
Today we'll spend the day on the beach. A surfing lesson is arranged and provided for those who want it, and boards, wetsuit and snorkels are available to hire. This afternoon we'll head inland towards the huge

6. The aim here is to make the text a little shorter so that it comes back to the left hand column, and to do this without rewriting it nor changing its formatting so that it looks different to the rest of the text. The approach used is known as *tracking*. Tracking is used to adjust the spaces between words and characters, and used well it will make text either longer or shorter without it looking too noticeable. Look in the Control Panel and ensure that the *Character Formatting Controls* button is selected (if it's darker than the other one, it is). Using the dropdown menu shown below, adjust the **Tracking** to *-5*.

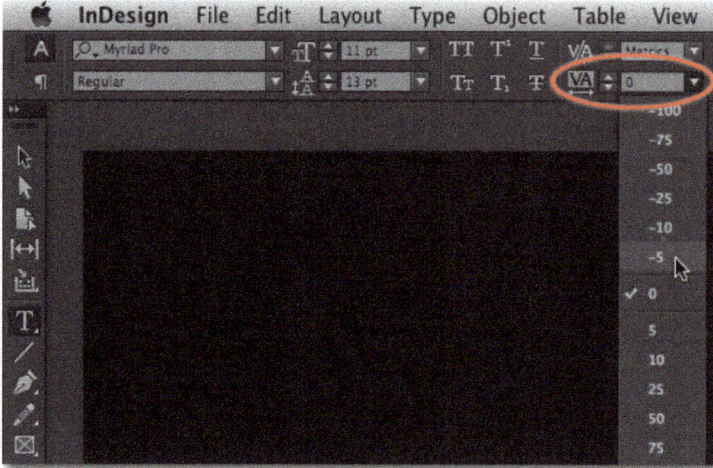

7. You might notice that the text appears to be a little closer together, but not enough to bring it back to the left hand column. If you try with *-10* tracking you'll sadly have the same result. In the dropdown menu there is no option for *-15**, but if you type that in the tracking value you'll see that this has the desired effect.

* *A tracking value of between -15 and +15 is generally regarded as within acceptable limits, but of course each circumstance is different and you have to use your own judgement.*

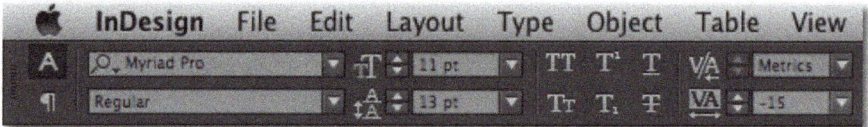

Day 3
Granada
This morning we'll climb the Mombacho volcano that
overlooks Granada, and also have time to spend at the
organic coffee farm and butterfly garden located there.
We'll spend a relaxing afternoon exploring the city on
foot (or by horse drawn carriage for those that wish),
taking in some of its beautiful colonial buildings including
the Cathedral de Granada, the Convento y Museo San
Francisco and the Palacio de la Cultura Joaquin Cuadro
Pasos. Everyone will then have some free time to continue
exploring, wandering the winding backstreets to discover
the hidden delights of this beautiful colonial gem.

8. This exercise is realistic in that you may have to adjust the
    tracking more than you'd wish to, given that the result, while
    not looking perfect, looks better than before. It's also realistic
    in that if you look back at page two you'll see that this has
    not completely fixed the problem of the overset text.

Days 14 -15
Little Corn Island
For the last two days of the trip we'll take a boat over
to Little Corn island, a picture postcard desert island.
Here there will be ample chance to snorkel, dive, swim,
walk around or simply soak up the laid-back vibe in a
hammock.

Day 16

9. The problem this time is the body text under *Day 5,* which
    again is slightly too long to fit in the previous column
    and is pushing all the remaining text down with it.

next couple of days.

Day 6
Omotepe island
The Isla de Omotepe is Nicaragua's jewel in the crown.
An island in the middle of a giant freshwater lake,
consisting of two huge volcanoes, connected by a thin

10. Whilst you could adjust the tracking to fix it, the other approach to consider is to very subtly adjust the height of the image on page one. Using the **Selection Tool,** click once on the frame containing the map image to select it.

Day 4
Granada to San Juan del Sur
Today we'll spend the whole morning relaxing at the
Laguna de Apoyo, a 200m deep crater lake. Surrounded

11. If you look just underneath the image you should notice a thin blue line. This indicates that a feature called *text wrap* is being used, whereby the image prevents the text from occupying its space and forces the text to wrap around it. Drag the central handle at the bottom of the image up a little to make the image a tiny bit less tall, thereby allowing the final line of the *Day 5* text to come back to the bottom of the right hand column of page one, fixing the problem of the overset text.

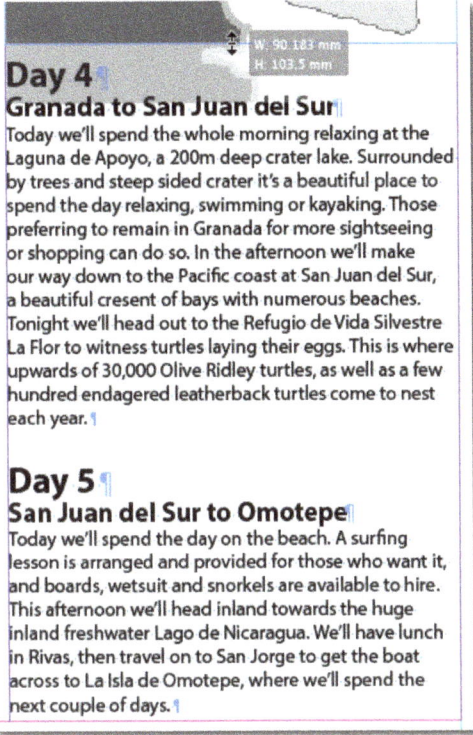

Day 4
Granada to San Juan del Sur
Today we'll spend the whole morning relaxing at the Laguna de Apoyo, a 200m deep crater lake. Surrounded by trees and steep sided crater it's a beautiful place to spend the day relaxing, swimming or kayaking. Those preferring to remain in Granada for more sightseeing or shopping can do so. In the afternoon we'll make our way down to the Pacific coast at San Juan del Sur, a beautiful cresent of bays with numerous beaches. Tonight we'll head out to the Refugio de Vida Silvestre La Flor to witness turtles laying their eggs. This is where upwards of 30,000 Olive Ridley turtles, as well as a few hundred endagered leatherback turtles come to nest each year.

Day 5
San Juan del Sur to Omotepe
Today we'll spend the day on the beach. A surfing lesson is arranged and provided for those who want it, and boards, wetsuit and snorkels are available to hire. This afternoon we'll head inland towards the huge inland freshwater Lago de Nicaragua. We'll have lunch in Rivas, then travel on to San Jorge to get the boat across to La Isla de Omotepe, where we'll spend the next couple of days.

Summary of new commands used
Edit>Edit in Story Editor

Summary of new panels used
Control Panel: Tracking

Vinales, Cuba

Visit Cuba

"THE MORE WE ADAPTED TO THE CUBAN PACE OF LIFE, THE MORE RELAXED WE BECAME"

Visit Cuba

GO! ADVENTURES.COM
START YOUR ADVENTURE

BOLIVIA

Salar de Uyuni tour

WHERE?
The Salar de Uyuni is in Bolivia's South West, bordering Chile's Atacama desert covering thousands of kilometers at high altitude.

WHY?
In a word, adventure. You'll set off in a four wheel drive with all the provisions you'll need as you cross across salt flats and cold deserts. You'll see bubbling sulphur springs, wild flamingoes, giant cacti and a buildings made of salt.

WHEN?
This new trip leaves the first tuesday of every month from March to October.

GO! ADVENTURES.COM

Vinales, Cuba

Visit Cuba

PERU

FROM ANDEAN PEAKS TO the roar of the Pacific Ocean, Peru has it all.

Experience the energy and diversity of what this country has to offer as we travel from the depths of the Amazon to the heights of Macchu Pichu.

For more information on our Highlights of Cuba tour, visit us at go-adventures.com or pick up our South America brochure from your travel agent.

GO! ADVENTURES.COM
START YOUR ADVENTURE

CREATING FLYERS, POSTERS & POSTCARDS

This chapter is about creating flyers, posters and postcards. There are six in total, each one a little more complex than the last. With the exception of the postcard that you'll create, all of the documents are single sided (whilst a flyer might well be double sided, we'll cover that subject in the chapter on creating leaflets). The flyers, posters or postcards are created for two fictitious organisations, *Visit Cuba* and *Go Adventures*. As with any real organisation, they have had logos designed, and they use particular typefaces and colours in their branding.

1) Creating An A5 Flyer

The first thing you'll create in InDesign is a simple, one page flyer*.

* *What you might call a "side" a printer would call a page: so a one page flyer is printed on one side, whereas a two page flyer would be printed on both sides of the paper.*

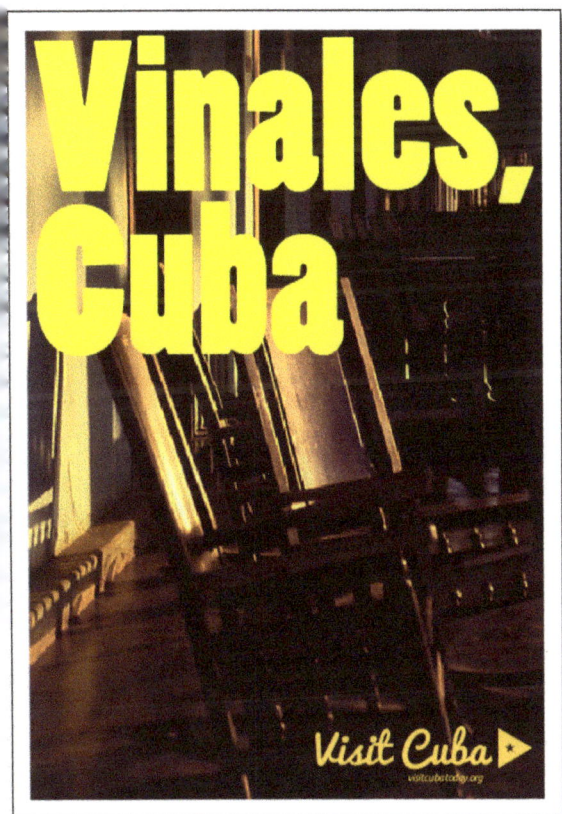

1. Choose *File>New>Document.*

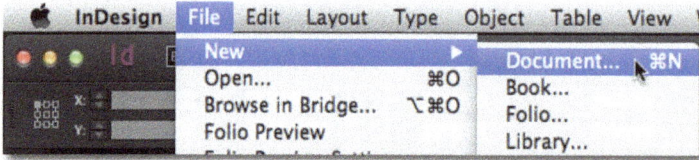

2. Check that the **Document Preset** is set to *Default.*
   If it's not, select it in the pop up menu.

3. Whilst you're in the *New Document dialogue box,* change the **Page Size,** from A4 to *A5* by clicking on the *Page Size dropdown menu.*

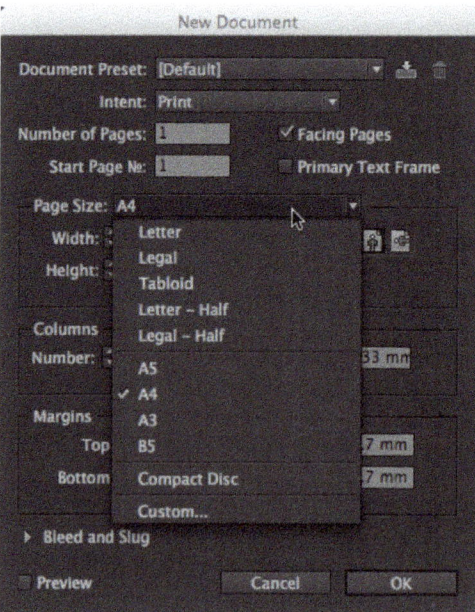

4. Whilst still in the New Document dialogue box, change all the *Margin* values to *5mm*. The easiest way to do this is to change the **Top** margin value and then click on the *padlock* to copy the value into the *Bottom, Left* and *Right* boxes. Then press the **OK button.**

5. You can now see your blank InDesign document. The black rectangle represents the edge of the document, and the pink/purple lines are *Margin Guides* (which you set to *5mm* from the edge of the document). These can be used in a variety of ways, but in this case you'll use them to define where the edge of your picture is going to be.

6. Select the *Rectangle Frame Tool* from the *Tools Panel.*

7. Once you've selected it, InDesign is expecting you to create a frame in which to put a picture or text. Notice that it has a plain crosshair at the moment. Position it over the intersection of the margin guides near the top left corner of the document and you'll see a little arrow, indicating that the cursor is accurately lined up with it.

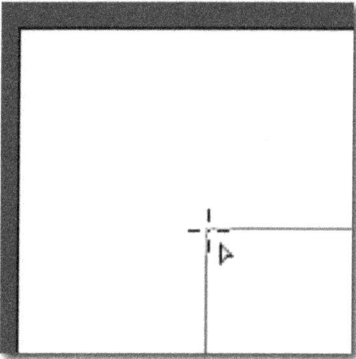

8. Press your mouse button down, and keeping it down, drag to the intersection of the margin guides near the bottom right of the page, letting go when you see the little arrow appear to let you know you're accurately lined up. Once you've let go, you'll have created your first frame.

9. Notice that you're still using the Rectangle Frame Tool, so if you either click, or click+drag, InDesign will try and create a new frame for you. To prevent this happening, change to the *Selection Tool* (found at the top of the Tools Panel) once you've drawn your frame*.

* *If you've already created extra frames, choose Edit>Undo to retrace your steps and remove them.*

10. Making sure you're using the **Selection Tool,** click on the frame you've just made. You can tell it's selected if you can see square blue *handles* around its edge. Notice the large *X* in the frame, indicating that the frame is currently empty.

* *As well as showing when a frame is selected, handles can also be used to resize frames.*

11. Choose *File>Place* to place an image into the frame.

12. From the dialogue box, find your *Creative Classroom Flyers* folder and select *visit-cuba-vinales-a5.jpg*.

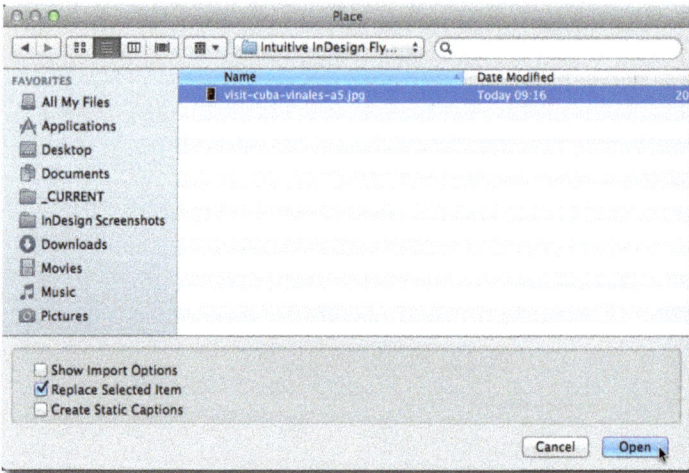

13. Press the **Open** button (or double-click) you'll see your frame is filled with the picture.

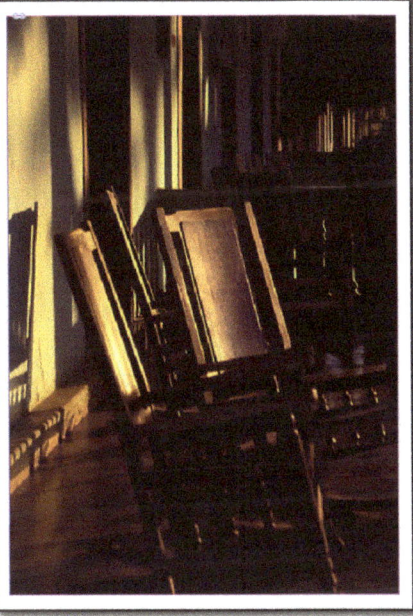

14. This document is to be one of a series of flyers advertising Cuba, each of which simply has a photograph and a place name. Each has been designed to show the text as large as possible. To achieve this, you'll create one large frame for the place name. Select the **Rectangle Frame Tool** once again. Starting just inside the edge of the previous frame, draw a frame like the one shown below. As you saw previously, there is a large X in the frame, indicating that it is currently empty. But this frame will shortly contain text.

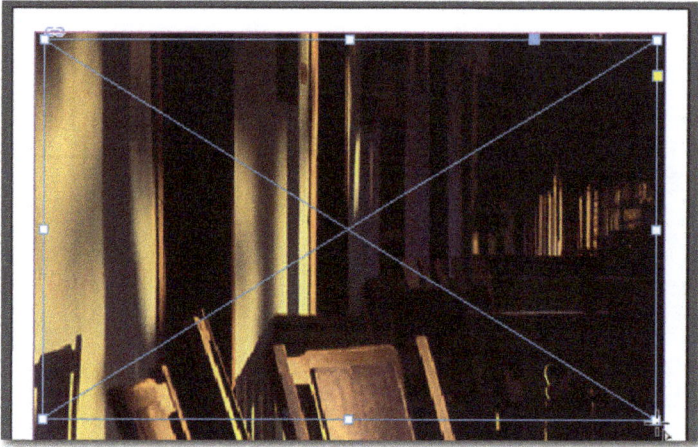

15. Select the **Type Tool** and click once on the new frame. You should now see that the X has disappeared, and instead contains a flashing cursor, indicating that InDesign is expecting you to type something.

16. Type the word "Vinales," (including the comma). You probably can't see the text very clearly, so type *[Command+2]*, a shortcut that will enable you to see the area you're working on at 200%. When you need to zoom back out, press *[Command+0 (zero)]* to zoom back out again.

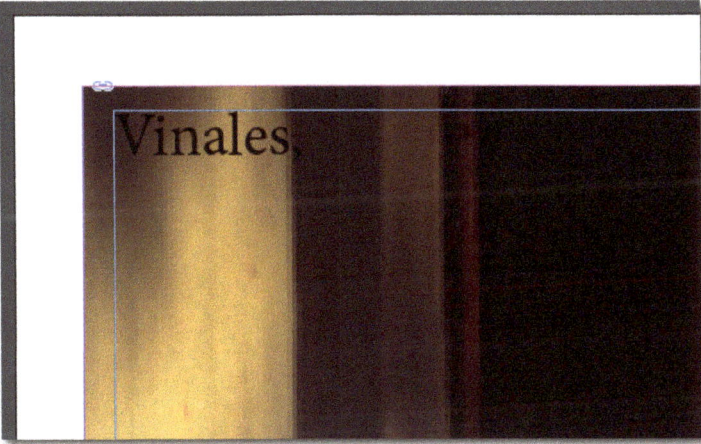

17. Notice that the **Control Panel** at the top of the screen is now showing information about the type. If you look at the left edge of the Panel, there are two buttons. Ensure that the **Character Formatting Controls** button is selected (if it's darker than the other one, it is).

18. Select all the text you've just typed either by dragging over it with your mouse, or by choosing **Edit>Select All.** Change the **Font** from Minion Pro to *Poplar Std.*

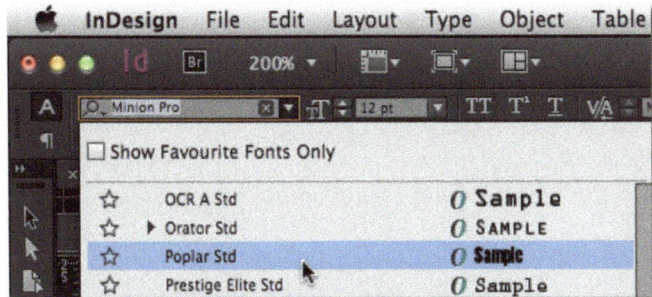

CREATING FLYERS, POSTERS & POSTCARDS

19. Change the size of the type from 12pt to *72pt* by choosing the drop down menu to the right of where it currently says 12pt.

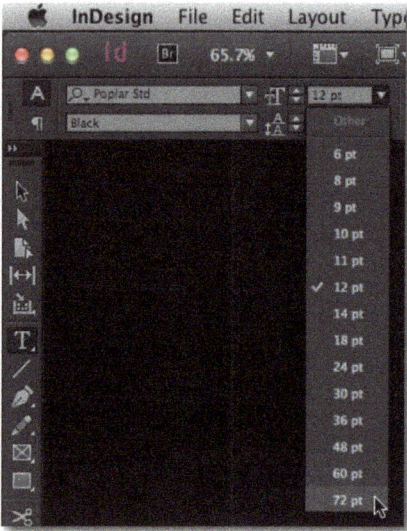

20. Even though you've just chosen the largest of all the preset sizes, the text should only about half fill the frame*. Adjust the size of the type to about *130pt* by typing that value directly into the **Font Size** area of the Control Panel.

If you're still looking at your document at 200% size, press Command+0 (zero) to zoom back out again.

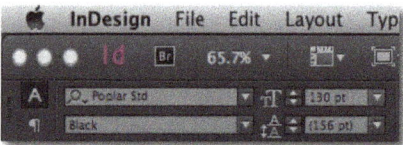

21. Depending on the size of your frame you may or may not see all of the text in the new typeface at the new size. If there's not enough room, you'll see an *Overset Mark* (a small red +) at the bottom right of your text frame.

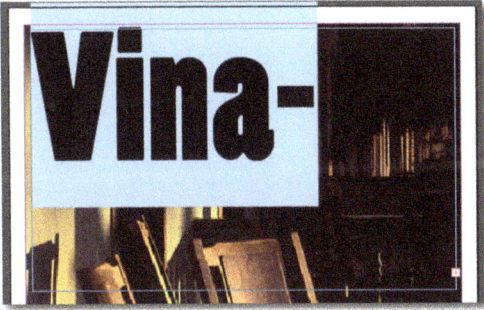

22. To fix it, make the type size smaller by pressing the **down arrow** in the **Control Panel** to the left of the font size. Similarly, if you want the text to be larger, increase the font size by using the **up arrow** in the same place.

23. Many of the features in InDesign use Panels that are docked to the side of the screen. Your first look at one of these is the **Swatches Panel,** which you'll use to change the colour of the text. To see what's inside the Panel, click once on the name of the Panel (in this case, click on where it says *Swatches*).

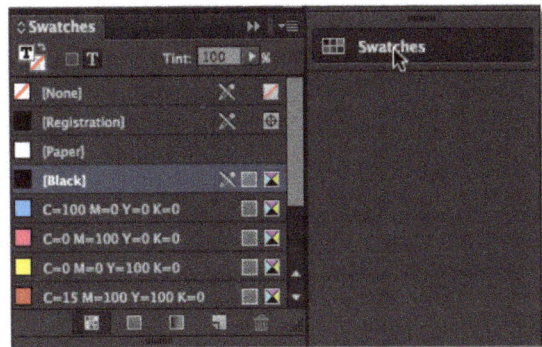

24. Notice that at the top left of the Panel there is a small black "T". This tells you that some text is selected, it is black, and that any changes in colour will affect the text and not the frame (more about this later).

25. Notice also that the black swatch has a faint highlight on it to indicate it's being used. Click on the *Yellow* swatch to change your text to that colour instead.

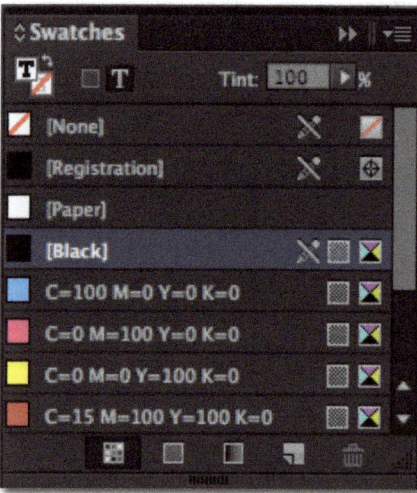

26. Change to the **Selection Tool.** If you want to move your frame somewhere else on the page, simply click and drag it. Make the frame less deep by clicking and dragging the square handle that you can see at the bottom of the frame, in the centre.

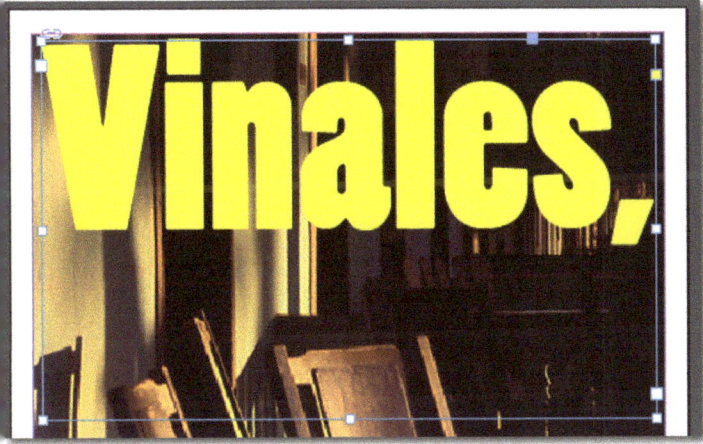

27. You can also use the Selection Tool to duplicate frames. You'll duplicate the frame containing "Vinales," so that you can quickly create the remainder of the text using the same font, size and colour. To do this, hold down the *Alt key* as you drag the text frame with the **Selection Tool,** noticing that the cursor icon changes to indicate that you'll be duplicating, as opposed to moving the text frame.

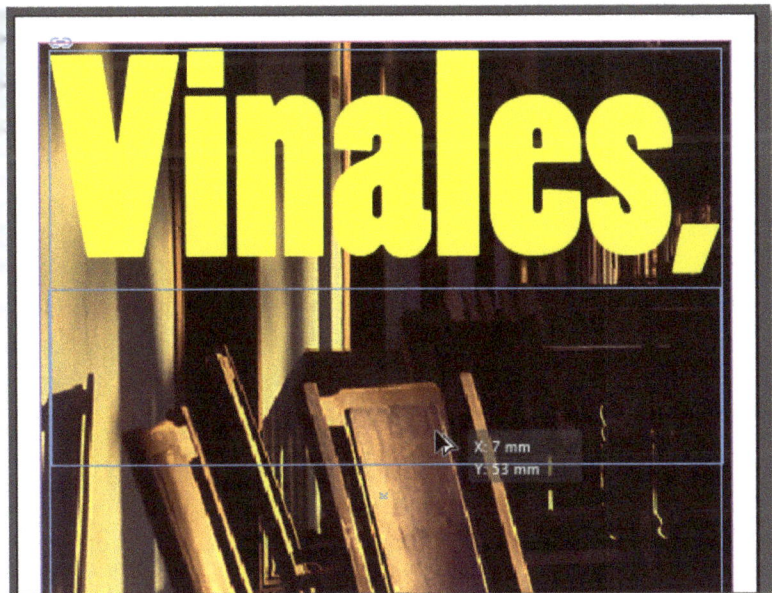

28. Once the duplicated frame is in place, choose the **Type Tool** from the **Tools Panel.** Drag over the "Vinales," text and type over it with the word *"Cuba."* If you want to reposition this text, change back to the **Selection Tool** and drag it to a different place, or for a more subtle change, alternatively nudge it up, down, left or right with the *Arrow keys* on your keyboard.

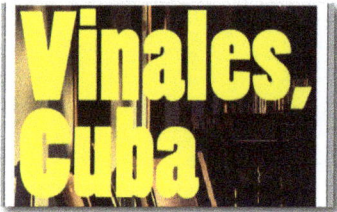

29. To bring in the *Visit Cuba* logo it would be possible to create a frame as you did before, then place the logo in as you did with the rocking chair picture. However, it can be much more effective with small images like logos to allow InDesign to create a frame for you whilst you import it. To use this second approach, ensure that you're using the **Selection Tool,** and that nothing is selected (click on a blank area outside the document if you need to deselect everything). Then choose **File>Place** and import the *visit_cuba_100yellow.eps* file. The logo will attach to your cursor.

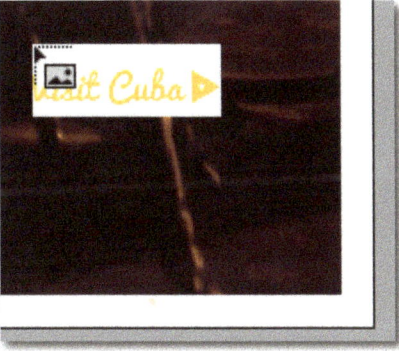

30. To place it in the document, click and drag in the bottom right
corner of the document, and you'll create a frame that's exactly
the same shape as the logo, at the size you choose. If you didn't
quite get the size you wanted, choose **Edit>Undo.** This removes
the logo from the page and re-attaches it to your cursor so you
can try it again. Once you're happy with the size of the logo, you
can drag it with the **Selection Tool** if you want to reposition it.

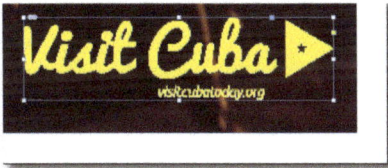

31. By default, when you bring in a logo or similar *vector* graphic (see
Images from Photoshop and Illustrator in the *Brief Notes* section) it
won't appear on your screen at full quality. To get a better idea how
your finished document will appear when it's printed, change to
Presentation Mode* by choosing ***View>Screen Mode>Presentation.***

* *If you're using InDesign CS4 or earlier you won't have Presentation Mode. Instead,
you can see the graphics in full quality by choosing **View>Display Performance>High
Quality Display.** You can use Preview mode **(View>Screen Mode>Preview)** to hide
elements that won't print, returning to Normal Mode using **View>Screen Mode>Normal.***

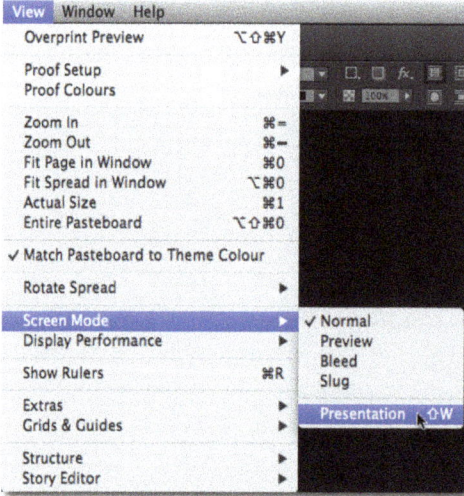

32. Presentation Mode changes InDesign to a full screen mode, hides everything that won't print and shows graphics at their full resolution. To leave Presentation Mode, press the **Esc key** at the top left of your keyboard.

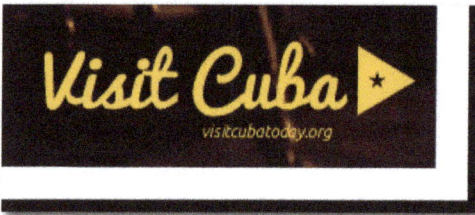

Summary of Menu commands

File>New>Document *[Command+N]*

File>Place *[Command+D]*

Edit>Select All *[Command+A]*

Edit >Undo *[Command+Z]*

View>Screen Mode>Presentation

Summary of Tools used

Rectangle Frame Tool

Selection Tool

Type Tool

Summary of shortcuts used

Command+2: view at 200% size
Command+0 (zero): Fit Page to Window
Alt + drag with Selection Tool: duplicate
Esc: leave Presentation Mode

Summary of Panels used

Swatches (to apply a colour to the text)
Control Panel (to change font and size of the text)

If things went wrong...

I kept creating more and more frames. *This is because when you're using a frame tool, InDesign assumes you will want to keep using it. So after you have created your frame, if you click or click and drag with the tool (for example to select, deselect or try and resize a frame) it will continue to create frames for you. If you change to the Selection Tool when you've created your frame(s) this won't happen. Select any frames you don't want with the Selection Tool and delete them by pressing the Delete key.*

I couldn't see all of my type. *Your frame wasn't big enough to accommodate all of the type, as indicated by the red Overset Mark in the bottom right corner. Either undo what you've done, or make the frame bigger by dragging one of the selection handles with the Selection Tool. Once you can see all your type, select it with the Type Tool and make it smaller. Then you can resize the frame back to the size you want it.*

I couldn't see the colour of the type change. *This is because (in the CS versions of InDesign) type that is highlighted is shown in its complementary colour. So, for example, black type will appear white, and yellow type will appear blue. Change to the Selection Tool to deselect the text and see the colour you've applied.*

2) Creating an A3 Poster

You're now going to create a poster that's similar to the flyer you have just created, but with two key differences. Firstly the picture goes right to the edge of the page, and secondly the text is more extensive.

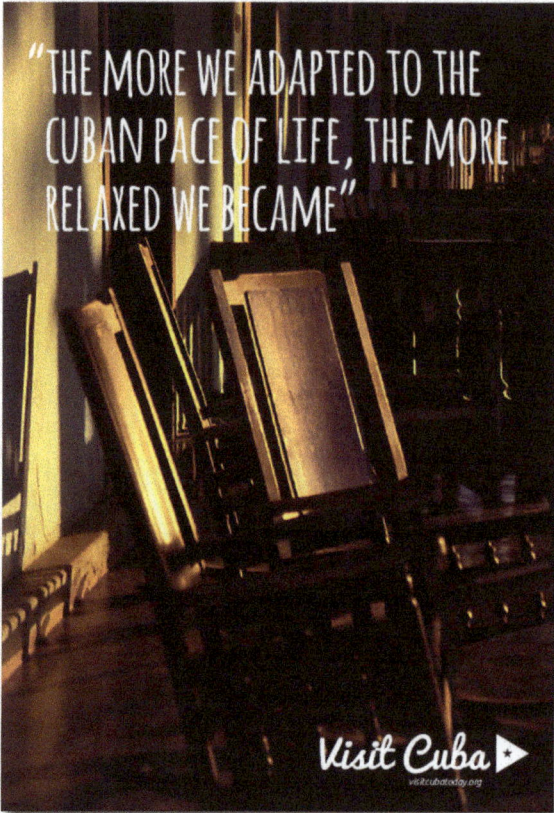

1. Choose **File>New>Document.**

2. Check that the **Document Preset** is set to *Default*.
    If it's not, select it in the pop up menu.

3. Change the **Page Size** from A4 to *A3*. At the bottom
    of the *New Document* dialogue box you should see a
    dropdown button next to the words **Bleed and Slug*.**

* *If you're using a version of InDesign prior to CC (any of the CS versions)
you'll instead press the* **More Options** *button towards the top right of the
New Document dialogue box to reveal the Bleed and Slug values.*

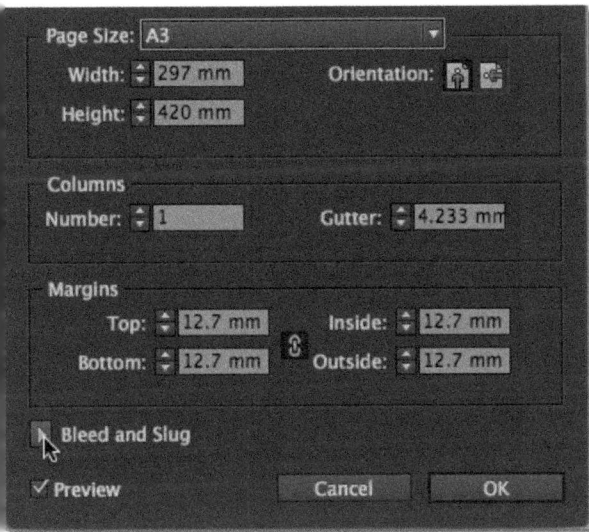

4. Once you can see the Bleed and Slug values, enter *3mm* for one of the *Bleed* values and click on the padlock to apply the same value to all edges of the document. Then press the **OK button.**

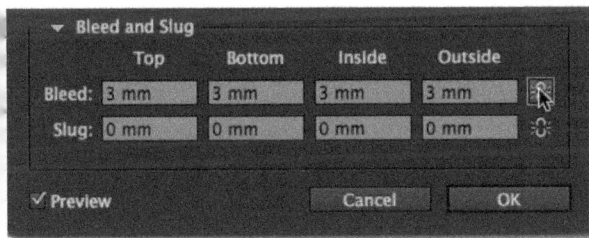

5. If you look at the edge of this document you'll see a red border outside the black border that you've seen on the previous document you created.

6. As you know, the black border indicates the edge of your document, but that's not the full story. When you send your InDesign document to a commercial printer they are often printed on sheets or rolls of paper that are larger than the document size. They are then trimmed down to size on a guillotine, whose blade is lined up with *Trim Marks* (see the diagram below).

7. The black border represents where the trimming should occur. However, as the guillotine blade runs through a stack of paper its blade may bend slightly, and your document may be trimmed slightly inside or outside the black line. To allow for this, any elements that need to appear right at the edge of a page need to continue, or 'bleed' over the edge. The Bleed Guide makes it straightforward to create bleeds, as objects snap to the guide. *3mm* is generally accepted as a suitable bleed amount for most work. Select the **Rectangle Frame Tool** and create a frame for the rocking chair picture, but this time drag from the red bleed guide outside the top left of the page and extend all the way down to the bleed guide outside the bottom right of the page.

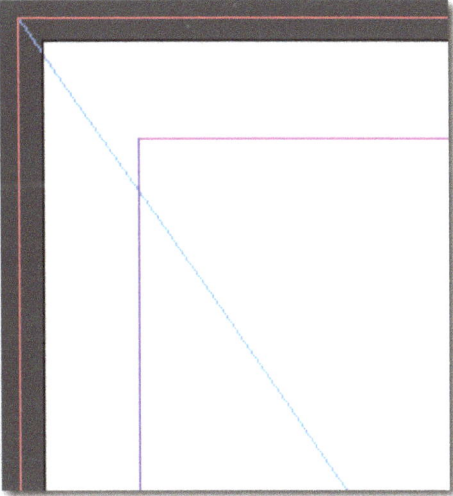

8. Change to the **Selection Tool** as you did earlier and choose
    File>Place to import the *visit-cuba-vinales-a3.jpg* image.

9.   As you did earlier, ensure nothing is selected and then import
     the *visit_cuba_white.eps* logo, positioning it at the bottom right
     of the page, aligned to the Margin Guides. As before, this vector
     graphic does not display in full quality. Earlier you viewed it in
     high quality by changing to presentation mode, but a way you
     can see it in full quality and keep working with it is by choosing
     View>Display Performance>High Quality Display.

10. Last time you created two separate frames for the display text, which
     gave you a flexible way of adjusting the two different pieces of text.
     More generally, text is created to be in a single frame, with attributes
     such as *Leading* and *Tracking* used to control its vertical and horizontal
     spacing. Create a new frame that snaps to the top, left and right margin
     guides, extending down about a third of the depth of the page.

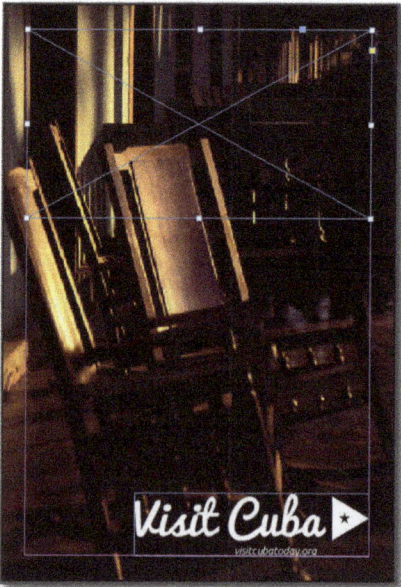

11. Click into this new frame with your **Type Tool,** and type the following quote in (including the quote marks, in lower case): *"the more we adapted to the cuban pace of life the more relaxed we became".* As this text is small you might find it easier to temporarily zoom in. To do this use the *Command + 2* shortcut again (use the *Command +0* shortcut to return to view the whole page).

12. Change the font to *Amatic*.* Adjust the **Font Size** to about *100pt.* Notice the value underneath the Font Size is *(120pt).* This is the *Leading* value, and describes the vertical space between the lines of type. The brackets indicate that the value is automatically calculated (by adding 20% on top of the font size).

* *You can of course use any font you wish, but I've created the branding for this company using this font. One of the reasons I've used it is because it's freely available for anyone to use. If you want to download the font, go to www.fontsquirrel.com and follow their instructions at www.fontsquirrel.com/help for help on how to download and install it.*

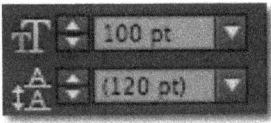

13. The default leading value is normally fine for general text, but for some fonts and typically at large sizes you might wish to override it. To bring the lines of type closer together, reduce the **Leading** value to around *100pt.*

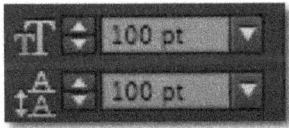

14. To make the upper case text slightly easier to read, you'll adjust the *Tracking* value, which allows you to adjust the amount of space between each character. Change the **Tracking** value to around *10,* which will add a subtle amount of space between each character. Then apply the *Paper (white)* swatch colour to the text.

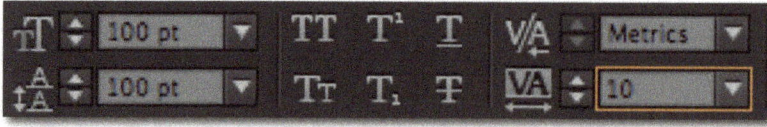

15. To indent the text so all the lines start inside the quote mark, place your cursor just after the opening quote mark and choose *Type>Insert Special Character>Other>Indent to here.* [Command + \]

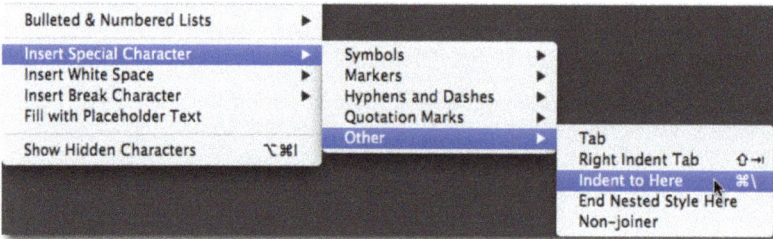

Summary of new Menu commands

Type>Insert Special Character>Other>Indent to here. *[Command + \]*
File>New Document: (Set up Bleed Guides)

Summary of new shortcuts used

Indent to here. *[Command + \]*

Summary of Panels used

Control Panel (to change leading and tracking)

3) Creating an A6 postcard

The next sort of document you're going to create will be a postcard. It's the sort of postcard you'll hopefully be familiar with, featuring a white border around a picture on the front, lines indicating where to write, and a guide to where to affix a stamp on the back. Whilst this is a fairly straightforward exercise, it would be a lot more complicated to do without making considered use of the Margin Guides.

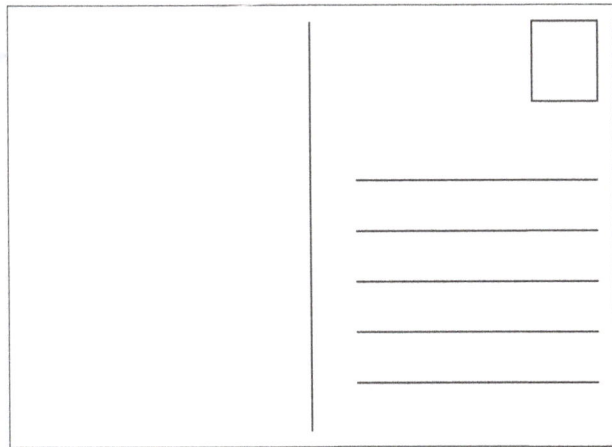

1. From the **File Menu** choose **New>Document** to create a new document. In the *New Document* dialogue box, you'll apply some settings to ensure this document is as easy to create as possible.

2. Change the **Number of Pages** to *2*. This is because to a printer, each 'side' of paper represents a page, so a postcard printing on both sides is a 2 page document.

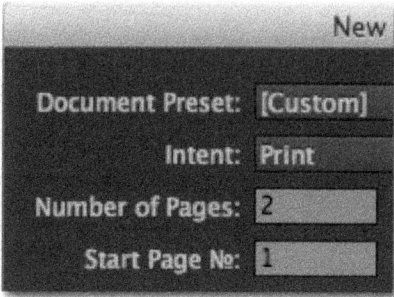

3. Turn **Facing Pages** *off.* Facing pages is suitable for documents that will have a spine, such as a book or a magazine*.

* *None of the documents you've created before have required facing pages, but it's not been mentioned until now to try and avoid imparting too much information at once.*

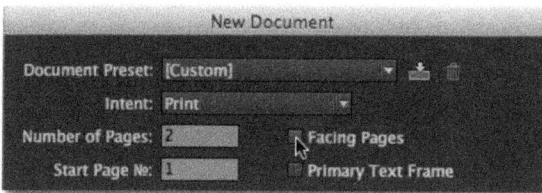

4. A typical postcard size is A6, but this is not available in InDesign's presets, so type these numbers in instead: **Width:***148mm;* **Height:***105mm*. Make sure the **Orientation** is set to *Landscape* (the button on the right). Using the same technique you've used before, change all the **Margin** values to *4mm*. Then press **OK.**

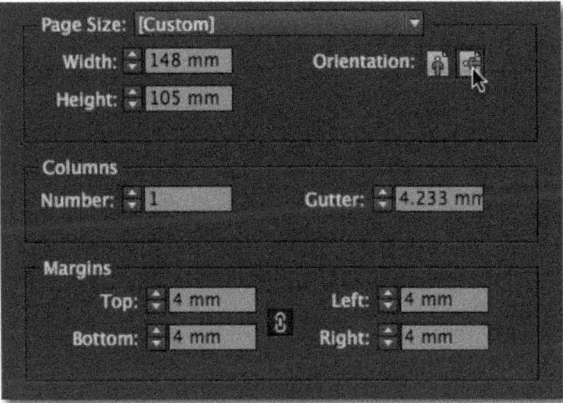

Page Size: [Custom]
Width: 148 mm   Orientation:
Height: 105 mm

Columns
Number: 1   Gutter: 4.233 mm

Margins
Top: 4 mm   Left: 4 mm
Bottom: 4 mm   Right: 4 mm

5. In this document you're going to make full use of the Margin Guides you've just set up. You're going to snap everything you create to them, making the process quicker, easier, more accurate and consistent. Select your **Rectangle Frame Tool** and draw a frame across the page, snapping to the Margin Guides at the corners (remember the arrow that appears if you're lined up with the guides).

6. Change to the **Selection Tool.** Choose **File>Place** and import *go-bolivia-a6.jpg*.

7. Deselect the frame by clicking somewhere outside the edge of the document, and change to Presentation Mode by choosing **View>Screen Mode>Presentation.** You should be able to see that the white space around the edge of the picture is consistent on every side. Press the **Esc** key to leave Presentation mode.

8. Using your **Selection Tool,** import the *go-adventures-white-strapline.ai* logo and place it in the bottom right corner of the page using the same technique you used when creating the *Visit Cuba* flyer and poster. If need be, adjust the size of the logo by dragging any of the corner handles (that look like squares) whilst holding down the ***Command*** and ***Shift*** keys simultaneously*.

* *To see it in full quality whilst you work with it, choose* **View>Display Performance>High Quality Display.**

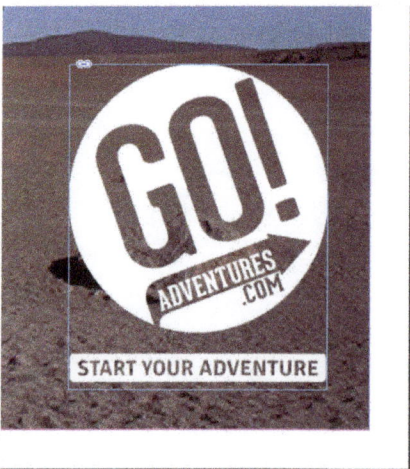

9. The front of the postcard is finished, so now you'll work on the back. Open the **Pages Panel** by clicking once on its name (it should be towards the top right of your screen). It shows all of the pages in your document, and you can go to a page by double clicking on its icon. **Double click** on the 2 icon to go to page 2. Then close the panel by clicking on its name once again.

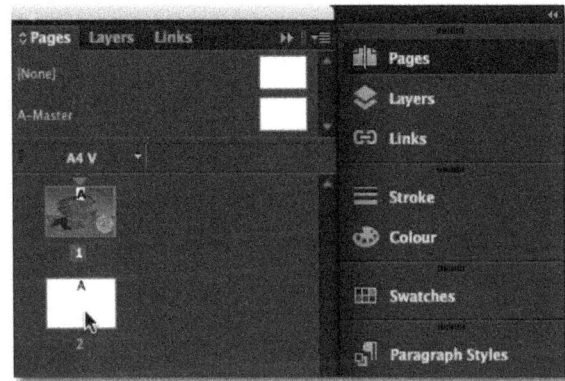

10. Page 2 is currently empty, but notice that the margin guides are the same as on page 1. This is because the Margin Guides you defined when you first created the document are applied by default to all its pages.

11. The screenshot below shows what the final postcard will look like. The first step is to create the frame that shows where the stamp will be stuck onto the postcard. Choose the **Rectangle Frame Tool** and create a frame of an appropriate shape, making sure you line up the top right corner with the Margin Guides.

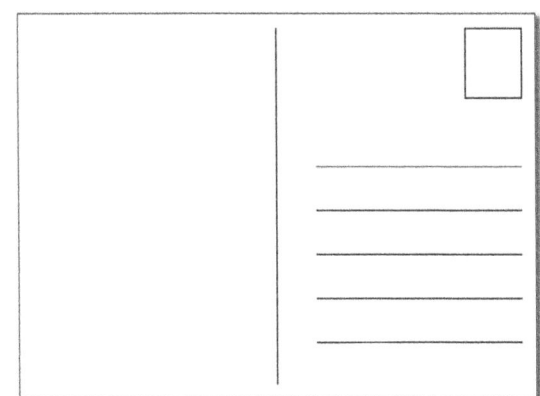

12. Before you change the colour of the frame it's worth knowing about how InDesign applies *fills* and *strokes* to objects. To do this you'll need to see the area in the Tools Panel that shows this to you. Unfortunately in recent versions of InDesign this area is so small that it's hard to clearly see what it's for, so the first thing to do is make it larger. To do this, click on the **tiny button** (that resembles a Fast Forward button) at the very top left of the Tools Panel which makes the panel two columns wide.

13. The area highlighted in the screenshot below describes the fill and stroke of the selected frame. The square on the top left describes its *fill* (the colour inside the frame) and the square on the bottom right describes its *stroke* (the colour around its edge). In this case, it's showing that both the fill and the stroke are *none* (or transparent).

14. When you click on the black swatch to change the colour of the frame it'll either be applied to the fill or the stroke, depending on which of the two squares is in the front. For example, if the fill square is in the front, this will be the result:

15. If, however, the stroke square is in front, this will be the result:

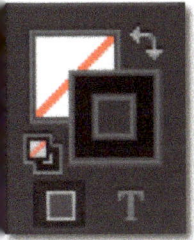

16. If you've inadvertently applied the black swatch to the fill, apply the *none* swatch to it instead by clicking in the area shown below, then click once on the *stroke square* to bring it to the front, before applying the black swatch again.

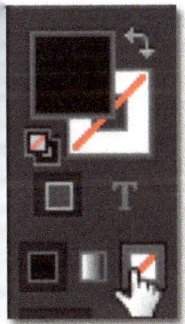

17. Next you'll create the vertical line in the centre of the postcard. Choose the *Line Tool* from the **Tools Panel.**

18. Line up your cursor with the pink margin guide (look for the arrow that indicates alignment), roughly in the centre of the page. Click and drag with your Line Tool in much the same way as you did with the **Rectangle Frame Tool,** only this time dragging directly downward. When you reach the margin guide at the bottom of the page, your line will probably not be completely straight. To constrain your line to make it straight, hold down the *Shift Key* and keep it down until you've let go of your mouse. If you didn't get the result you wanted, choose **Edit>Undo** and try again.

19. Look at the Fill and Stroke area of the Tools Panel. If the stroke of your Line is *none,* apply the *black* swatch to the stroke, like you just did to the stamp frame.

20. To position the line exactly in the (horizontal) centre of the page, select
it with the **Selection Tool** and drag slowly towards the horizontal centre
of the page. When the line is aligned centrally you should see a magenta
(pink) guide appear, running from the top down to the bottom of the
page. This is in addition to the guide that runs from the left to the right
of the page, which tells you that the line is aligned vertically central.

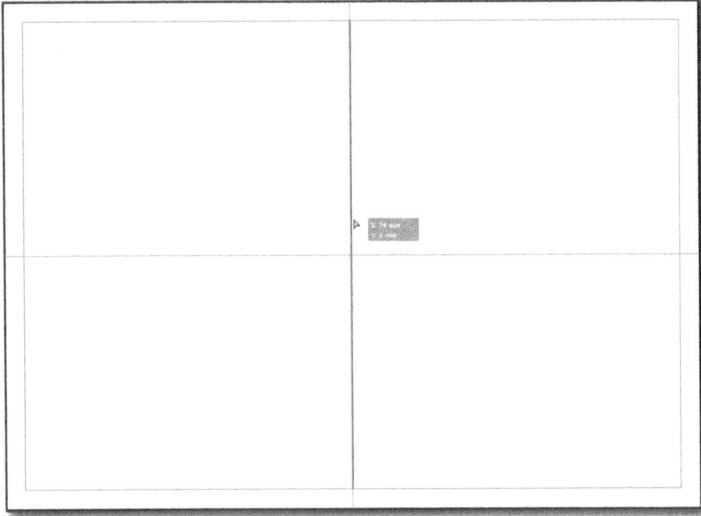

21. To create the first horizontal line, drag with the **Line Tool** from the guide
on the right hand side to the left. When you get near to the line you've
just drawn, hold down the **Shift Key** as you let go of the mouse, as before.

22. Ensure, as above, that the line's Stroke is *black*. You're now going to make several copies of this line at the same time. Change back to the **Selection Tool** and choose *Step and Repeat* from the **Edit Menu.**

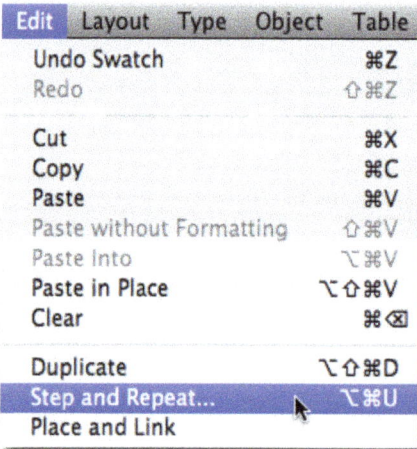

23. In the Step and Repeat dialogue box enter a **Count** value of *4,* a **Vertical offset** of *12mm,* and **Horizontal offset** value of *0mm* and then check the *Preview* checkbox. The preview shows 4 extra lines under the original, each one offset by 12mm. If at this point you would like to adjust the number of lines or how far they are separated, press the arrows next to the appropriate values and you'll see the preview change. Press the **OK button** when you've got the results you want.

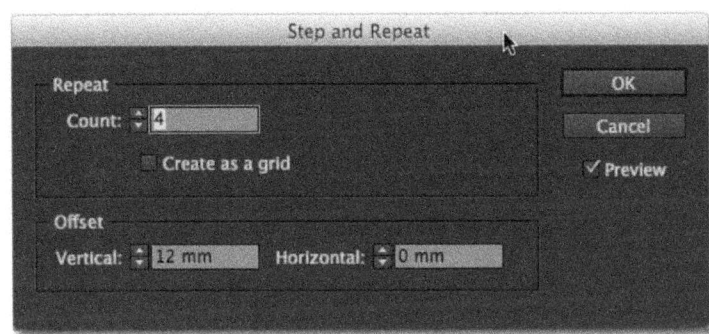

24. Check what the finished postcard looks like by deselecting everything, then changing to Presentation Mode. If any strokes are still *none* they will not show up in this Mode, as it only displays things that will appear when the document is printed. Notice how the stamp's frame is exactly the same distance from the edge of the postcard as both the vertical and horizontal lines. This was relatively easy to achieve by using the *4mm* Margin Guides; without it, this would have been a much more difficult task.

Summary of new menu commands used

Edit>Step and Repeat *[Command+Alt+U]*

Summary of new Tools used

Line Tool

Summary of new Panels used

Pages
Tools Panel: Fill and Stroke

Summary of new shortcuts used

Shift key: to keep lines straight

If things went wrong...

I accidentally created additional lines. *As with the Rectangle Frame Tool, you will continue to use the tool until you change to another tool – so you may unwittingly create additional lines. Either Undo or change to the Selection Tool and select and delete the extra lines.*

I couldn't create straight lines. *Make sure you continue to hold down the Shift key until after you've let go of the mouse button.*

I couldn't find my lines after I'd drawn them. *This is because the black colour hadn't been applied to the Stroke. It's a good idea to check this before you deselect the line, as it can be hard to locate if there is no stroke applied to it.*

The Step and Repeat Dialogue box wouldn't let me duplicate my lines. *This is probably because the offset values that were already in the dialogue box were too big to work on your document. If this happens, uncheck the Preview checkbox, adjust the values to the ones specified earlier, then check the Preview checkbox again.*

4) Creating a single page A5 Flyer

For this document you're once again going to use Margin Guides, within which you'll position various elements that will create a flyer. You'll make use of a feature called *Create Guides* that can really help you when designing pages from scratch. This will be your first look at working with a significant amount of text, and you'll learn how to place it in a document, about more complex formatting, and how to copy that formatting across to other text.

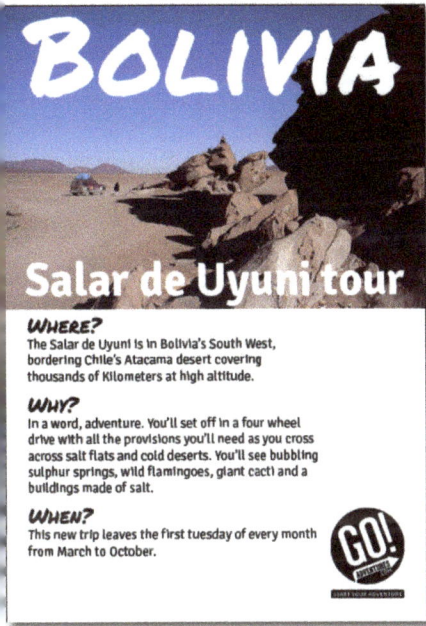

1. Create a new document. In the *New Document* dialogue box, turn off **Facing Pages,** change the **Page Size** to *A5,* make all the **Margins** *8mm* and create a *3mm* **Bleed** guide.

2. From the *Layout menu* choose **Create Guides.**

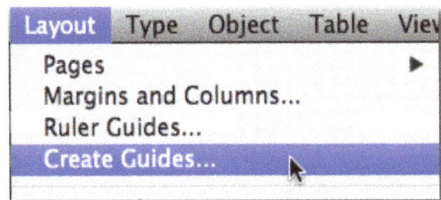

3. This feature places guides on the page, easily enabling you to break the page up into halves, thirds, quarters and so on. In the *Create Guides* dialogue box, choose *2* **Rows,** *4* **Columns** and set a *4mm* **Gutter** for each.

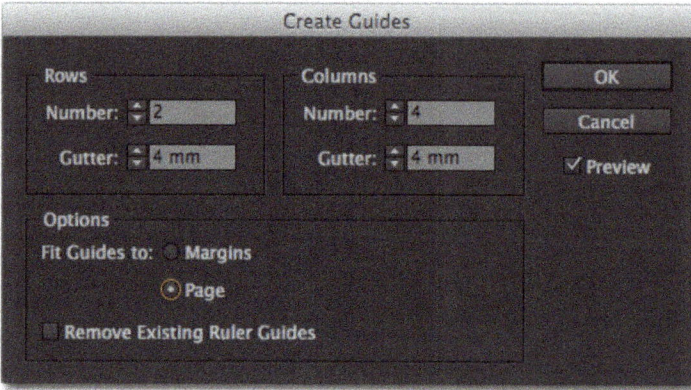

4. Using a combination of the bleed guides and the guides you've just created, draw a frame with the **Rectangle Frame Tool** that covers the top half of the page.

5. Change to the **Selection Tool** and import the *Bolivia-Uyuni-A5.jpg image.*

6. So far the images you've placed into InDesign have been carefully cropped so that you haven't had to get into repositioning or resizing them. But this image is more realistic in that it will need to be adjusted to fit properly. Notice that at the moment the edge of the Frame is *blue.* This indicates that the *Frame itself* is selected. However, if you double-click on the image you will now see a brown frame*.

*For users of InDesign older than CS5, change to the **Direct Selection Tool** (the white arrow) instead to adjust the picture as described above, then revert back to the **Selection Tool (the black arrow).**

7. The brown frame indicates that the *picture itself* is selected. This is why the brown frame is not exactly the same shape and size as the blue frame. If you press and hold down the mouse, any area of the picture that's outside the blue Frame will be seen, but will be ghosted out*.

*PC users might find they need to move their mouse slightly to see the remainder of the image.

8. If you want to reposition the picture, drag your mouse and the picture will move within the frame. If you want to resize your picture, drag one of the brown corner handles, but make sure you hold down the **Shift Key** as you drag to keep the shape of the picture in proportion.

9. Once you're finished adjusting the image, create a new frame on top of it that aligns with the Margin Guides and covers about a third of the depth of the picture.

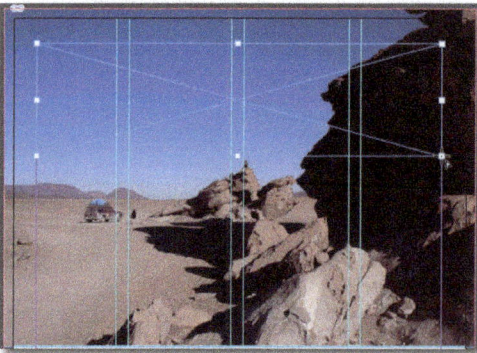

10. Click on the Frame with the **Type Tool** and type *"bolivia"* (in lower
    case) into the frame. Drag over the text to select it and change the
    Font to *Permanent Marker** and the **Font Size** to *100pt,* increasing it
    using the up arrow to the left of the font size to make it fill as much
    of the width of the frame as possible. If you feel the text would
    look better with either more or less space between the letters,
    adjust the Tracking. Change the colour of the text to *White.*

* *Permanent Marker is available from the Font Squirrel website, as mentioned previously.*

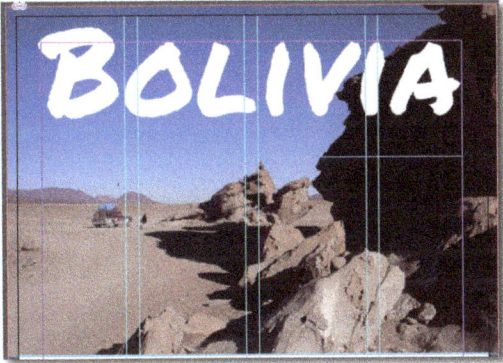

11. Create another frame near the bottom of the image, aligning
    it with the Margin Guides as you did earlier. Type *"Salar de
    Uyuni Tour"* and change the **Font** to *Signika*,* the **Weight** to
    Bold and adjust the **Size** and **Tracking** to make it fit across the
    width, as above. Change the colour of the text to *White.*

* *Signika is also available from the Font Squirrel website.*

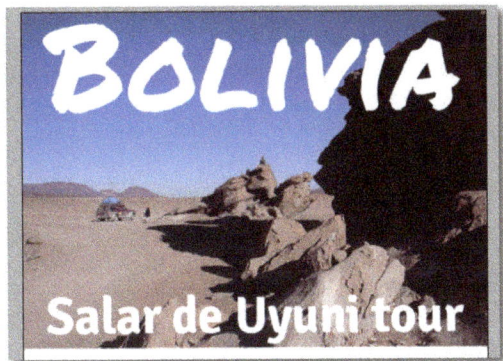

12. Create a third frame, this one aligning to the guides so that it starts half way down the page, and extends from the margin guide on the left, across three-quarters of the page and down to the margin guide at the bottom.

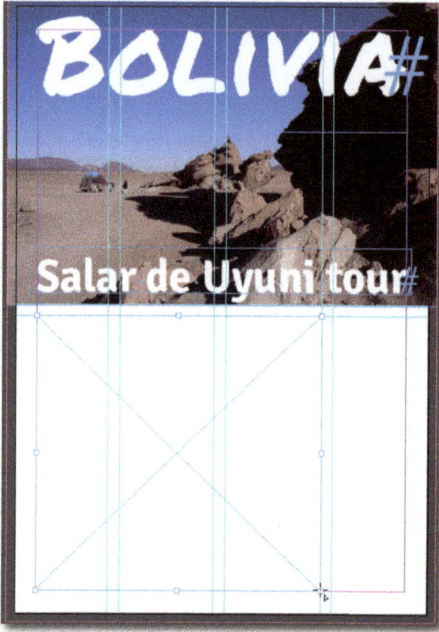

13. Click in the new frame with the **Type Tool.** Instead of typing anything, this time you're going to import some text that's already been typed.

14. Just as with a picture, to import text choose the **File>Place** command. Select the *go-bolivia-uyuni-sales.txt* file and press the **Open** button. The text flows into the frame that your cursor was in.

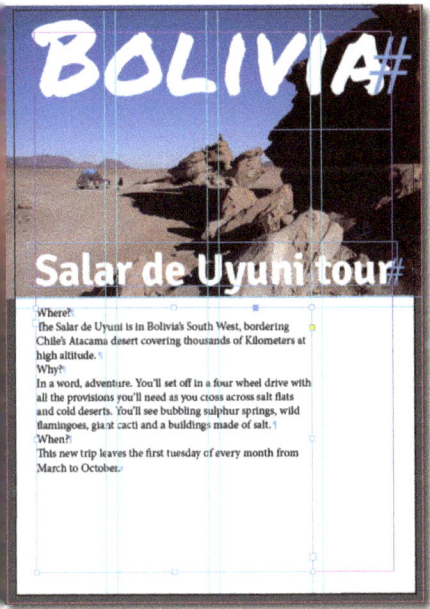

15. The changes you've made so far to text have included changing the Font, and adjusting the type's Size, Weight, Leading and Tracking. These are all *Character Formats.* At the risk of pointing out the obvious, this means that the changes you make will only affect the characters that are selected. This is in contrast with *Paragraph Formats,* which you'll shortly use to affect a whole paragraph. To be able to see this a bit more clearly, it will help to use a command that will show you where the paragraphs begin and end.

16. Choose **Type>Show Hidden Characters.** You'll then see characters that, whilst they will not print, are nevertheless an essential component of text. Spaces are indicated by a simple dot (this is a useful way to find double spaces in text) and a paragraph symbol is one of these: ¶. This shows you where a paragraph ends (one appears every time you hit the **Return key** whilst typing). For now the important thing to grasp is that everything in between two of these paragraph symbols is a paragraph.

Where?
The Salar de Uyuni i
Chile's Atacama dese
high altitude.
Why?

17. The most straightforward way to select a whole paragraph of text, is to quadruple-click on it (or, click in it four times in quick succession) with the **Type Tool.** Select the second of the long paragraphs by **quadruple-clicking** on it.

Where?
The Salar de Uyuni is in Bolivia's South West, bordering Chile's Atacama desert covering thousands of Kilometers at high altitude.
Why?
In a word, adventure. You'll set off in a four wheel drive with all the provisions you'll need as you cross across salt flats and cold deserts. You'll see bubbling sulphur springs, wild flamingoes, giant cacti and a buildings made of salt.
When?

18. Change the **Font** to *Signika,* the **Weight** to *Regular* and the **Size** to *13pt.*

Signika 13 pt
Regular (15.6 pt)

19. When using the **Type Tool** if you look at the **Control Panel** you'll see there are two icons at the top left of the Panel. These are *buttons:* the top one gives you access to the *Character Formatting* options, and the bottom one gives you access to the *Paragraph Formatting* options. You've just applied some of the Character options, now you'll change one of the Paragraph ones, so press the *¶ button.*

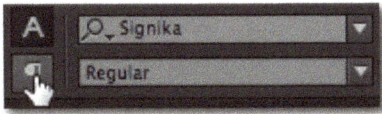

20. Uncheck **Hyphenate** to prevent the text in this paragraph
    from automatically having a hyphen applied to it.

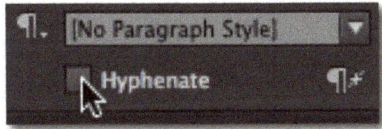

21. With the paragraph still selected, choose the *Eyedropper*
    Tool from the **Tools Panel** and click once on the paragraph
    you've just worked on. This takes the formatting from this
    paragraph and allows you to apply it to other paragraphs*

* *This is fine for short documents, but for longer documents you've be advised to use*
  Paragraph Styles, which is beyond the scope of this book, but is covered in detail in
  our "Creating Leaflets with InDesign" and "Creating Newsletters with InDesign" books.

The Salar de Uyuni is in Bolivia's South West,
bordering Chile's Atacama desert covering
thousands of Kilometers at high altitude.

22. Using the paragraph symbols to guide you, using the **Eyedropper,**
    click and drag carefully through each of the longer paragraphs
    in turn to apply the same formatting to each of them.

Where?

The Salar de Uyuni is in Bolivia's South West,
bordering Chile's Atacama desert covering
thousands of Kilometers at high altitude.
Why?

In a word, adventure. You'll set off in a four wheel
drive with all the provisions you'll need as you cross
across salt flats and cold deserts. You'll see bubbling
sulphur springs, wild flamingoes, giant cacti and a
buildings made of salt.
When?

This new trip leaves the first tuesday of every month
from March to October.

23. With your **Type Tool** select the paragraph that simply consists of the word *"Why?"* Press the **Character Formatting** button, change the **Font** to *Permanent Marker,* and the **Size** to around *20pt.*

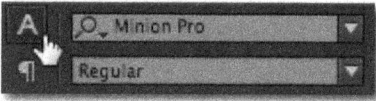

24. Press the ¶ button to access the paragraph formatting options and apply a **Space Before** value of *2mm* to increase the space above the heading.

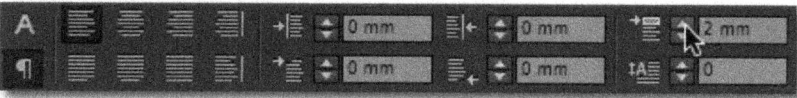

25. Use the **Eyedropper** as you did before to apply the formatting to the other two short paragraphs (*"Where?"* and *"When?"*)

WHERE?
The Salar de Uyuni is in Bolivia's South West, bordering Chile's Atacama desert covering thousands of Kilometers at high altitude.

WHY?
In a word, adventure. You'll set off in a four wheel drive with all the provisions you'll need as you cross across salt flats and cold deserts. You'll see bubbling sulphur springs, wild flamingoes, giant cacti and a buildings made of salt.

WHEN?
This new trip leaves the first tuesday of every month from March to October.

26. To finish the flyer, change to the **Selection Tool,** and making sure nothing is selected choose **File>Place.** Select the *go-adventures-black.ai* logo and position it at the bottom right of the page. Use **Presentation Mode** to look at the finished flyer at full quality.

Summary of new Menu commands

File>Place (for text instead of a picture) *[Command+D]*

Layout>Create Guides

Type>Show Hidden Characters *[Command+Alt+I]*

Summary of new Tools used

Eyedropper Tool

Summary of Panels used

Control Panel (to adjust Hyphenate and Space Before)

5) An A5 flyer with a cut out

This flyer uses an image that has been cut out in Photoshop – something you can't do in InDesign – but of course you can import these images and use them in your work. As you can see, having an image that is not rectangular makes it look a great deal different from everything you've created so far.

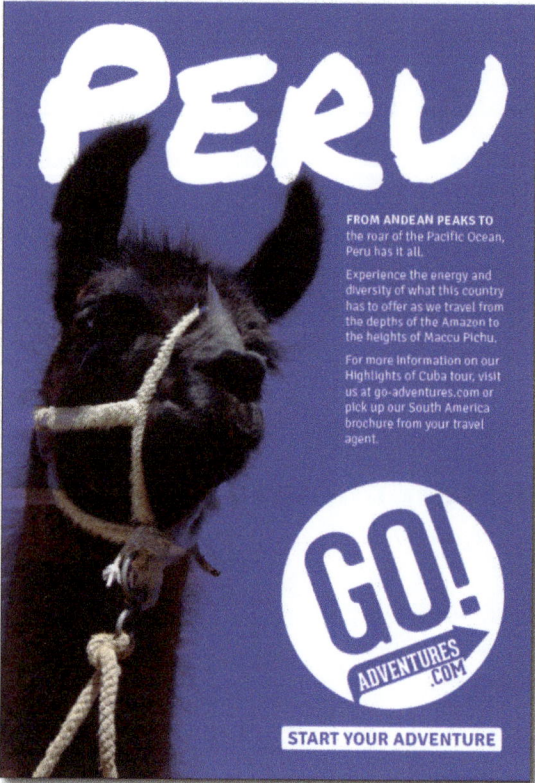

1. Create a new document. In the *New Document* dialogue box, turn off **Facing Pages,** change the **Page Size** to *A5,* make all the **Margins** *8mm* and create a *3mm* **Bleed** guide.

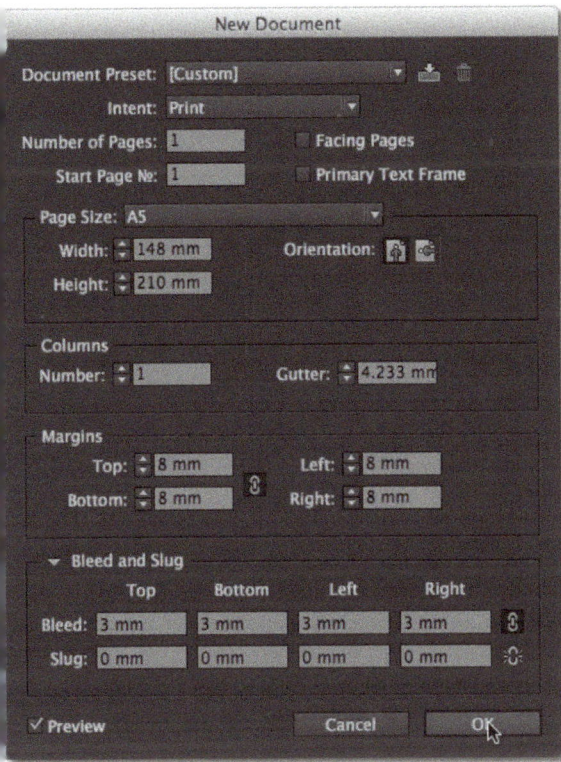

2. Snapping to the (red) bleed guides, draw a frame with the **Rectangle Frame Tool** that covers the entire page. Change to the **Selection Tool** and change the **Fill colour** of the frame to *dark blue*.

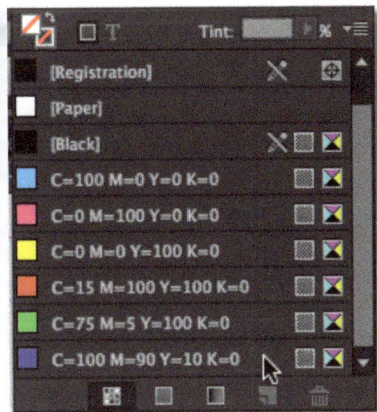

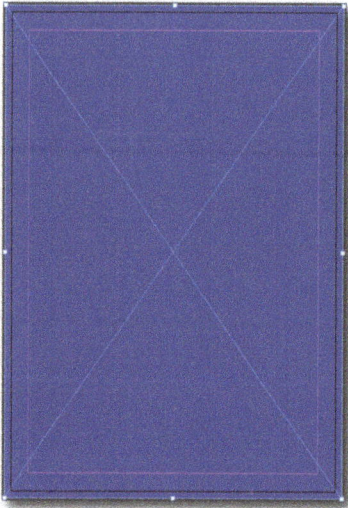

3. Once again you'll use Guides to help you design your page. From the **Layout menu** choose **Create Guides,** and choose *8* **Rows,** *3* **Columns,** set a *0mm* **Gutter** for each and make sure the guides fit to the **Margins.**

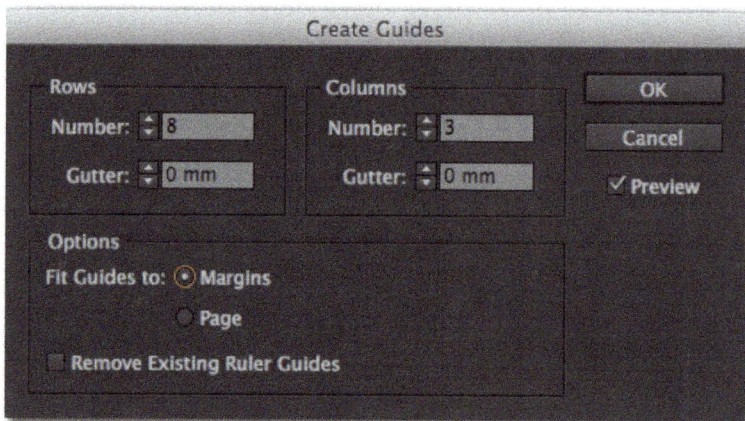

4. As you have done previously, using the **Rectangle Frame Tool,** create a frame across the top of the page, aligned to the top, left and right Margin Guides, and extending about a quarter of the depth of the page. Change to the **Type Tool,** type "Peru" into the frame and fill the width of the frame with the type (using *Permanent Marker,* colour *White* at a size of roughly *170pt).* Adjust the position of the frame with the Selection Tool if you want to.

5. Notice how the guides divide up the page into a grid of twenty four rectangular areas. Create another frame that more of less aligns to the area defined by the grid, as shown below.

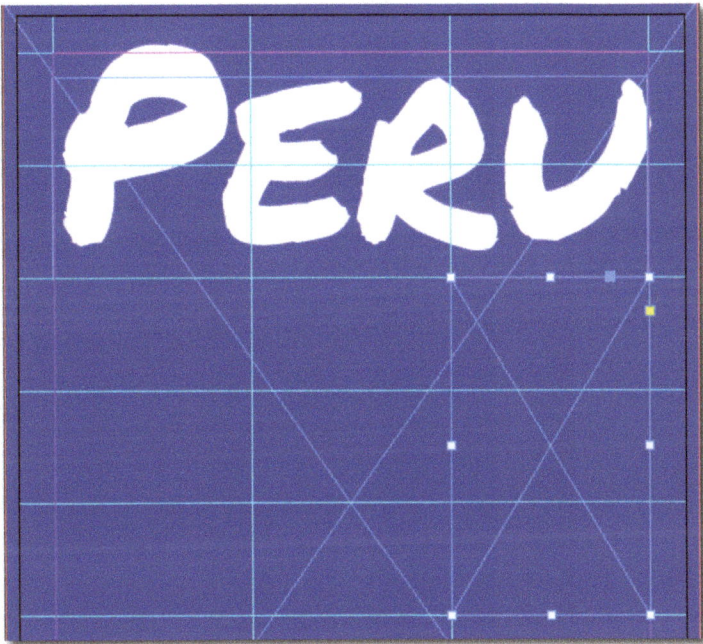

6. Click in the frame with your **Type Tool** and choose **File>Place** to import the *go-peru-sales.txt* file.

7. Click five times to select all of the text, and change its character formatting as follows: **Font:** *Signika;* **Weight:** *Light;* **Size:** *10pt;* **Tracking:** *10.* Adjust its paragraph formatting as follows: turn off **hyphenation** and apply a *2mm* **Space Before.**

8. To add emphasis to the start of the text, select the first four words, change their **Weight** to *Bold,* and press the **All Caps** button (to the right of the font size).

9. As you did before, change to the **Selection Tool,** click off the edge of the page to ensure nothing is selected, and place in the *go-adventures-white-strapline.ai* logo towards the bottom right of the page. Adjust the size of the logo by dragging any of the corner handles (that look like squares) whilst holding down the **Command** and **Shift** keys simultaneously. Try and size the logo so that it is roughly three grid squares deep.

10. You're about to import an image of a Llama that has been cut out using a *layer mask* in Photoshop. This means that its background has been hidden, and that even though you'll be importing the whole image, some parts of it will be transparent. Just as it can be easier to place a logo using the **Selection Tool** (without creating a frame for it first), this can also be the case with cut out images. Choose the Selection Tool and ensure nothing is selected. Choose **File>Place** and import *llama-cutout.psd*.

11. As with the previous logos that you've imported, click and drag to position the Llama so that it fits around the other elements on the page, resizing if necessary by dragging a corner handle whilst holding down the **Command** and **Shift** keys.

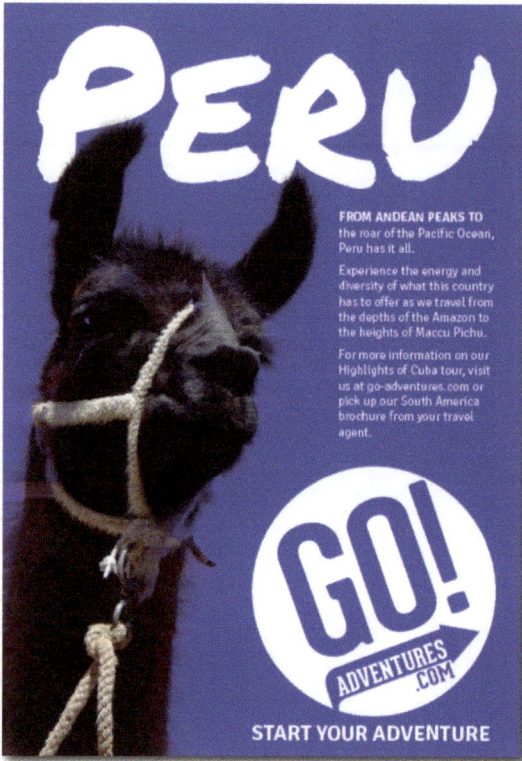

Within the flyer image: PERU — FROM ANDEAN PEAKS TO the roar of the Pacific Ocean, Peru has it all. Experience the energy and diversity of what this country has to offer as we travel from the depths of the Amazon to the heights of Maccu Pichu. For more information on our Highlights of Cuba tour, visit us at go-adventures.com or pick up our South America brochure from your travel agent. GO! ADVENTURES.COM START YOUR ADVENTURE

12. Images that contain transparent elements (like the transparent pixels that surround the body of the Llama) can sometimes affect the output of adjacent text when images are printed. For that reason it's advisable to make a couple of changes to the text in the document, which won't affect the design, but should prevent potential problems occurring. Firstly, select the frame on the right containing the descriptive text and choose **Object>Arrange>Bring to Front.** This is because text in front of transparent objects shouldn't be affected.

13. Of course you could also do this to the *Peru* text at the top, but if you want to keep the text behind the image for creative reasons you'll need to use a different approach. Select the frame containing the Peru text with the Selection Tool and choose **Create Outlines** from the **Type menu.** This text has now been converted into a vector graphic, so it's no longer strictly text and won't be affected by the transparency in the image (as it's no longer text, this also means that to make it bigger of smaller you'd have to scale it as you would a logo).

New Menu Commands used

Object>Arrange>Bring to Front *Command+Shift+]*
Type>Create Outlines *Command+Shift+O*

6) A5 flyer with a transparent panel

The final document you'll create will be a modified version of the first document you created – the A5 flyer for Visit Cuba.

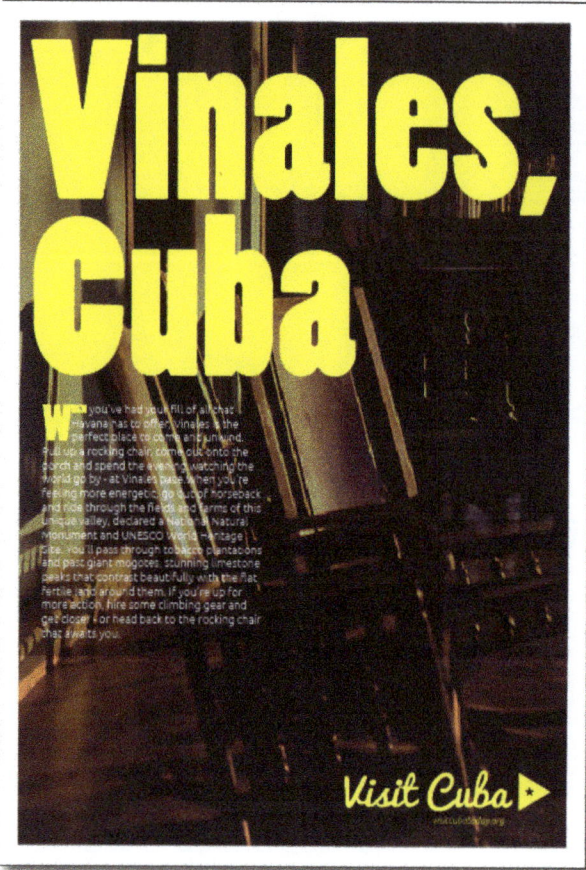

1. From the **File Menu** choose *Open,* and in the dialogue box choose the A5 Vinales flyer you created earlier. Again from the **File Menu** choose *Save As,* and save a copy with a different name so that you don't overwrite your initial work.

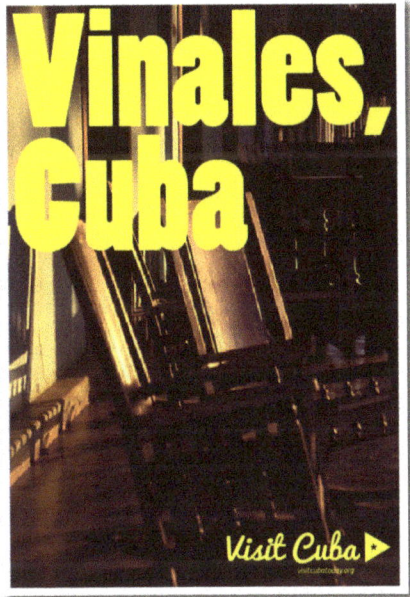

2. With the **Rectangle Frame Tool,** create a new frame underneath
the display text that's roughly half the width of the page
and extending roughly two-thirds of the way down it.

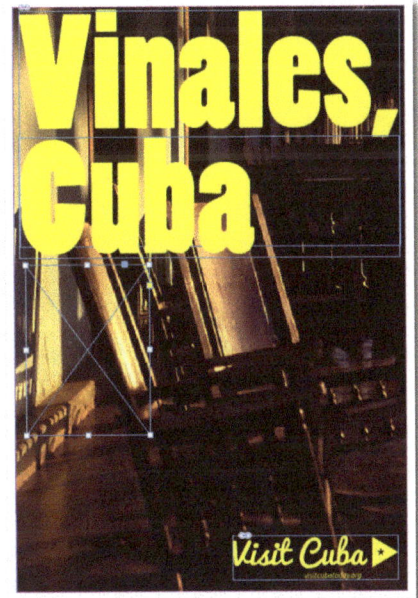

3. Click in the frame with your **Type Tool** and choose **File>Place** to import the *visit-cuba-vinales-a5.txt*

4. Click five times to select all of the text, and change its character formatting as follows: **Font:** *Ubuntu;* **Weight:** *Light;* **Size:** *8pt.*

* *Ubuntu is available from the Font Squirrel website, as mentioned previously.*

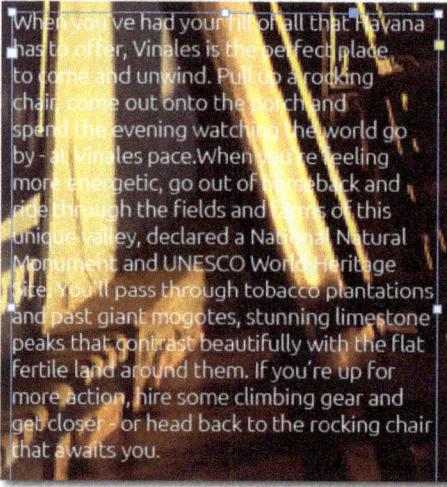

When you've had your fill of all that Havana has to offer, Vinales is the perfect place to come and unwind. Pull up a rocking chair, come out onto the porch and spend the evening watching the world go by - at Vinales pace.When you're feeling more energetic, go out of horseback and ride through the fields and farms of this unique valley, declared a National Natural Monument and UNESCO World Heritage Site.You'll pass through tobacco plantations and past giant mogotes, stunning limestone peaks that contrast beautifully with the flat fertile land around them. If you're up for more action, hire some climbing gear and get closer - or head back to the rocking chair that awaits you.

5. Adjust its paragraph formatting by turning off **Hyphenation.** To add emphasis to the start of the text, apply a ***Drop Cap*** to the first three lines of the text, by typing the number *3* in the area shown below.

6. This certainly makes the start of the text distinctive from the text that follows, but it would look better if it repeated elements that had been previously used, notably the *Poplar* font, the uppercase text and the yellow colour. To do this, highlight the first word of the text, change the **Font** to *Poplar Std,* press the **All Caps** button and change the **Swatch** to *Yellow.*

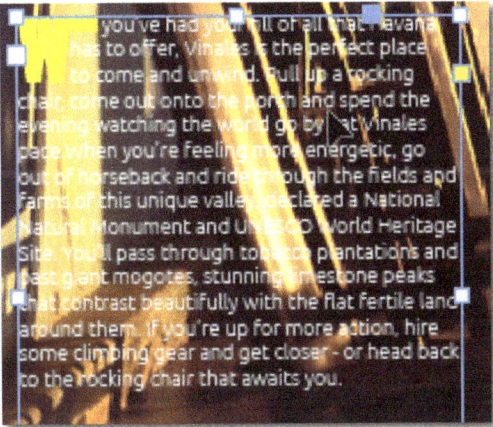

7. If you look carefully at the text you might find it slightly difficult to read over the top of the image. A way to overcome this is to place a semi-transparent block of colour underneath the text. To do this, use the **Rectangle Frame Tool** to create a frame that aligns to the top, left and right margins of the document, and extends down just below the text. Change the **Fill** colour of this frame to *Black.*

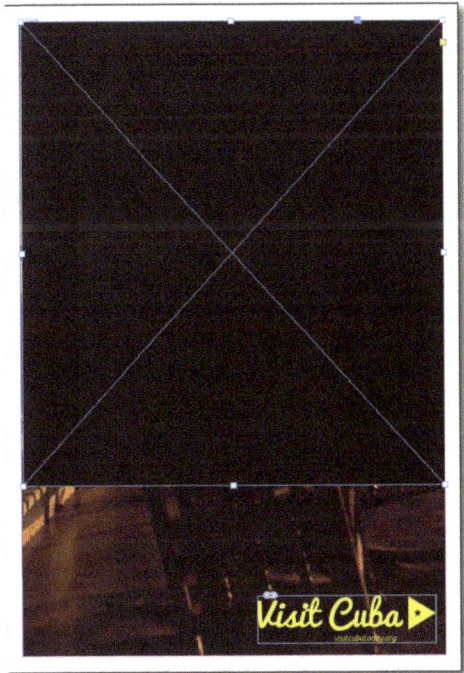

8. Clearly the results so far are not great, in that, as the new frame is the latest thing you've created, it's placed on top of the three text frames. To adjust this, from the **Object menu** choose ***Arrange>Send Backward.*** This places it further back in the stacking order.

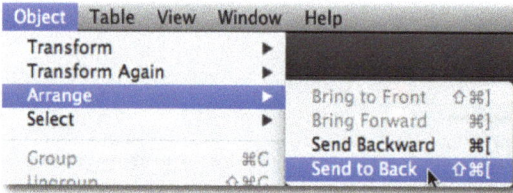

9. Repeat this as many times as necessary to position the black frame behind the text, yet still in front of the image.

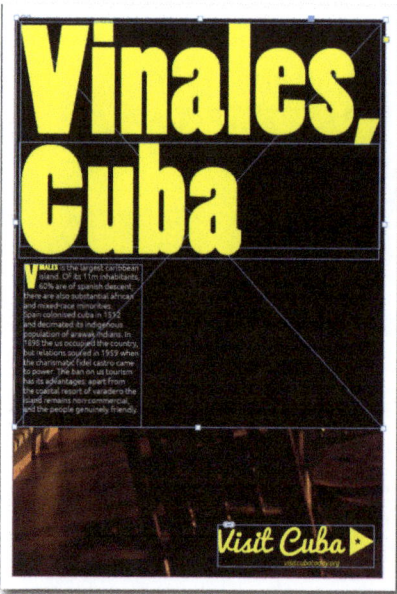

10. To make this look a bit more subtle, from the **Window menu** choose **Effects.** Click on the drop down menu that says *"Normal"* and change the blending mode to *Darken.* The blending mode controls how transparency is calculated – in this case, by combining the elements in a way that always produces a darker result.

11. Drag the slider found underneath the word **Opacity** to around *30%*, which should hopefully make the text easier to read without losing too much of the image detail underneath.

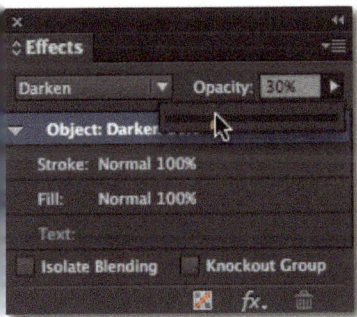

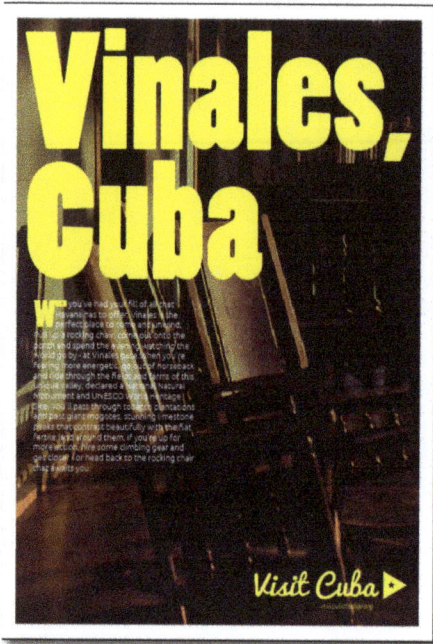

New commands used

Object>Arrange>Send Backward *Command+[*
Window>Effects *Command+Shift+F10*

From Aruba to Zanzibar Plan your dream escape
Ocean Hotels — Visit www.ocean-hotels.com for inspiration

From Aruba to Zanzibar Plan your dream escape
Ocean Hotels — Visit www.ocean-hotels.com for inspiration

From the Turquoise coast of Turkey to the Carribean coast of Cuba, we know we've got somewhere in the world that's just right for you.

Find your perfect escape with us.
Visit **www.ocean-hotels.com** for inspiration.

Ocean Hotels

DISCOVER Cultural Tours
Discover Japan with us
To receive our Japan brochure
Call 023445 3456123 or visit
www.discover-tours.com

Discover Japan with us
DISCOVER Cultural Tours

Discover Angkor with us
DISCOVER Cultural Tours

Pacific Coast, Mexico. Wish you were here?
Ocean Hotels

Discover Europe with us
From deserted Greek islands to street markets in Turkey, we'll show you the very best that Europe can offer even the most seasoned traveller. Leave it all to us, and discover it with us.

To receive our Europe brochure call **02344 3456123**
or visit **www.discover-tours.com**

DISCOVER Cultural Tours

CREATING ADVERTS

This chapter is about creating adverts. There are eight in total, each one more complex than the last. The adverts are created for two fictitious companies, *Ocean Hotels* and *Discover Cultural Tours.* As with any real company, they have had logos designed, and they use particular typefaces and colours in their branding. When placing an advert in a publication you will buy a space of a certain size (which will be a proportion of the publication's page, for example a quarter of the page), and that size will be the dimensions used when creating the advert.

1) A B&W advert for Ocean Hotels

The first thing you'll create in InDesign is a simple black and white advert for *Ocean Hotels.*

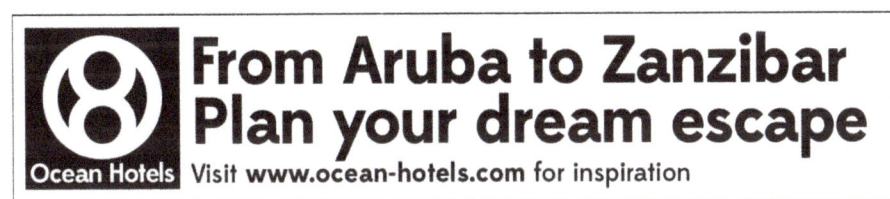

1. From InDesign's **File menu** choose **New>Document**.

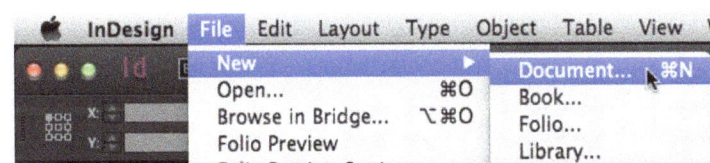

2. Look at the top of the *New Document* dialogue box to check that the *Document Preset* is set to *[Default].* If it's not, select it from the pop up menu you can see there.

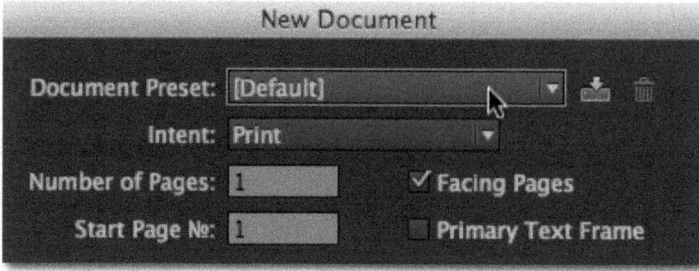

3. When creating an advert you're governed by the size of the ad space that you or someone from your organisation has bought. These are all imaginary adverts for imaginary companies, but they will be produced to a variety of specifications that will be mentioned at the beginning of each exercise. This advert is for a black and white publication, and the size of the advert is to be *145mm* wide by *30mm* high.

4. In the *New Document dialogue box,* firstly uncheck **Facing Pages,** then change the **Width** to *145mm* and the **Height** to *30mm*.

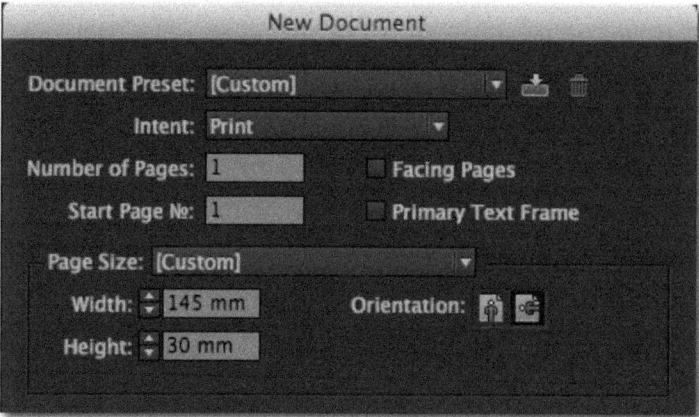

5. Next, change all the **Margin** values to *2mm*. The easiest way to do this is to change the **Top** margin value and then click on the padlock to copy the value into the *Bottom, Left* and *Right* boxes. Then press the **OK button.**

5. You can now see a blank InDesign document. The black
    rectangle represents the document's edge, and the pink/
    purple lines are its *Margin Guides*. These guides can be used
    in a variety of ways, but in this case you'll use them to define
    where the edge of the Ocean Hotels logo is going to be.

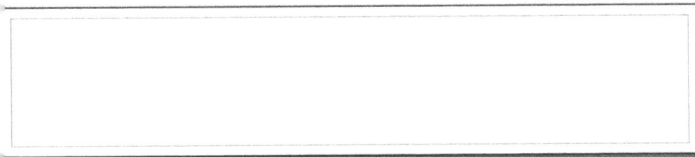

7. The first action you'll take to create this advert is to bring in the Ocean
    Hotels logo. To do this, firstly choose the **Selection Tool** by clicking
    on it at the top of the **Tools Panel** on the left of your screen.

8. Next, choose **Place** from the **File menu.**

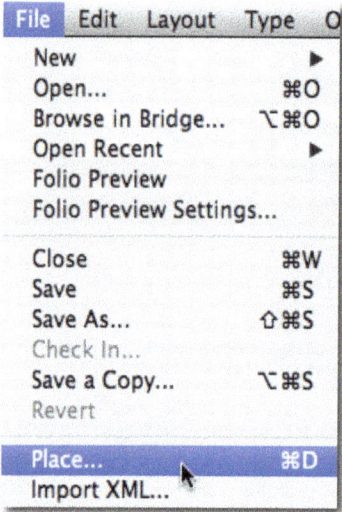

File Edit Layout Type O

New	▶
Open...	⌘O
Browse in Bridge...	⌥⌘O
Open Recent	▶
Folio Preview	
Folio Preview Settings...	
Close	⌘W
Save	⌘S
Save As...	⇧⌘S
Check In...	
Save a Copy...	⌥⌘S
Revert	
Place...	⌘D
Import XML...	

9. From the dialogue box that appears, find the *Creative Classroom Adverts* folder and from within that select the *ocean_hotels_wob.eps* file.

10. The logo will attach to your cursor.

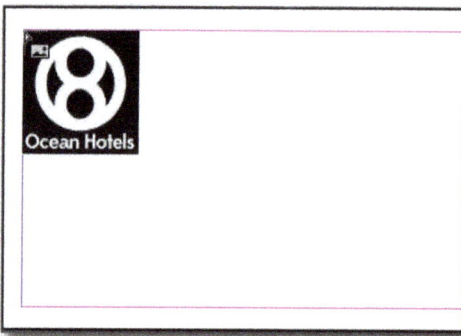

11. To place it in the document, click and drag from near the top right corner of the document where the pink/purple margin guides meet, diagonally down to the right until your cursor aligns with the margin at the bottom of the advert. This approach ensures that you will create a frame that's exactly the same shape as the logo, at whatever size you choose. If you didn't quite get the size you wanted, choose **Edit>Undo** to remove the logo from the page and reattach it to your cursor so you can try again.

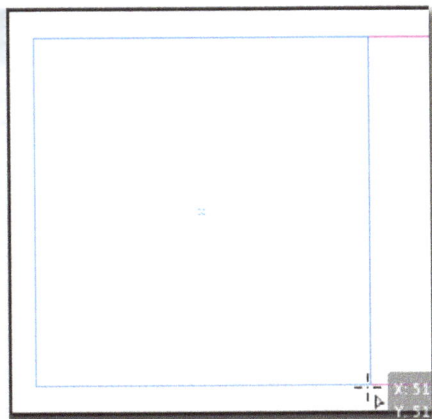

12. By default, when you bring in a logo or similar vector graphic (see *Images from Photoshop and Illustrator* in the *Brief Notes* section) you'll not see it at full quality. To get a better idea how it'll look when it's printed, choose **View>Display Performance>High Quality Display***.

* *You might find that working in high quality display mode slows your computer down. If it does and you want to return to the default mode, choose* **View>Display Performance>Typical Display.**

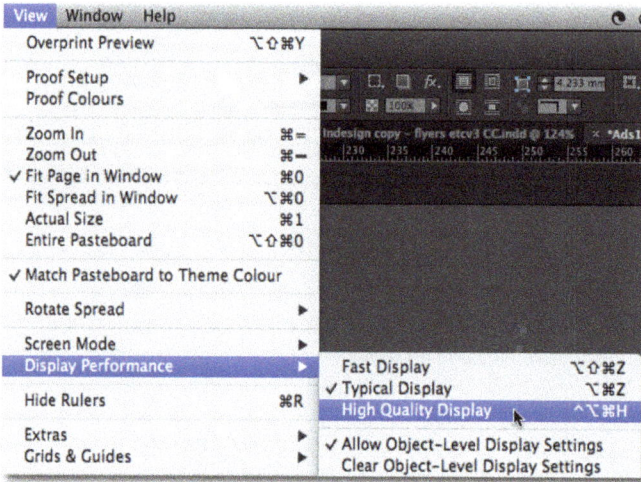

13. To create the large text for this first advert you'll firstly
need to create a frame to put it in*. To do this, firstly select
the ***Rectangle Frame Tool*** from the **Tools Panel.**

** Everything in InDesign is placed inside a frame. Even though you didn't create
the frame for the logo you just imported, InDesign created it for you.*

14. Now you're using the Rectangle Frame Tool, InDesign is expecting you
to create a frame in which to put a picture or text. Notice that it has a
plain crosshair at the moment. Align it to the top margin guide*, leaving
a similar amount of space to the right of the logo as there is on its left.

** Notice that when you place the crosshair on the margin, a little arrow
appears to let you know you're accurately lined up with it.*

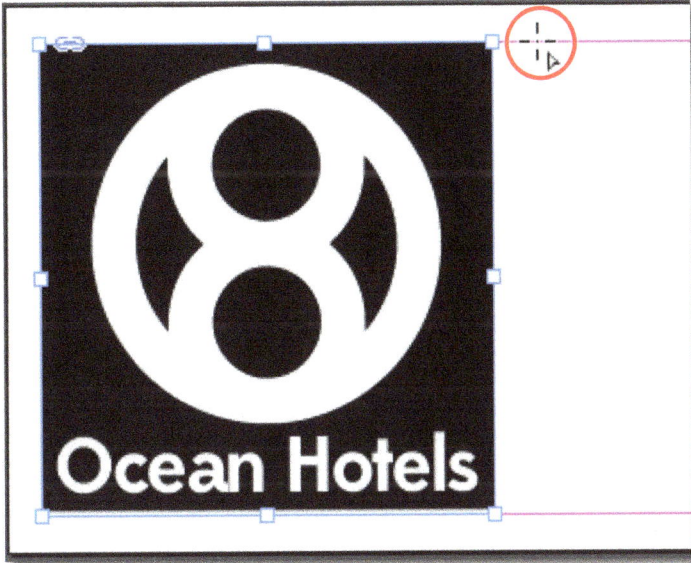

15. Press your mouse button down, and keeping it down, drag to the intersection of the margin guides near the bottom right of the advert, letting go when you see the little arrow appear to let you know you're accurately lined up. Once you've let go, you'll have created an empty frame.

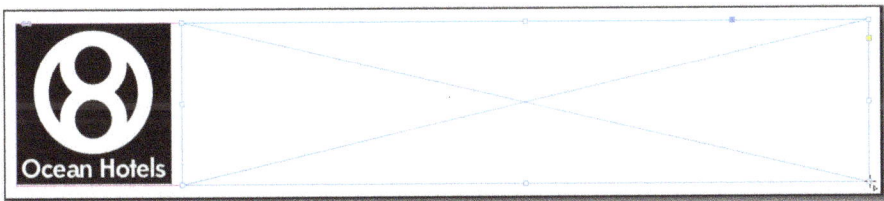

16. Notice that you're still using the Rectangle Frame Tool, so if you either click, or click+drag, InDesign will try and create a new frame for you. To prevent this happening, change back to the **Selection Tool** once you've drawn your frame*.

* *If you've inadvertently created extra frames, choose* **Edit>Undo** *to retrace your steps and remove them.*

17. Making sure you're using the **Selection Tool,** click on the frame you've just made. You can tell it's selected if you can see square *handles* around its edge. Notice the large *X* in the frame, indicating that the frame is currently empty.

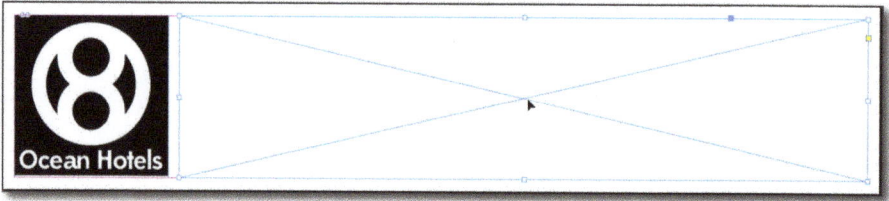

18. Select the *Type Tool* from the **Tools Panel.**

19. Click on the newly created frame with the **Type Tool.** You should now see that the X has now disappeared, and instead contains a flashing cursor, indicating that InDesign is expecting you to type something.

20. Type the words *"From Aruba to Zanzibar"* then press the *Return* key on your keyboard to start a new paragraph. Type the words *"Plan your dream escape."*

21. Notice that the **Control Panel** at the top of the screen is now showing information about the type. If you look at the left edge of this panel, there are two small buttons. Ensure that the (topmost) **Character Formatting Controls** button is selected (if it's darker than the other one, it is).

22. You're about to change the look of the text by changing the font, amongst other attributes. Within the brand guidelines I've created for this company I've chosen a specific font (the one that's used in the logo). This is a font that you're unlikely to have, but I've used it for several reasons. I've chosen it firstly because I think it works well. Secondly because it's a font that anyone can obtain (because the font designer has generously made it available for download at a *choose your price rate*). And thirdly because even though it might be a bit frustrating to have to download and install a font, it's likely to be something that you'll either need or want to do as your design skills progress. But if for whatever reason you'd rather not install a font at this stage, feel free to use a different font, but bear in mind that the other text settings you'll use will differ from the ones specified below (and the advert will look different, too). Select all the text you've just typed either by dragging over it with your mouse, or by choosing **Edit>Select All.** Change the **Font** from Minion Pro to *Edmondsans**, and the **Weight** to *Bold*.

* *If you want to download the font, go to www.losttype.com/ font/?name=edmondsans (and please consider a donation). For instructions on how to install fonts, visit www.fontsquirrel.com/help*

23. Increase the size of the type by pressing the up arrow that's to the left of the **Font Size** *(where it says 12pt)* until you see an *Overset Mark* (a small red +) at the bottom right of your text frame. The Overset Mark tells you there isn't room for all the type in the frame. To fix this, make the font size smaller again by pressing the down arrow.

24. Notice there is a value underneath the Font Size which is in brackets. This is the *Leading* value, and describes the vertical space between the baselines of the type (the invisible lines that the text "sits" on). The brackets indicate that the leading value is automatically calculated (by adding 20% on top of the font size). So depending on the size of your text, the leading value should be around 32-34pt. The automatic value is normally fine for general text, but for some fonts and typically at large sizes you might wish to override it, as you'll do now. To bring the lines of type closer together, reduce the **Leading** value to around the same size as your font size.

25. A method that's widely used to give type such as this more impact is to reduce its *Tracking* value, which allows you to adjust the amount of space between each character. Change the **Tracking** value to around *-30,* which will subtly reduce amount of (horizontal) space between each character.

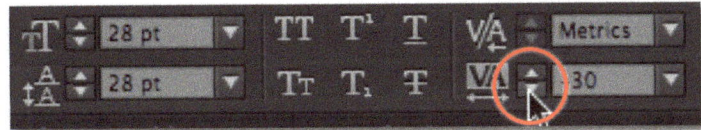

26. As well as making the type look a little more punchy, it also means it takes up less space, so you can increase its font size to around *30pt.*

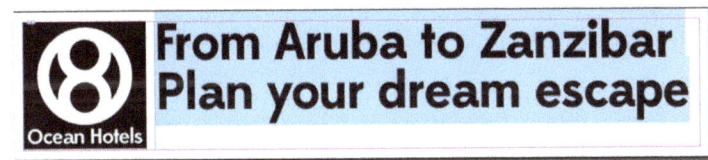

27. To fine tune your advert you're going to make sure that the type aligns as well as possible with the logo, to help make it appear that they should belong together. You'll firstly ensure that the *x-height* (the height of most lowercase characters, like an "x") of the top line of type lines up with the top of the upper black circle in the logo. This is a great deal easier with something to guide you. If you look carefully at your screen you should see little rulers above and to the left of your page.

28. Using your **Selection Tool,** click on the ruler at the top of the page. Drag your mouse down, and you should see that you're dragging a light blue guide from the ruler. Drag it roughly into position as shown below.

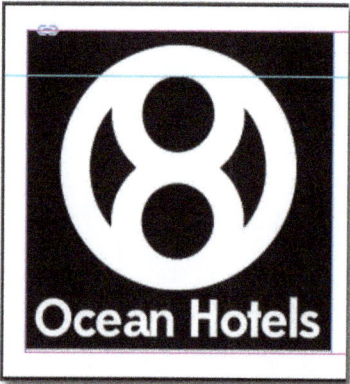

29. If the x-height of the top line of your type doesn't line up with the guide, you can either drag the text frame up or down with your **Selection Tool,** or do the same by pressing the *up* or ***down arrow*** keys on your keyboard.

30. Using the same approach you just used, drag another
guide down from the ruler so that it aligns with the
bottom of the lower black circle in the logo.

31. To ensure that the *baseline* (the line on which the text "sits") of your
lower line of type aligns with the circle select the whole of the lower
line of type with the **Type Tool** and adjust its *Leading* value (if need be).

32. When you're trying to precisely arrange different lines of type, one approach is to do what you've just done and keep it in the same frame, adjusting its positioning using leading. An alternative approach is to place different lines of type in different frames, which is what you'll do next. Before you do this, reduce the size of the frame you've just been working with so that it's no bigger than it needs to be. To do this, choose the **Selection Tool** and use it to drag any of the square *handles* at the edges of the frame. If you make the frame too small to contain the type you'll see an *overset mark* (a red "+") appear towards the bottom right of the frame. If this happens, simply make the frame larger again.

33. Using the **Rectangle Frame Tool,** create another frame whose left edge aligns to the left of the previous frame and extends to the right margin guide, and down to the edge of the document.

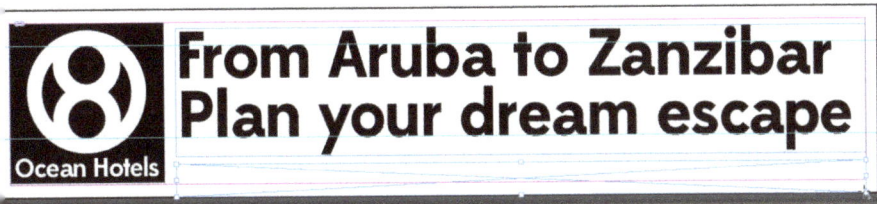

34. As you've done before, click in this new frame with the **Type Tool.**
When you see a flashing cursor appear, type *"Visit www.ocean-hotels.com for inspiration."* Select all the text you've just typed and
change the **Font** to *Edmondsans,* and the **Weight** to *Medium.*

35. Select the website address and change the weight of the font to *Bold.*

36. Using the **Selection Tool** as before, drag a final guide down from
the ruler so that it aligns with the baseline of the text in the logo.
This time, align the baseline of the text in the new frame by nudging
the frame up and down using the **arrow keys** on your keyboard.

37. To have a better look at your finished advert you can use *Preview mode (**View>Screen Mode>Preview**)* to hide elements that won't print, returning to *Normal Mode* using ***View>Screen Mode>Normal.***

38. Save the completed advert by choosing ***Save*** from the **File menu,** choosing an appropriate file name and location for your work.

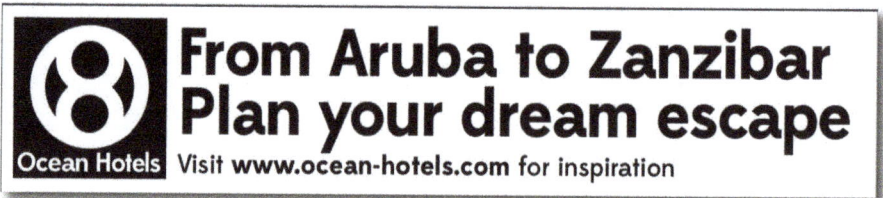

Summary of Menu commands

File>New>Document *[Command+N]*
File>Place *[Command+D]*
Edit>Select All *[Command+A]*
Edit >Undo *[Command+Z]*
View>Display Performance>High Quality Display
View>Display Performance>Typical Display

Summary of Tools used

Rectangle Frame Tool
Selection Tool
Type Tool

Summary of Panels used

Control Panel (to change font and size of the text)

If things went wrong...

I kept creating more and more frames. *This is because when you're using a frame tool, InDesign assumes you will want to keep using it. So after you have created your frame, if you click or click and drag with the tool (for example to select, deselect or try and resize a frame) it will continue to create frames for you. If you change to the Selection Tool when you've created your frame(s) this won't happen. Select any frames you don't want with the Selection Tool and delete them by pressing the Delete key.*

I couldn't see all of my type. *Your frame wasn't big enough to accommodate all of the type, as indicated by the red Overset Mark in the bottom right corner. Either undo what you've done, or make the frame bigger by dragging one of the selection handles with the Selection Tool. Once you can see all your type, select it with the Type Tool and make it smaller. Then you can resize the frame back to the size you want it.*

2) A "WOB" advert for Ocean Hotels

Your second advert will be almost identical to the first, but rather than being black on a white background it'll be white on a black background (often described as a "WOB").

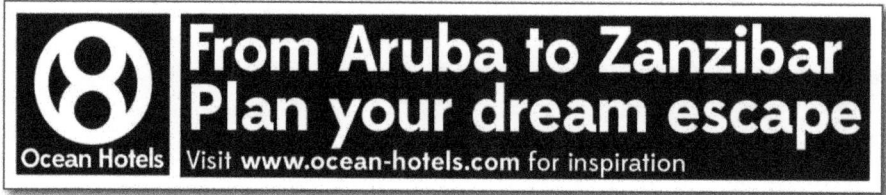

1. As this advert will be almost identical to the first, the easiest way to create it will be to save a copy of your first advert, then work on that. If your previous advert isn't still open in InDesign, choose **File>Open,** locate it where you saved it and open it.

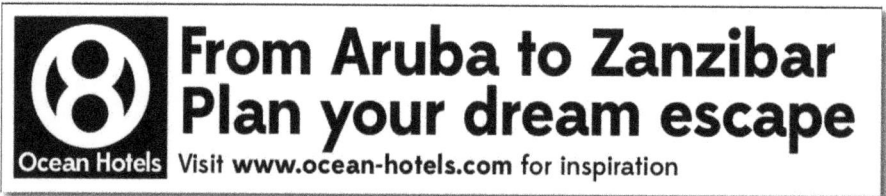

2. Choose **File>Save As.** In the *Save As* dialogue box, save it by a different name but in the same location.

3. All the text you've just created will become white, and placed on a black background. That means that you'll firstly need to create that background for the logo and text to be seen against. To do this, choose the **Rectangle Frame Tool** from the **Tools Panel** and drag with it from the document's top left corner to its bottom right to create a frame that covers the whole document.

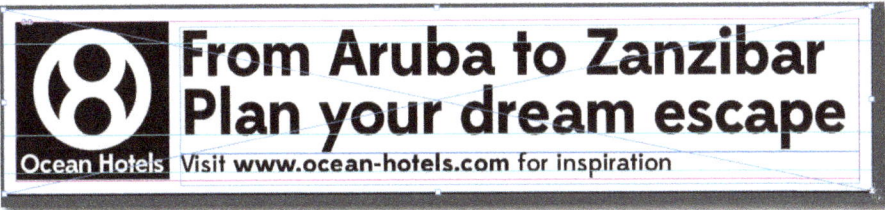

From Aruba to Zanzibar
Plan your dream escape
Ocean Hotels Visit www.ocean-hotels.com for inspiration

4. To change the rectangle's colour you'll need to see the area in the Tools Panel that describes the colours of frames. However in recent versions of InDesign this area is so small that it's hard to clearly see what it's for, so the first thing to do is make it larger. To do this, click on the **tiny button** (that resembles a Fast Forward button) at the very top left of the Tools Panel which makes the panel two columns wide.

5. The area highlighted in the screenshot below describes the colour of the selected frame (make sure the rectangular frame is selected before continuing). The square on the top left describes its *fill* (the colour inside the frame) and the square on the bottom right describes its *stroke* (the colour around its edge). In this case, it's showing that both the fill and the stroke are *none* (or transparent).

6. To change the frame's colour to black, firstly click on the word *Swatches* on the right of your screen to expand the **Swatches Panel,** then click on the *[black]* swatch.

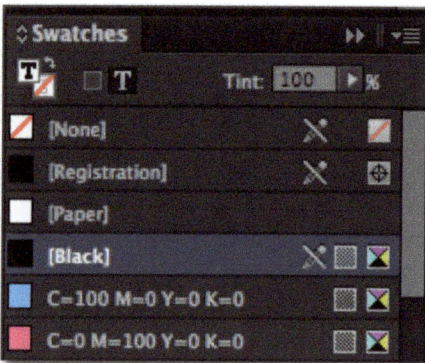

7. The black swatch will either have been applied to the fill or the stroke of the frame, depending on which of the two squares was in the front. For example, if the fill square was in the front, this will be the result:

8. If, however, the stroke square was in front, this will be the result:

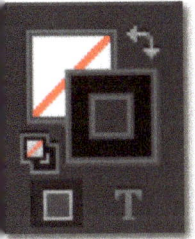

9. If you've inadvertently applied the black swatch to the stroke, apply the *[none]* swatch to it instead by clicking in the area shown below, then click once on the *fill square* to bring it to the front, before applying the black swatch again.

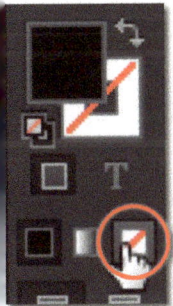

10. As you might well be thinking, even though you want a black fill to create the background colour for your advert, introducing that colour now is going to make things more confusing as you won't be able to see the existing black letters over the top of it. So even though black is the colour you'll want to use, for now, go to the **Swatches Panel** again and apply the *Red* swatch to the frame instead.

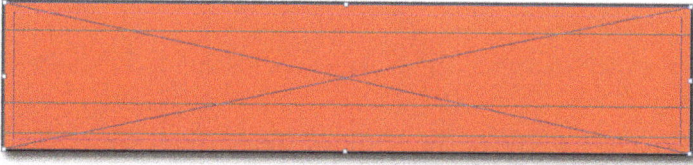

11. Even though the frame's colour is different from the text, you still can't see the text. This is because in InDesign there is what's known as a *stacking order.* The last thing that you create will be positioned in front of the previous thing you created. So the red frame is in front of the text, obscuring it from view. To change that, in the **Object menu** choose **Arrange>Send to Back.** This places the red frame at the back of the stacking order and enables you to see the text and the logo because they are now above it.

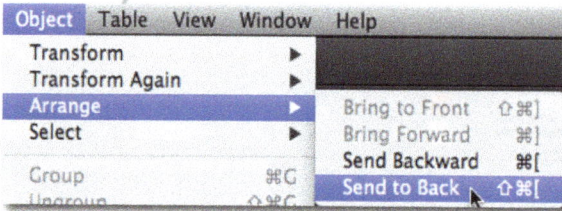

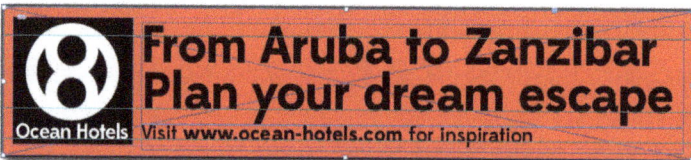

12. Using your **Type Tool,** click once on the large text as if you are going to edit it. Then from the **Edit menu** choose *Select All* to select all of the text in the frame.

13. Look back at the colour area of Tools Panel and notice that it now contains a black "T." This indicates that the currently selected text is black, and that if you changed the colour it would affect the text instead the frame.

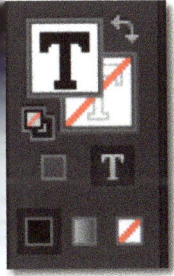

14. Go to the **Swatches Panel** to apply the *Paper* (white) swatch to the text.

15. Select the text in the frame underneath and make that white as well.

16. Using the **Selection Tool,** carefully click on the red background frame (try to avoid selecting the frames containing text) and change its fill colour to *Black.*

17. Using the square handles on the edges of the frame, bring the edge of the frame in so that they align to the pink/purple margin guides at the top, bottom and right of the document.

18. Try and create the same gap between the edge of the logo and the left edge of the black background frame by dragging the handle on its left.

19. Using the **arrow keys** on your keyboard, nudge your text frames a little to the right to create a subtle yet consistent gap between the text and the edge of the black frame. If you need to, use the **Type Tool** to adjust the size, tracking or leading of the text to help achieve this.

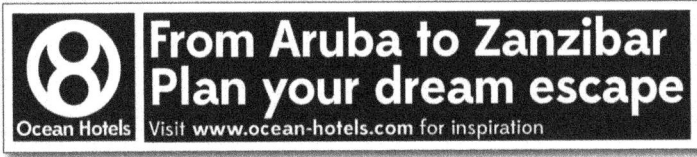

20. As you did with the previous advert, use *Preview mode* **(View>Screen Mode>Preview)** to have a look at the finished advert, returning to *Normal Mode* using **View>Screen Mode>Normal.**

Summary of new menu commands

File>Open *[Command+O]*
File>Save As *[Command+Shift+S]*
Object>Arrange>Send to Back

Summary of new panels used

Swatches Panel

3) A colour advert for Ocean Hotels

Your third advert will introduce colour and a photograph as well as a logo.

From the Turquoise coast of Turkey to the Carribean coast of Cuba, we know we've got somewhere in the world that's just right for you.

Find your perfect escape with us.
Visit **www.ocean-hotels.com** for inspiration.

Ocean Hotels

1. From the **File menu** choose **New** to create a new document. Check that the *Document Preset* is set to *Default*. If it's not, select it in the pop up menu at the top of the dialogue box. Uncheck *Facing Pages,* then change the *Width* to *195mm* and the *Height* to *116mm*. Change all the **Margin** values to *5mm* by changing change the **Top** margin value and then click on the padlock to copy the value into the *Bottom, Left* and *Right* boxes. Then press the **OK button.**

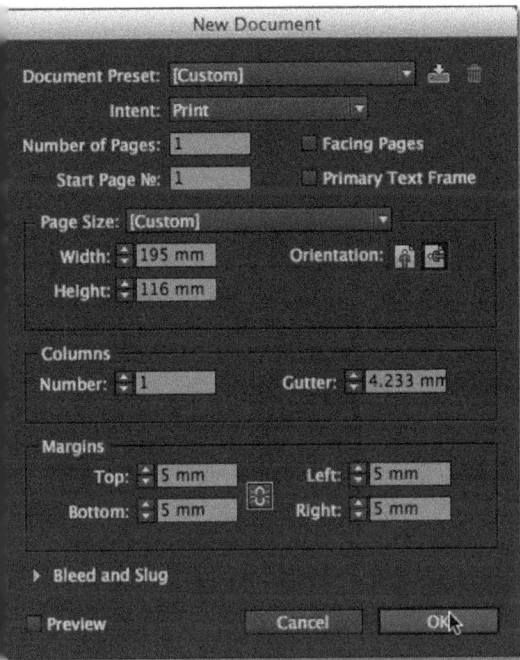

2. The first thing you'll do to create this advert is to create a frame for the photograph. Click and drag with the **Rectangle Frame Tool,** aligning to the top, left and right page edges and continuing down about two thirds of the way down the page.

3. Change to the **Selection Tool,** then choose **File>Place** and import the *OH_mexico1.jpg* image. Press the **Open** button and you'll see your frame is filled with the picture.

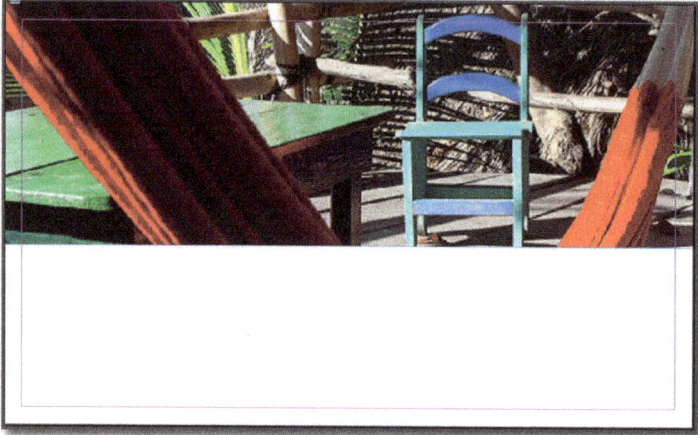

4. To bring in the *Ocean Hotels* logo you'll employ the approach you used with the first advert. Using the **Selection Tool,** ensure that nothing is selected by clicking once on an empty part of the page, and choose **File>Place** to import the *ocean_hotels_blue_reversed.eps* logo by attaching it to your cursor.

5. Click and drag to place it in the bottom right corner of the document, attempting to leave the same amount of space between the picture and the logo as there is at the edge of the page.

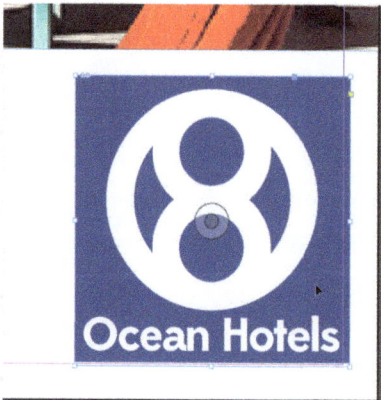

6. Drag with your **Selection Tool** if you want to reposition the logo. If you want to resize the logo you can drag any of the corner handles (that look like squares) whilst holding down the **Command** and **Shift** keys simultaneously. As you discovered previously, you can make the logo display better by selecting **View>Display Performance>High Quality Display.**

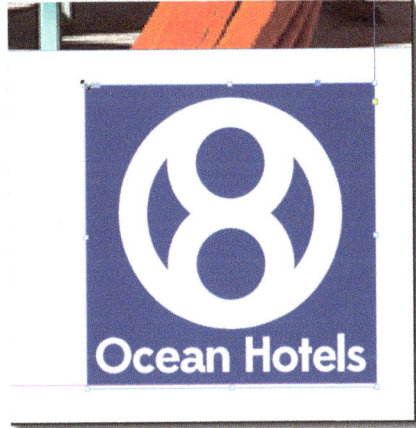

7. Next you'll create a frame for the text. Try to make it align to the top of the logo, to the left and bottom margin guides, and leaves a similar amount of space on its right before the left edge of the logo.

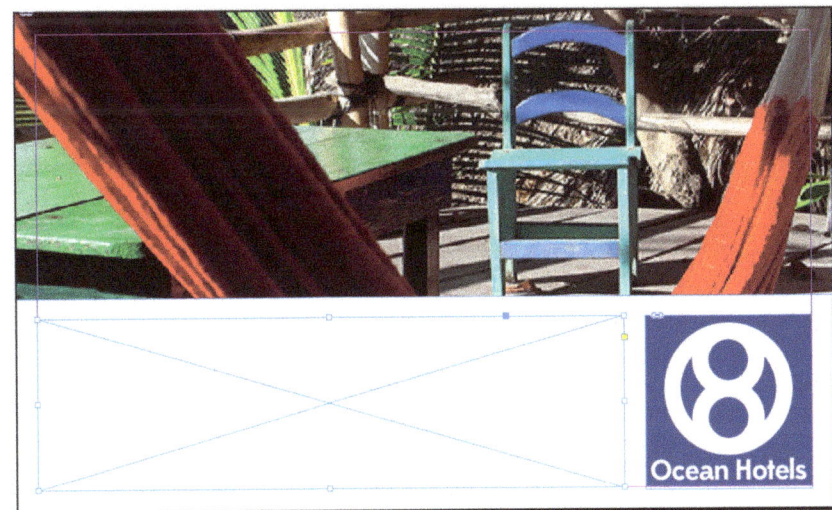

8. Click in the frame with the **Type Tool** and type the following text: *"From the Turquoise coast of Turkey to the Caribbean coast of Cuba, we know we've got somewhere in the world that's just right for you."* Press the **Return key** then type "Find your perfect escape with us." Press the **Return key** again and type *"Visit www.ocean-hotels.com for inspiration."*

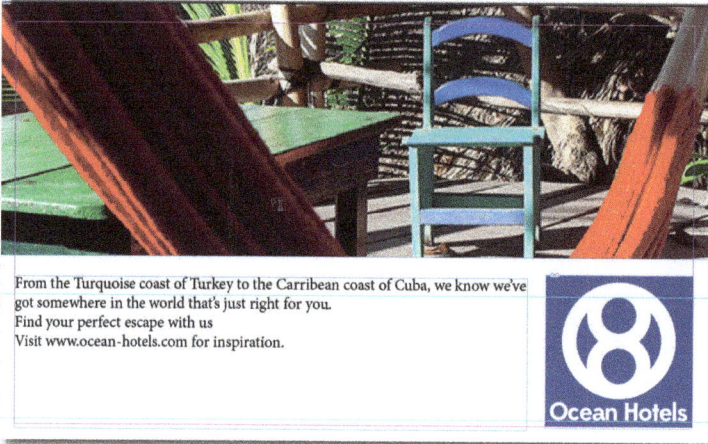

9. As you have done before, select all the text you've just typed either by dragging over it with your mouse, or by choosing **Edit>Select All.** Change the *Font* from Minion Pro to *Edmondsans,* the *Weight* to *Medium,* the *Size* to *17pt* and the *Leading* to *19pt.* Change the web address to **Bold.** Apply the *Blue* swatch to the text.

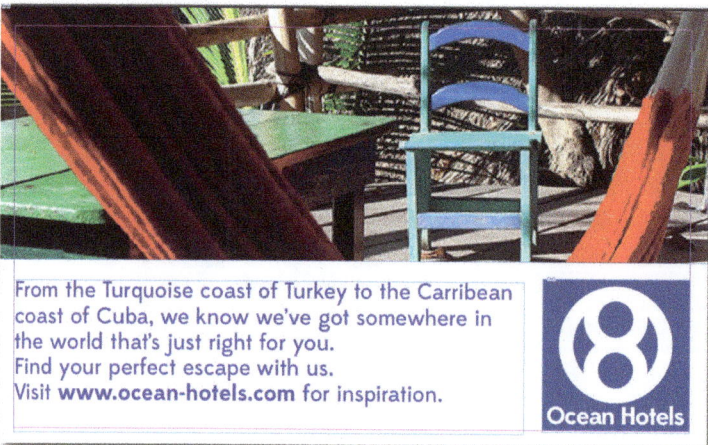

10. Using the **Selection Tool** as you did previously, drag two guides down from the ruler, one that aligns with the top of the blue circle in the logo and one that aligns with the baseline of the text in the logo.

11. Align the baseline of the first line of text to the topmost guide by selecting the frame and nudging it up or down using the **arrow keys** on your keyboard.

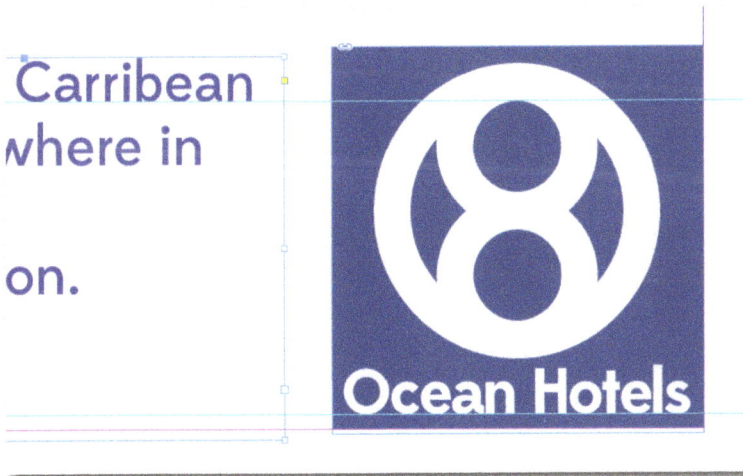

12. Finally, increase the **Leading** of the *"Find your perfect escape with us."* type so that the baseline of the final line of type aligns to the baseline of the text in the logo.

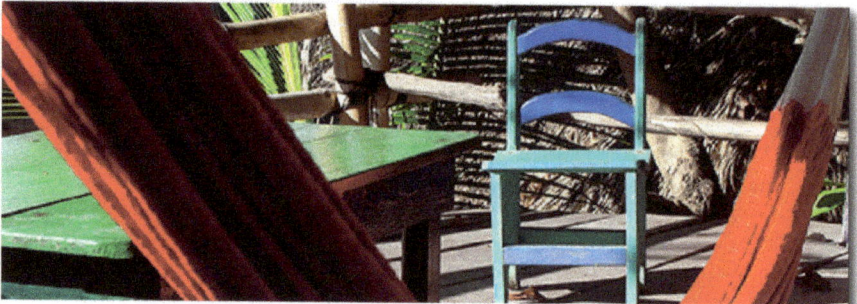

Summary of new shortcuts used

Scaling a frame and its contents simultaneously:

Command key + Shift key + drag corner handle

4) An advert for Discover Cultural Tours

This next advert will teach you how to apply rounded corners to a frame and how to sample and use colours from a photograph.

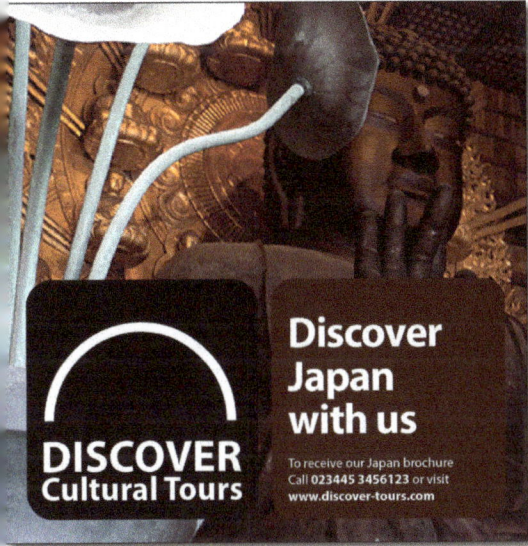

1. From the **File menu** choose **New** to create a new document. As before, start with the *Default* document preset and uncheck *Facing Pages*. Change both the **Width** and the **Height** to *70mm* and all the **Margin** values to *3mm* before pressing the **OK button.**

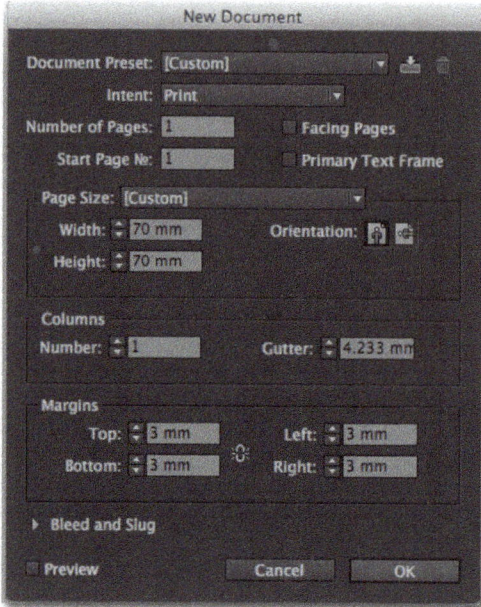

2. As you have done before, create a frame that snaps to all the edges of the document and choose **File>Place** to import *Discover_japan_nara.jpg*.

3. So far the images you've placed into InDesign have been carefully cropped so that you haven't had to learn about repositioning or resizing them. But this image is more realistic in that it will need to be adjusted to fit properly. From the **Object menu** choose *Fitting>Fill Frame Proportionally.* This resizes the image so that it fits the frame as best it can without changing the proportion of the image nor leaving any white space in the frame.

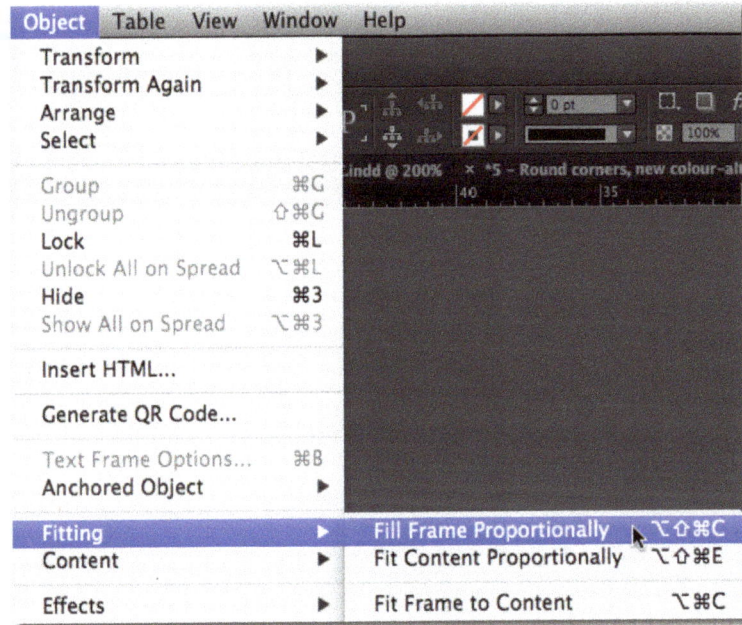

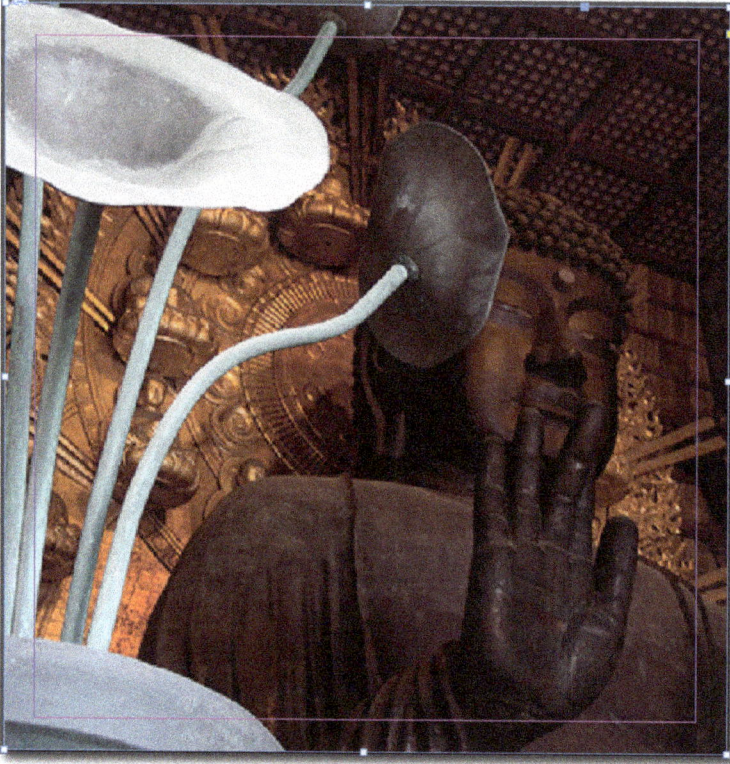

4. Notice that at the moment the edge of the frame containing the
    images is *blue*. This indicates that the *frame itself* is selected. However,
    if you double-click on the image with the **Selection Tool** you will
    now see a *brown* frame instead*. This indicates that the *picture itself*
    is selected. This is why the brown frame is not exactly the same
    shape and size as the blue frame. As the page is probably filling
    your screen you may need to zoom out a little in order to see the
    brown frame. To do this, hold down the **Command key** and press
    the *minus key* a couple of times. To make the page fill the screen
    again, hold down the **Command key** and press the *Zero key.*

* *For users of InDesign prior to CS5, change to the **Direct Selection Tool** (the
  white arrow) instead to adjust the picture as described above, then revert
  back to the **Selection Tool** (the black arrow) when you've finished.*

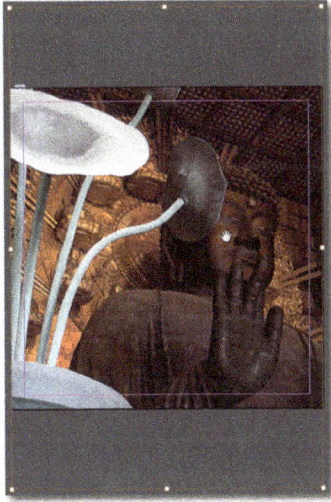

5. With the brown frame selected, if you press and hold down your mouse button, any area of the picture that's outside the blue frame will be seen, but will be ghosted out.

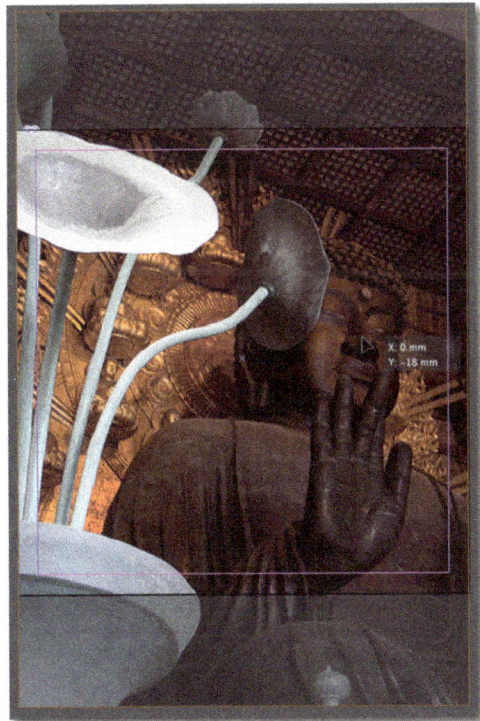

6. If you want to show a different part of the picture, drag up or down your mouse to reposition it.

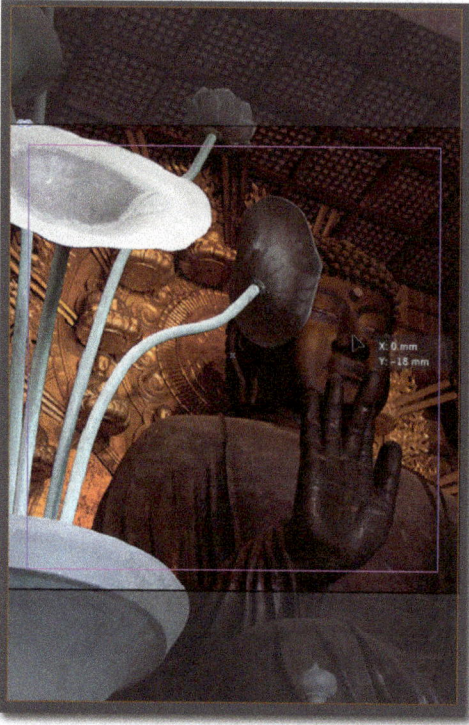

7. Once you've finished working with the picture, deselect it by clicking somewhere outside the edge of the page. Next, import the *discover-logo-wob-round.ai* logo so that it attaches to your cursor. Click and drag with the loaded cursor so that the logo almost covers the bottom left quarter of the advert. If you want to resize it, drag any of the handles whilst holding down the **Command** and **Shift keys.**

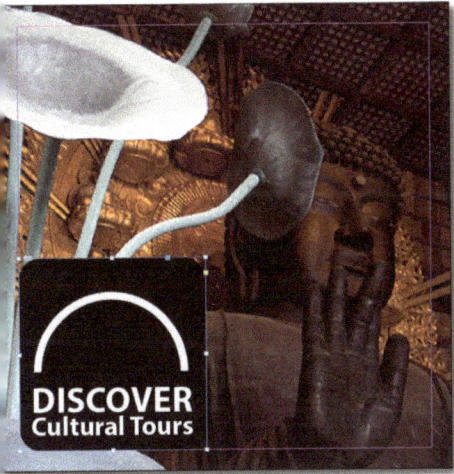

8. The next step is to create an empty frame of the same size and shape as the logo (including the rounded corners). Drag with the **Rectangle Frame Tool** whilst holding the **Shift key** to create a perfectly square shape. Use the **Command** and **Shift keys** as described above to resize it, looking out for the green *smart guides* to help you align the two objects together.

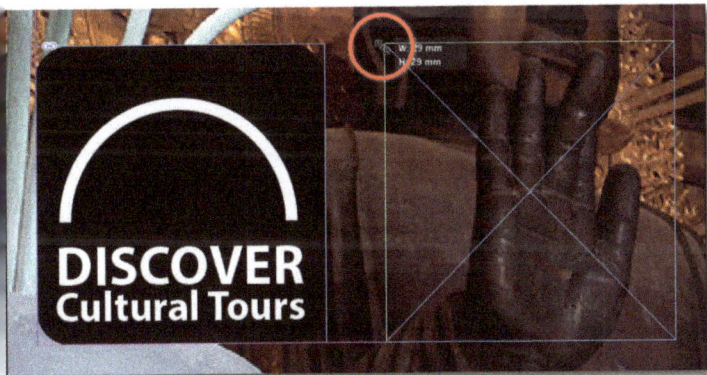

9. If you want to increase or decrease the space between the frames, resize one using the method described above, then resize the other whilst trying to keep your cursor aligned to the corner handle that you're dragging it with; a green smart guide should appear when the two objects are the same height.

10. To apply rounded corners to the empty frame, choose **Corner Options** from the **Object menu.** In the dialogue box that appears ensure that the padlock icons appear locked, then click on any of the icons to the right of the numbers to apply a rounded effect.* Adjust the numbers to somewhere around 3-4mm to match the roundedness of the logo.

    * *Prior to InDesign CS5 the dialogue box was simpler, but will still enable you to achieve the same effect.*

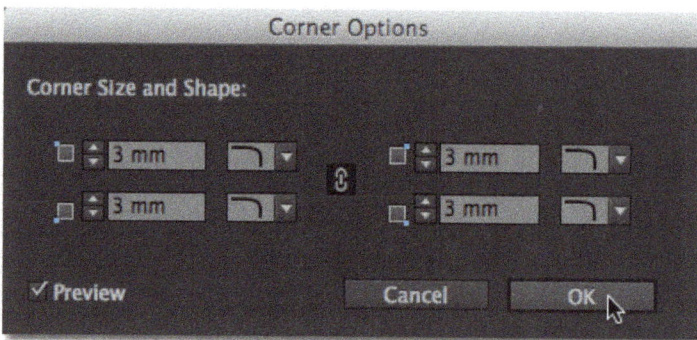

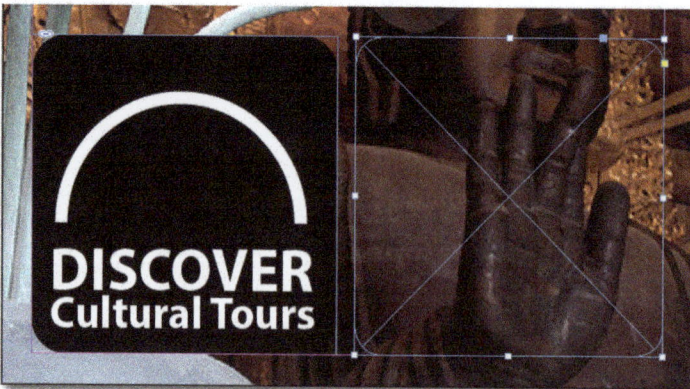

11. So far the only colours that you've used have been provided for you. Very often you'll want to use a colour that works well with the image, and a good way to do that is to sample a colour from an image on the page. To do this, ensure the new frame you've just created is selected, and then choose the *Eyedropper Tool* from the **Tools Panel.**

12. Notice that the eyedropper's pipette is currently *white.* Click with the eyedropper on an area of colour in the image that you think you might want to use. Notice when you do that, that firstly the frame colour changes to match, and that secondly the pipette becomes *black,* as if it's sucked the colour up from the picture.

13. If you want to use the colour you've sampled the best approach is to add it to your list of swatches. To do this, firstly open the **Swatches Panel,** then click with the **Eyedropper Tool** onto the *new swatch button* near the bottom right of the **Swatches Panel,** to keep it for future use. However if you want to sample again simply hold down the *Alt key* and notice that the eyedropper's pipette becomes white again, enabling you to sample a different area of colour.

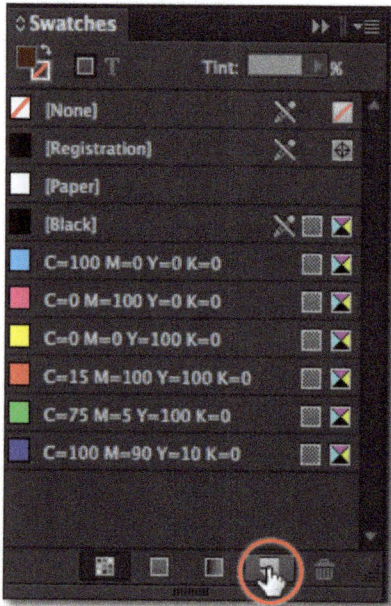

14. Once you've changed the colour of the frame to a colour you want to use, change to the **Rectangle Frame Tool.** Create a frame for the advert's text on top of the coloured panel you've just created.*

* Having a separate text frame can make it easier to control and adjust the position of the text.

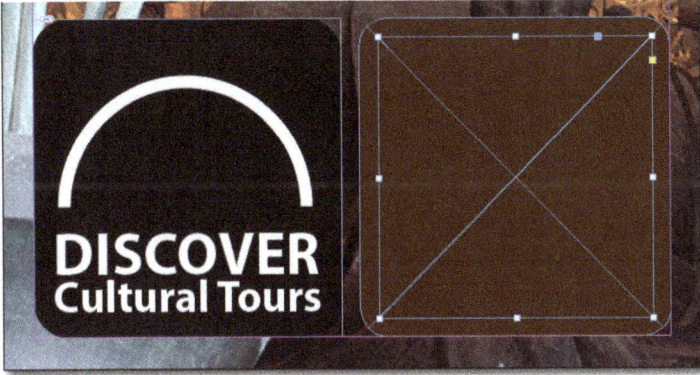

15. Click in the frame with the **Type Tool** and type the following text: *"Discover Japan with us"*. As you have done before, select all the text you've just typed either by dragging over it with your mouse, or by choosing **Edit>Select All**. Change the **Font** from *Minion Pro* to *Myriad Pro*, the **Weight** to *Bold,* the **Size** and **Leading** to around *16pt* and the **Tracking** to *-25*. Apply the *Paper/White* swatch to the text.

16. Place your cursor before the word "with" and press the **Return key** to force it down onto a separate line.

17. Using your **Selection Tool** in combination with the **up** and **down arrows** (and using a guide if you need to), adjust the position of the text frame so that the x-height of the top line of the text roughly aligns to the top of the arc in the logo. Then reduce the size of the text frame so that it is as small as you can make it whilst still leaving room for all of the text.

18. Create a separate frame for the text that will appear below the text you've just worked on. Then type the following text in*, and once you've done so try to make it fit in a way that aligns well with the logo and uses the same fonts as above (use a combination of different weights to add contrast):
"To receive our Japan brochure
Call 023445 3456123 or visit
www.discover-tours.com"

* *As the default font size is 12pt you might find that you've run out of room before you've typed all of the text. If that happens, choose Edit>Select All to select all of the text and reduce its size to around 6pt.*

19. To finish the advert, look carefully at all the elements and decide if any of them need to be changed. Reposition the picture inside the frame, change the colour of the rounded frame or amend the type if necessary.

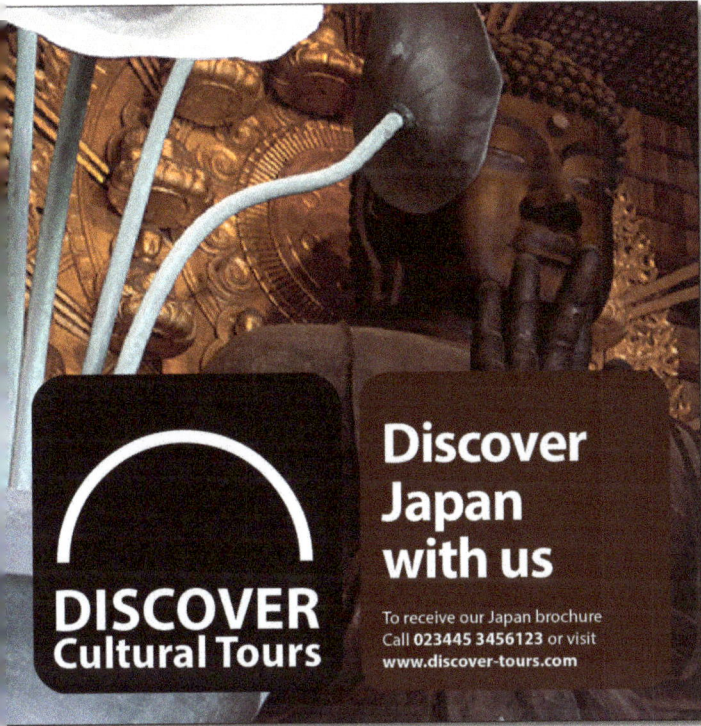

New Commands used

Object>Fitting>Fill Frame Proportionally
Object>Corner Options

New Tools used

The Eyedropper Tool.

5) Re-purposing the previous advert

Whilst the next advert is a very different shape to the previous one, the techniques employed in creating it are almost the same. So here you'll learn a way to repurpose elements you've created for one advert to be used in another one.

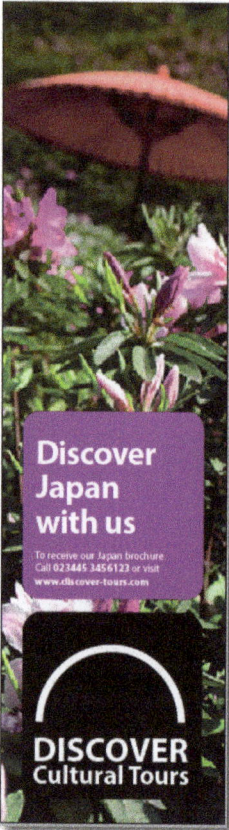

1. From the **File menu** choose **New** to create a new document. As before, start with the *Default* document preset and *uncheck* **Facing Pages.** Change the **Width** to *40mm* and the Height to *140mm* and all the Margin values to *4mm* before pressing the **OK button.**

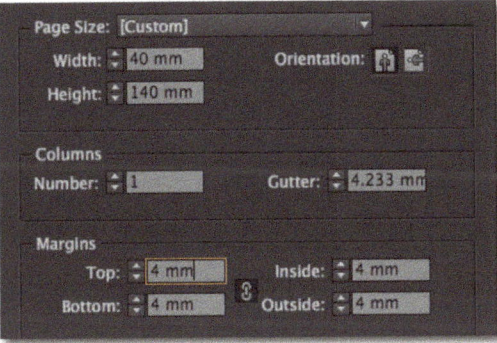

2. As with the previous advert, create a frame that snaps to all the edges of the document. Then choose **File>Place** to import *Discover_japan_kyoto.jpg*.

3. Select the image's frame with the **Selection Tool** and from the **Object menu** choose **Fitting>Fill Frame Proportionally.**

4. Bearing in mind that the bottom half of the image will shortly be mostly covered up, explore how best you can crop and size the image by double clicking on it, like you did previously. In addition to repositioning the image, if you want to resize it, drag one of its brown corner handles, but make sure you hold down the **Shift Key** as you drag to keep the shape of the picture in proportion.

5. An alternative to repeating all the previous steps used to create the last advert is to open the previous advert and copy the logo, coloured frame and text frame across to this one before resizing them using the **Command** and **Shift** keys. To do this, firstly choose **File>Open** and select the advert you just created.

6. In the previous advert, select the coloured frame by clicking on it with the **Selection Tool,** then hold down the **Shift** key as you select each text frame in turn. With everything selected, choose *Group* from the **Object menu.** This will make the resizing of both the coloured frame and the text frames less awkward because as they are now grouped if you move or resize them they will behave as if they are one object.

7. From the **Edit menu** use the *Copy* command to copy the group to the clipboard. Go back to the new advert by clicking on its tab towards the top of the screen, then use the *Paste* command from the **Edit menu** to paste the group into the new advert.

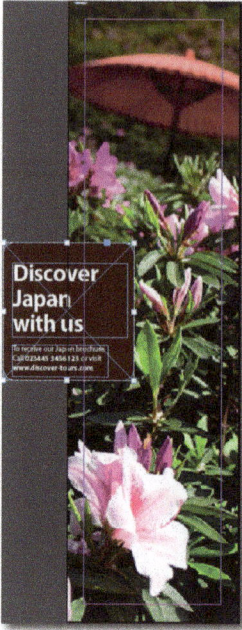

8. Copy and paste in the logo from the previous advert as
   well, then reposition and resize them both, using the
   Command and **Shift keys*** where necessary.

* *It's entirely possible to resize frames containing text in this way, but be
aware that you may end up with some fairly strange point sizes.*

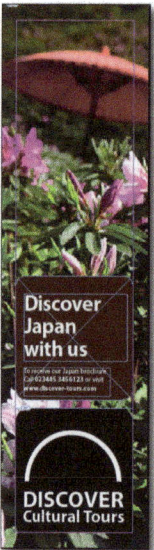

9. You're about to work with the coloured frame. It'll be easier to work with if it's not grouped with the text frame(s). If the coloured background frame is grouped with the text frame(s), select the group with the **Selection Tool** and choose *Ungroup* from the **Object menu** before proceeding.

10. Finally, make sure that only the coloured background is selected* and then use the **Eyedropper** to sample a more suitable colour for it from the image, remembering that you can use the **Alt key** if you don't get the result you hoped for first time.

* *Click off the edge of the document to deselect everything, then click back on the background frame.*

Summary of new commands used.
Edit>Copy
Edit>Paste
Object>Group
Object>Ungroup

6) An advert using a transparent element

Whilst the next advert is similar to the previous two that you've created, this features a transparent background as opposed to a solid one.

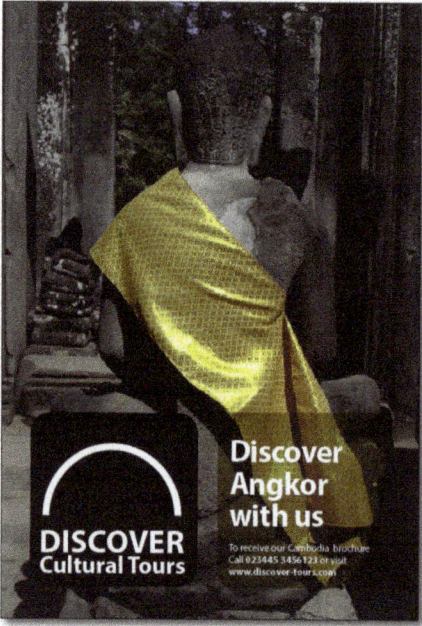

1. From the **File menu** choose **New** to create a new document. As before, start with the *Default* document preset and *uncheck* **Facing Pages.** Change the ***Page Size*** from *A4* to *B5.* Leave the Margin values at their *12.7mm* default and press the **OK button.**

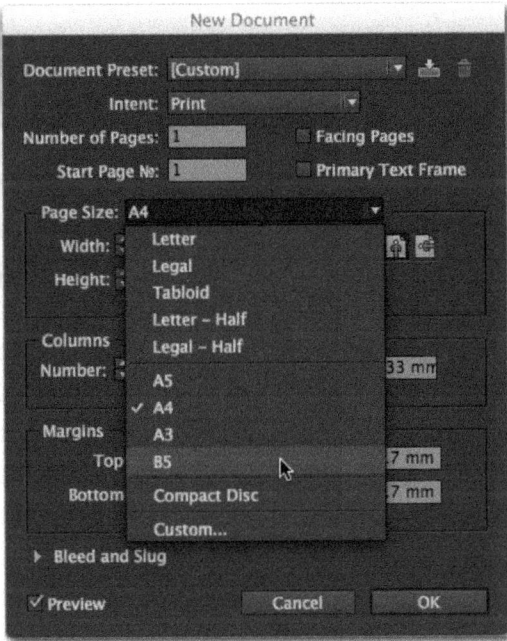

2. Either creating from scratch, or by copying elements from previous adverts, get all the frames in place*. The photograph for the background image is *Discover_cambodia1.jpg*.

*Remember that it might be easier to group the text frames with the background coloured frame before you copy and paste them, and that you might want to ungroup them before you continue working on them.

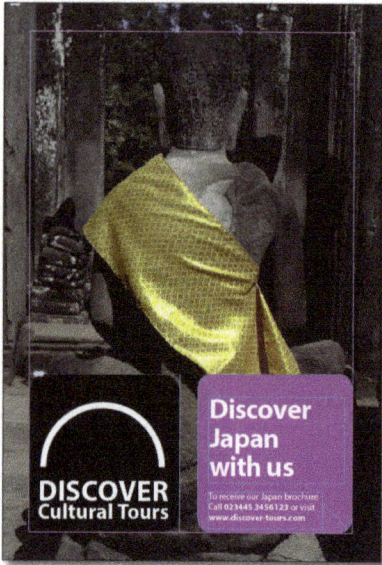

3. If you've copied elements from one of the previous adverts, change the "Discover Japan with us" text to "Discover Angkor with us." Change the "To receive our Japan brochure" to "To receive our Cambodia brochure." You will need to widen the smaller text frame or make the text smaller in order to accommodate the longer word.

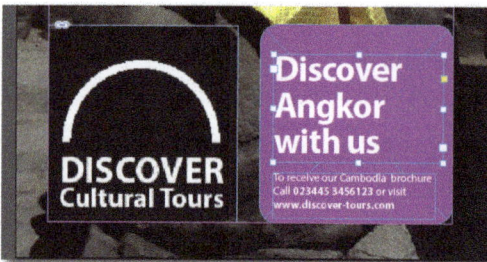

4. Using the **Selection Tool,** select the background frame, then use the **Eyedropper Tool** to sample an appropriate colour.

5. To make it look a bit more subtle, from the **Window menu** choose **Effects.** Click on the drop down menu that says *"Normal"* and change the blending mode to *Multiply.*

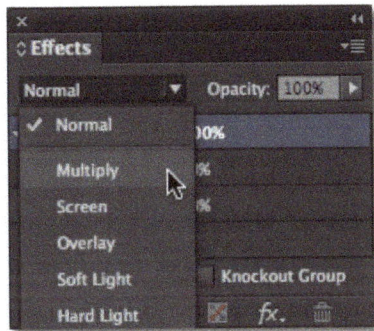

6. The blending mode controls how transparency is calculated – in this case, by combining the elements in a way that should produce a subtly darker result. If the effect is too strong, drag the slider found underneath the word *Opacity* to less than *100%,* change to a different *blending mode* or try it with a different sampled colour.

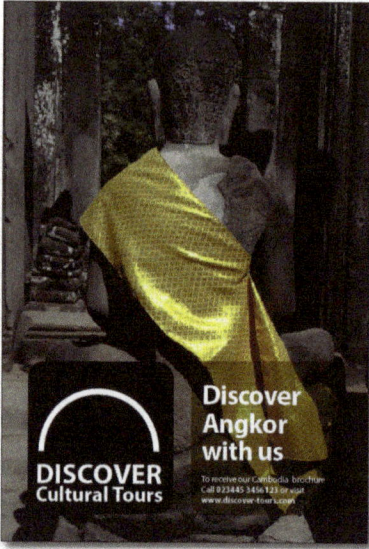

Summary of New Commands used

Window>Effects

7) An advert using an effect

The penultimate advert uses another type of effect to soften the look of a coloured background frame – directional feather, available since version CS3 of InDesign.

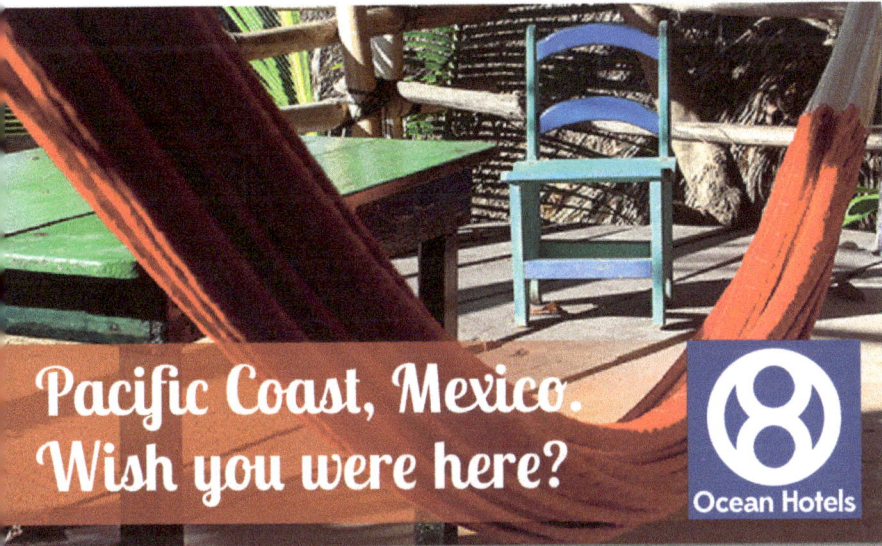

1. From the **File menu** choose **New** to create a new document. As before, start with the *Default* document preset and *uncheck* **Facing Pages.** Change the **Width** to *195mm* and the **Height** to *116mm.* Change the Margin values to *5mm* all the way round and press the **OK button.**

2. Using the techniques you've learned, create all of the elements you can see on the finished advert. The photograph for the background image is *OH_mexico2.jpg* the logo is *ocean_hotels_blue_reversed. eps,* the colour has been sampled from the images and the font is *Lobster Two Bold.** If you create the background coloured strip after you've placed the logo in, you'll need to use ***Object>Arrange>Send Backward*** to move the coloured strip behind the logo.

* *You can of course use any font you wish, but I've created the branding for this company using this font. One of the reasons I've used it is because it's freely available for anyone to use. If you want to download the font, go to www.fontsquirrel.com and follow their instructions at www. fontsquirrel.com/help for help on how to download and install it.*

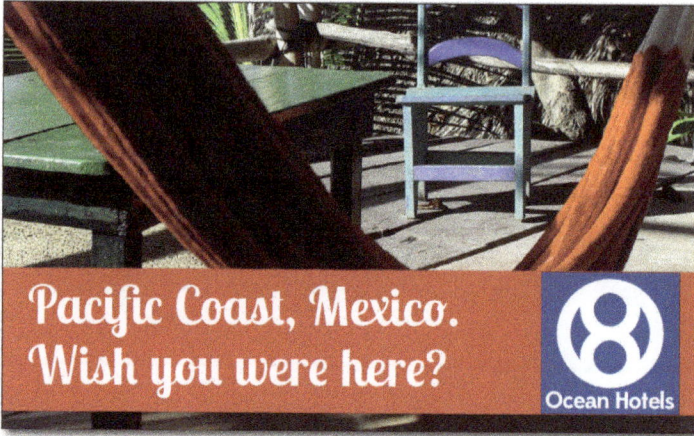

3. Once you've sampled a colour for the background frame, make sure it extends all the way across the advert from edge to edge. Using the **Effects Panel,** leave the blending mode at *Normal* but reduce the *Opacity* to make it semi-transparent.

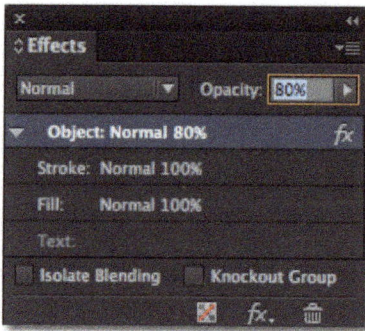

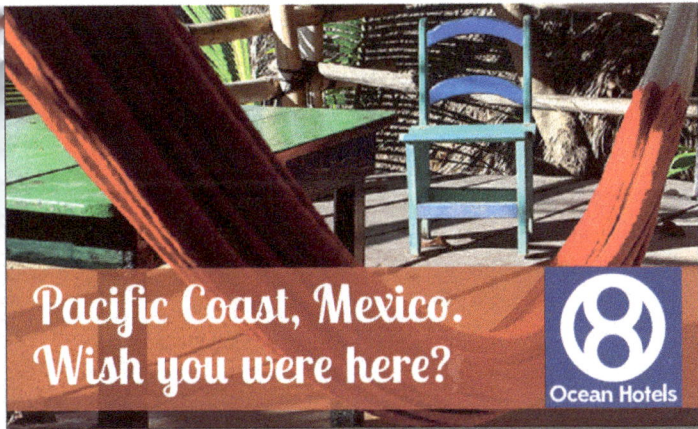

4. From the *dropdown menu* at the top right of the **Effects Panel** choose *Directional Feather.* Ensuring that the *preview* is checked, try increasing the *Right* value to gradually fade the colour in from the right of the advert.

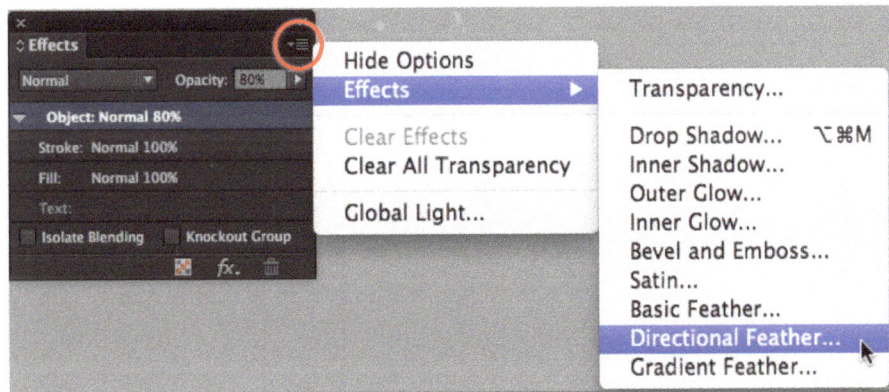

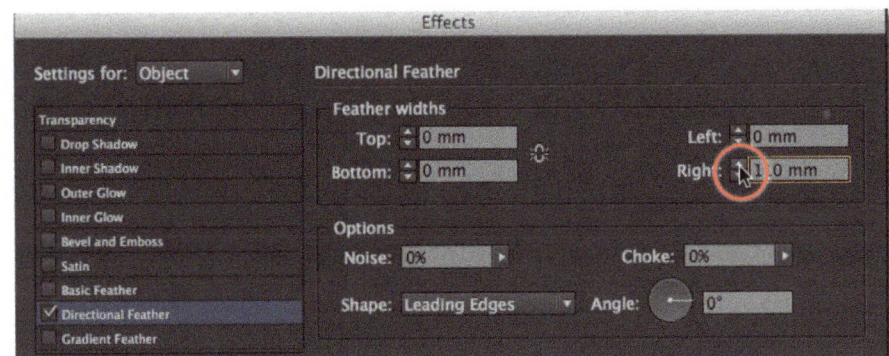

5. Continue to adjust the *Opacity,* the *Directional Feather* and the background colour until you're happy with the final result.

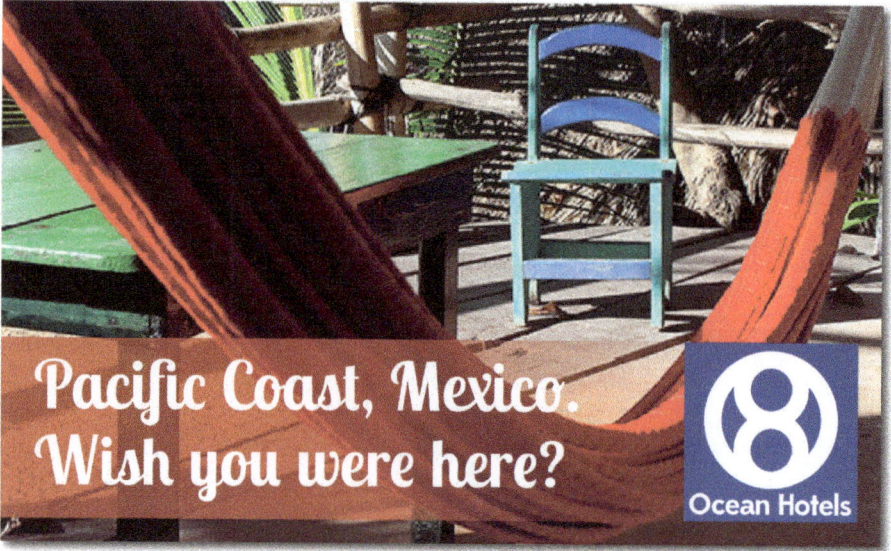

Summary of new commands used

Object>Arrange>Send Backward
Effects Panel: Directional Feather

8) An advert with multiple photos

The final advert introduces some techniques you can use to quickly create equally sized and spaced frames, import multiple images into them, and quickly crop the images into place.

1. From the **File menu** choose **New** to create a new document. As before, start with the *Default* document preset and *uncheck* **Facing Pages.** Change the **Width** to *210mm* and the **Height** to *99mm.* Change the Margin values to *8mm* all the way round and press the **OK button.**

2. You already know how to create most of this advert using a combination of the techniques you've learned so far, so I'll outline what you don't yet know. So far you've only worked with one photograph at most on an advert, whereas for this there will be six, all exactly the same size and equally spaced.

3. Before you bring all of the photographs in it will help to have a guide in position. Drag a guide from the ruler at the top of the page as you've done before to roughly a third of the way down the page, then click on it with the **Selection Tool.** Notice that it changes colour from light blue to dark to indicate that it is selected.

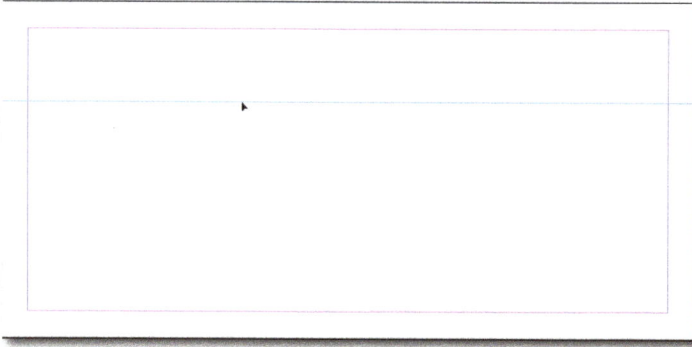

4. Look at the bottom left of the **Control Panel** at the top of the screen and notice that there is a *Y* value for this guide. This indicates how far something is positioned down the page. Type over the value so that it is exactly *38mm*.

5. To finish the advert you'll now import several images at once to create a montage. How you'll do this will depend on which version of InDesign you're using. If you're using InDesign CS5 or later you can skip on to the next step. If you're using version CS4 you'll need to skip to step *10*. If you're using a version of InDesign prior to CS4 you'll need to create the frames manually*.

* *To help you do this, go to the **Layout menu,** choose **Create Guides,** and create 6 column guides with an appropriate Gutter between them. Then create 6 frames with the **Rectangle Frame Tool,** place in all of the images from the Advert 8 folder, and skip to step 12.*

5. You'll now create six equally sized frames at once using InDesign's *Gridify* feature, available since version CS5. Using the **Rectangle Frame Tool,** click and drag from the top left margin guide, across to the right margin guide and down to the guide you just created, *but when you get there don't release your mouse button.* Instead, press the **right arrow** key five times (to create a total of 6 columns). When you release the mouse button you'll have created a total of six frames, all ready to receive images.

7. While the frames are all selected you can round all their corners at the same time by using the **Corner Options** command from the **Object menu.**

8. To import pictures into the frames, firstly choose the **Selection Tool** from the **Tools Panel,** ensure that no frames are selected, then choose **File>Place** and choose all six pictures in the *Advert 8 folder* All of the images become attached to your cursor – note the number next to it, telling you how many you have. Press the **up** or **down arrow key** to cycle through the images to find the one you want, and when you want to place it into an empty frame, simply click on it.

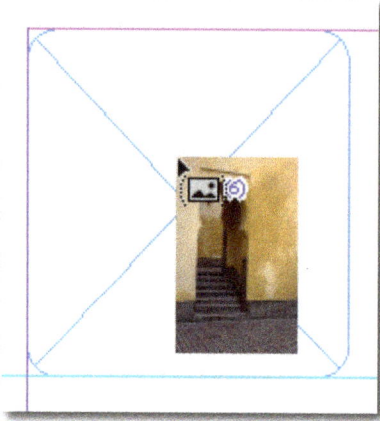

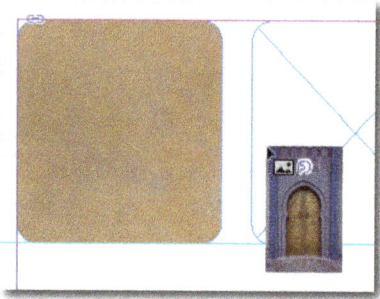

9. Once you've filled all of the frames with images, if you have any images still attached to your cursor, press the **Esc** key repeatedly to remove any leftover images.

10. If you're using InDesign CS4 there is an alternative way to create a grid of images (if you're using CS5 or later, skip to step 12). It requires the use of several consecutive keyboard shortcuts, so I would recommend that you read the instructions through before starting. Making sure you're using the **Selection Tool** and that no frames are selected, choose **File>Place.** Within the *Advert 8* folder click on the first image to select it, then hold down the **Shift key** and click on the last image to select all of the images at once. Once you've pressed the **Open button** the images will appear attached to your cursor, with the number *6* next to it, indicating that you have 6 images loaded on your cursor. Hold down the **Command** and **Shift** keys and notice that your cursor changes to something that resembles a grid.

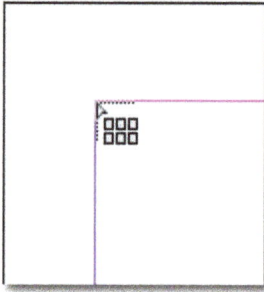

11. Click and drag from the top left margin guide, across to the right margin guide and down to the guide you just created. When you have drawn one large frame, let go of the Command and Shift keys, but *keep the mouse button held down*. Press the ***Right Arrow key*** five times (to create 6 columns) then finally release the mouse button. You'll see that the images are all in position, all in equally sized frames. While the frames are all selected you can round all their corners at the same time by using the **Corner Options** command from the **Object menu.**

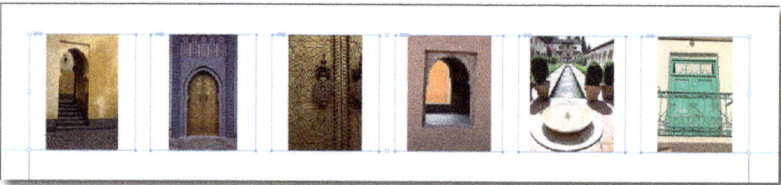

12. If need be, use your **Selection Tool** to click and drag over all of the frames at once to select them all, then choose **Object>Fitting>Fill Frame proportionally.** This resizes each image so that it fits the frame as best it can without changing the proportion of the image nor leaving any white space in the frame.

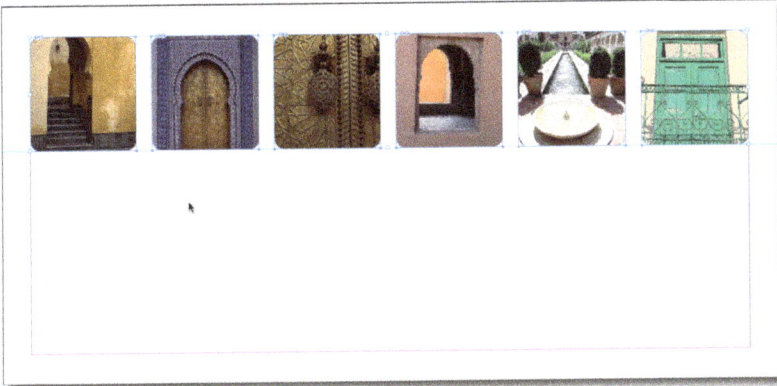

13. It may be that some of the images would look better with further adjustment. To do this, double-click with the **Selection Tool** to adjust any of them in the usual way.

14. Finish this last advert by applying a combination of the techniques you've learned by working through the exercises.

Discover Europe with us

From deserted Greek islands to street markets in Turkey, we'll show you the very best that Europe can offer even the most seasoned traveller. Leave it all to us, and discover it with us.

To receive our Europe brochure call **02344 3456123** or visit **www.discover-tours.com**

DISCOVER
Cultural Tours

Baracoa: Essential Info

WHY GO?

WHAT TO DO

GETTING THERE

IMMIGRATION

ACCOMMODATION

WHEN TO STAY

FOOD

FOR MORE

Visit Cuba
visitcubatoday.org

CUBA: ESSENTIAL INFO

GETTING THERE

GETTING AROUND

IMMIGRATION

WHEN TO STAY

FAR MORE

Visit Cuba
visitcubatoday.org

Tour Information
HIGHLIGHTS OF NICARAGUA, 2013

Day 1
Arrive in Managua

Day 2
Managua to Granada

Day 3
Granada

Day 4
Granada to San Juan del Sur

Day 5
San Juan del Sur to Ometepe

Tour Information
HIGHLIGHTS OF NICARAGUA, 2013

Day 6
Ometepe Island

Day 7
Ometepe to Granada

Day 8
Masaya and Leon

Day 9
Esteli

Day 10
Matagalpa

Day 11
Matagalpa link

Day 12
Managua to Volcan Masaya

Day 13
Big Corn Island

Day 14 –15
Little Corn Island

Day 16
Managua, home

HAVANA

For more information about any of the destinations mentioned here, and a complete guide to visiting Cuba, visit our website, www.visitcubatoday.org.

Visit Cuba
visitcubatoday.org

Visit Cuba
visitcubatoday.org

TRINIDAD

SANTIAGO

VINALES

Discover Asia with us

Asia

Laos

Cambodia

DISCOVER Cultural Tours

Vietnam

Ladakh

Japan

Thailand

CREATING LEAFLETS

This chpter is about creating leaflets. There are five in total, each one a little more complex than the last. The first two documents are single sided, and the final three have multiple pages that are arranged in different ways. The leaflets are created for two fictitious organisations, *Visit Cuba* and *Discover Cultural Tours*. As with any real organisation, they have had logos designed, and they use particular typefaces and colours in their branding.

1) A single sided leaflet for Visit Cuba.

The first document you'll create is a simple single sided leaflet. You'll learn about nDesign's essential tools, and how to bring images and text into a document.

Baracoa: Essential Info

WHY GO?
Beautiful, green, quirky, funky, Baracoa has it all. Isolated on a beautiful coastline and surrounded by lush hills and valleys, once you've arrived here you'll not be in a hurry to leave. What it lacks in size it more than makes up for with spirit. It's the perfect place to retreat to for a few days when you want to escape the hustle and bustle of Havana. Stay in one of the many Casa Particulares, feast of seafood straight from the ocean and hike through a lush teeming green landscape.

GETTING THERE
Flying is the easiest way to get to Baracoa, but booking ahead is essential unless you're shedule is very flexible. Cubana currently flies from Habana to Baracoa on Thursdays and Sundays, and on Sunday there is also a flight from Santiago de Cuba. If you'd rather travel by bus, Viazul have a daily afternoon service to Baracoa from Guantánamo and Santiago de Cuba.

ACCOMODATION
Hotels in Baracoa include Hotel El Castillo and Villa Gaviota Baracoa. There are also a wide selection of Casa Particulares, which are a perfect way to get to see the place through the eyes of a local. Recommended Casa Particulares include Casa Azul Baracoa, Casa Colonial Ykira and Casa Colonial Yalina y Gustavo.

FOOD
Many Casa Particulares will cook food to order, but there's plenty of places around town to tempt you out. The old established Paladar el Colonial continues to deliver its unique Baracoan take on Carribean cuisine, but there are a growing range of great places to eat and drink like O Poeta and Al's.

WHAT TO DO
The Museo Municipal, found in the Fuetre Matachin fortress, explains the history of Cuba's oldest settlement, including exhibits on Che Guevara and the local chocolate factory. The Museo Arqueológico is worth seeing for its location alone. Found in Las Cuevas del Paraíso, the archeological exhibits are displayed in caves that were once used as burial chambers. The 19th century church of Nuestra Señora de la Asunción contains the Cruz de la Parra, a wooden cross said to been erected by Columbus in 1492.

HIKING
In his journal, Christopher Columbus wrote about El Yunque, the hill across the bay from Baracoa. It's an 8km hike from the town, and the sights from the top as well as the wildlife you'll see along the way make it a trip well worth making. Local travel agent Cubatur offer a guided trip most days. Another popular hike through the lush local wilderness is to the Cueva del Aguas, a cave that contains a freshwater swimming hole.

FOR MORE
For more information on Baracoa before you go, visit our website. Once there, local travel agencies Cubatur and Ecotur are the places to visit.

Visit Cuba ▶

visitcubatoday.org

1. From InDesign's **File menu** choose *New>Document*.

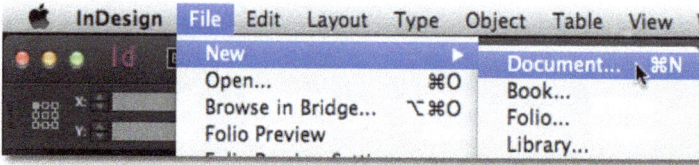

2. Look at the top of the *New Document* dialogue box to check that the *Document Preset* is set to *[Default]*. If it's not, select it from the pop up menu you can see there.

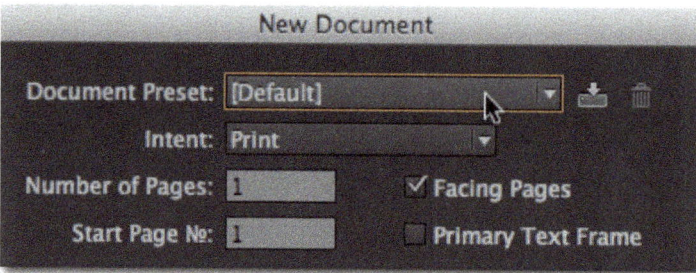

3. There are a great deal of useful options in the *New Document dialogue box,* many of which you'll explore shortly, but to keep things simple to start with, simply stick with the default settings and press the **OK button.**

4. As you look at the new InDesign document, notice the black rectangle around its edge. This represents the edge of the document, and the pink/purple lines are *Margin Guides*. These can be used in a variety of ways, but in this case you'll use them to align everything on your leaflet so that there is a consistent white space around its edge.

5. All of InDesign's tools are found in the panel at the left of the screen – the **Tools Panel.** Select the **Rectangle Frame Tool** from here by clicking on it .

6. Once you've selected the **Rectangle Frame Tool,** InDesign is expecting you to create a frame in which to put a picture or text. Notice that it has a plain crosshair at the moment. Position it over the intersection of the margin guides near the top left corner of the document and you'll see a little arrow, indicating that the cursor is accurately lined up with it.

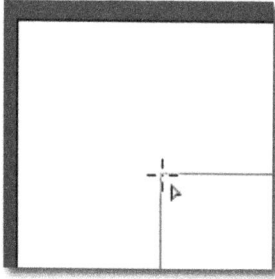

7. Press your mouse button down, and keeping it down, drag across to the margin guide at the right hand side of the page, and going down about a quarter of the page's depth. Release the mouse button when you see the little arrow appear to let you know you're accurately lined up. Once you've let go, you'll have created an empty frame.

8. Notice that you're still using the Rectangle Frame Tool, so if you either click, or click+drag, InDesign will try and create a new frame for you. If you've already created extra boxes, choose *Edit>Undo* to retrace your steps and remove them.

9. Notice the large *X* in the frame, indicating that it is currently empty. But this frame will shortly contain text. Select the *Type Tool* and click once on the new frame. You should now see that the X has disappeared, and instead contains a flashing cursor, indicating that InDesign is expecting you to type something.

10. Type the words *"Baracoa: Essential Info".* You probably can't see the text very clearly, so type *[Command+2]*, a shortcut that will enable you to see the area you're working on at 200%*. If you want to amend the text, simply drag over it with the **Type Tool** and retype as you would in any other text editing program.

* *When you want to come back out, press [Command+0 (zero)] to see the whole page again.*

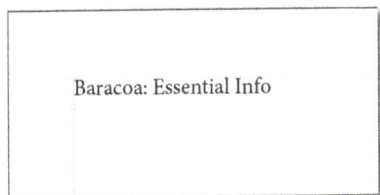

Baracoa: Essential Info

11. As you're using the **Type Tool** the context sensitive *Control Panel* at the top of the screen is now showing information about the type. If you look at the left edge of the Panel, there are two buttons. Ensure that the *Character Formatting Controls* button is selected (if it's darker than the other one, it is).

12. Select all the text you've just typed either by dragging over it with your mouse, or by choosing **Edit>Select All.** Change the **Font** from Minion Pro to *Poplar Std.*

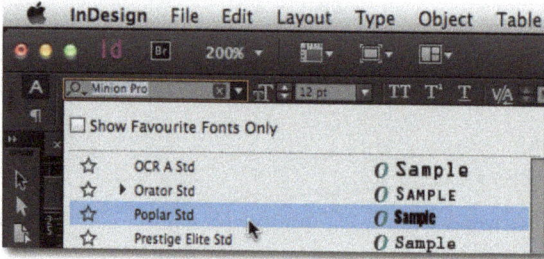

13. Change the size of the type from 12pt to *72pt* by choosing the drop down menu to the right of where the point size is displayed. Even though you've just chosen the largest of all the preset sizes, the text should still not quite fill the frame.*

* *If you've not already done so, press **[Command+0 (zero)]** to see the whole page again.*

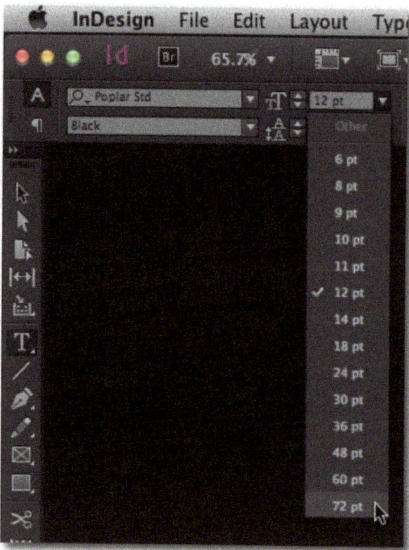

14. To make the upper case text slightly easier to read, you'll adjust its *tracking* value, which allows you to adjust the amount of space between each character. Change the **Tracking** value to *10,* which will add a subtle amount of space between each character. When you do this, it's likely that some of the text will move down to the next line*

* *If your frame isn't deep enough to accommodate two lines of text, you'll see an Overset Mark (a small red +) at the bottom right of your text frame, telling you that there isn't room to display all the text.*

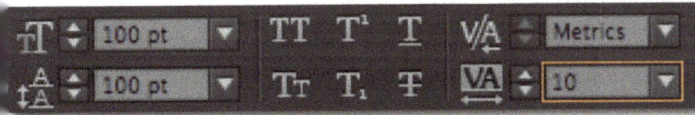

15.

16. Reduce the size of the type (by pressing the down arrow to the left of where the font size is displayed) until it all appears again on one line.

17. Many of the features in InDesign use *panels* that are docked to the side of the screen. Your first look at one of these is the **Swatches Panel,** which you'll use to change the colour of the text. To see what's inside the panel, click once on its name (in this case, click on where it says *Swatches*).

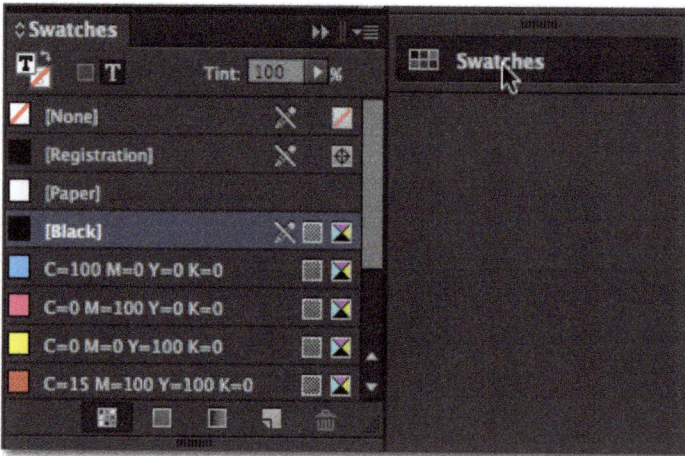

18. Notice that at the top left of the Panel there is a small black "T". This tells you that some text is selected, it is black, and that any changes in colour will affect the text and not the frame (more about this later).

19. Notice also that the black swatch has a faint highlight on it to indicate it's being used. Click on the *Red* swatch to change your text to that colour instead.

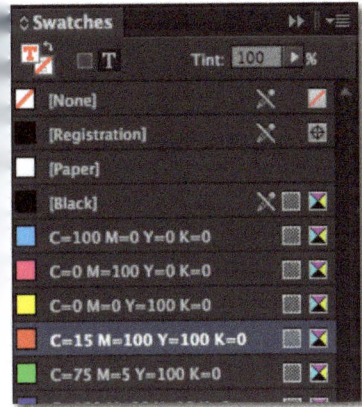

20. Switch to the **Selection Tool.** This tool is used to select frames, move them and resize them. Use the **Selection Tool** to reduce the height of the text frame by clicking on the *handle* that you can see in the centre of the bottom of the frame, and by dragging upwards.

21. Choose the **Rectangle Frame Tool** again from the **Tools Panel.** Draw a second frame, this time starting from just underneath the text frame, aligning to the left and right Margin Guides, and continuing down to almost half way down the page.

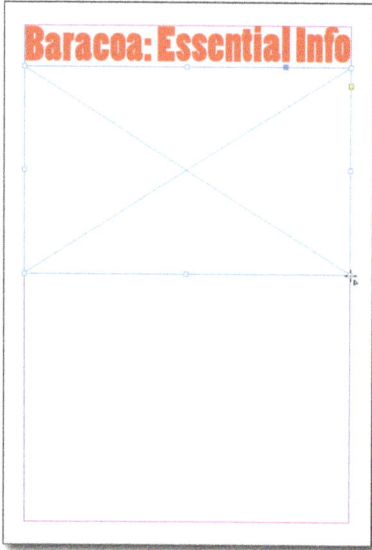

22. Choose the **Selection Tool** again from the Tools Panel and click on the frame you've just made. Choose *File>Place* to place an image into the frame. When the dialogue box appears, find the *Creative Classroom Leaflets* folder and select the *visit-cuba-baracoa-car.jpg* image. Press the **Open** button (or double-click) you'll see your frame is filled with the picture.

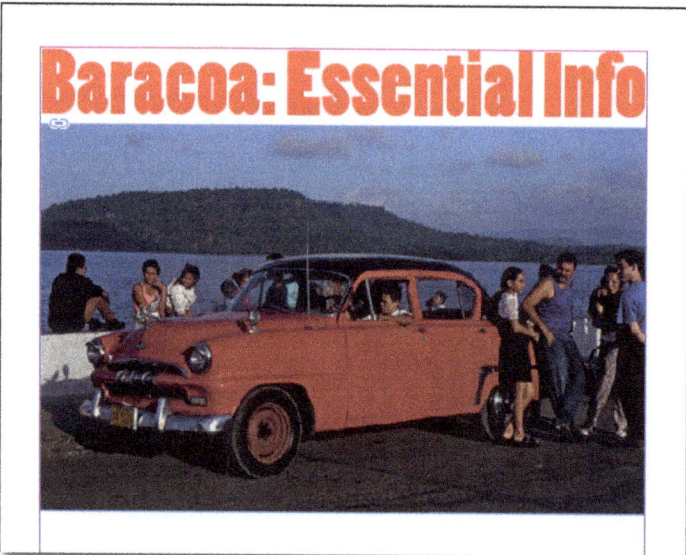

23. Using the **Rectangle Frame Tool,** create another frame for the main text to go in that starts a little under the picture frame and aligns to the left, right and bottom Margin Guides.

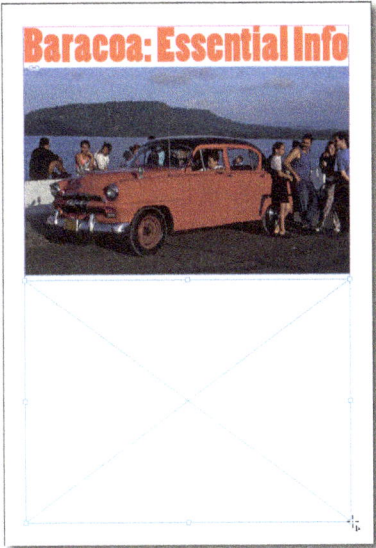

24. Click in the new frame with the **Type Tool.** Instead of typing anything, this time you're going to import some text that's already been typed.

25. Just as with a picture, to import text choose the **File>Place** command. Select the *visit-cuba-baracoa-essentials.txt* file and press the **Open** button. The text flows into the frame that your cursor was in.

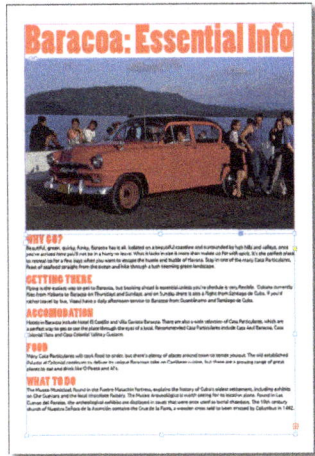

26. You might notice that the text comes in pre-formatted; this is not typical practice in InDesign, but it's being used here to keep things moving forward. In a subsequent exercise you'll learn how to format text from scratch using *Paragraph Styles.*

27. You might also notice that the text looks a little hard to read as it flows from the left of the frame all the way across to the very right. It will look far more readable if the text frame is split into two columns. To do this, choose **Object>Text Frame Options,** and once in the dialogue box change the number of **Columns** to *2.*

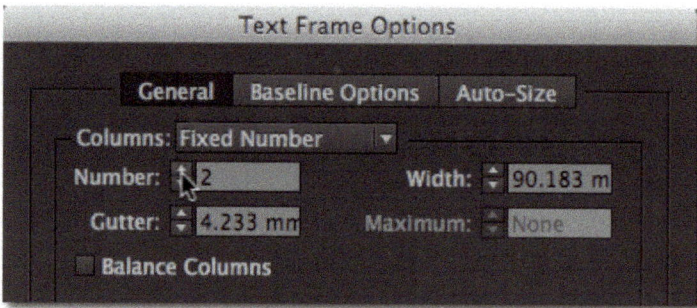

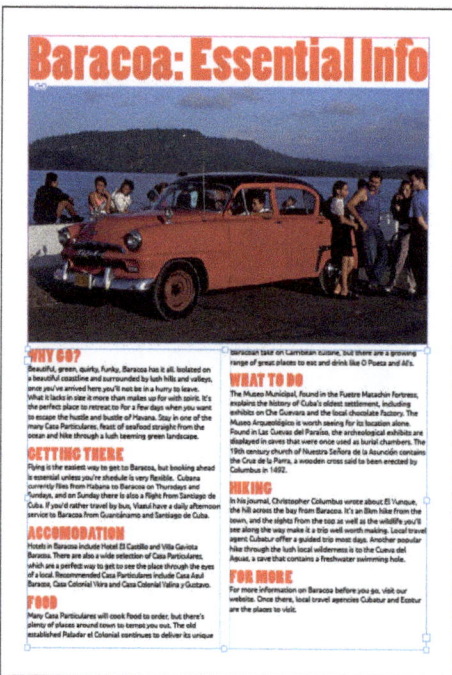

28. To bring in the *Visit Cuba* logo it would be possible to create a frame as you did before, then place the logo in as you did with the red car picture. However, it can be much more effective with small images like logos to allow InDesign to create a frame for you whilst you import it. To use this second approach, ensure that you're using the **Selection Tool,** and that nothing is selected (click on a blank area outside the document to deselect everything). Then choose **File>Place** and import the *visit_cuba_indesign_red.eps file.*

29. The logo will attach to your cursor. To place it in the document, click and drag near the leaflet's bottom right corner, and as you drag you'll be creating a frame that's exactly the same size and shape as the logo. If you don't get the result you wanted, choose **Edit>Undo** to take the logo off the page and re-attach it to your cursor so you can try again.

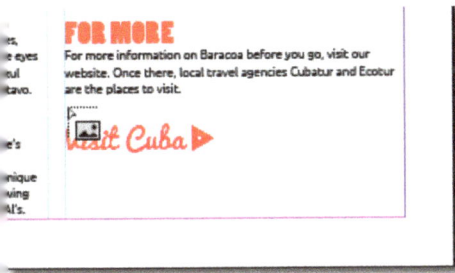

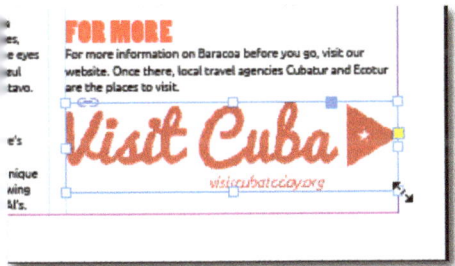

30. Drag with your **Selection Tool** if you want to reposition the logo.

31. By default, when you bring in a logo or similar vector graphic (see *Images from Photoshop and Illustrator* in the *Brief Notes* section for more information) you'll not see it displayed at full quality. Change to *Presentation Mode* by choosing **View>Screen Mode>Presentation.** This changes InDesign to a full screen mode, hides everything that won't print and shows graphics at their full resolution. To leave Presentation Mode, press the ***Esc key*** at the top left of your keyboard.

* *If you're using InDesign CS4 or earlier you won't have Presentation Mode. Instead, you can see the graphics in full quality by choosing **View>Display Performance>High Quality Display.** You can use Preview mode **(View>Screen Mode>Preview)** to hide elements that won't print, returning to Normal Mode using **View>Screen Mode>Normal.***

Baracoa: Essential Info

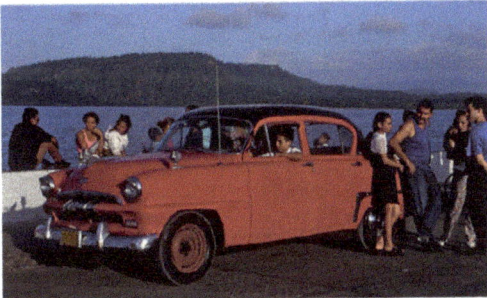

WHY GO?
Beautiful, green, quirky, funky, Baracoa has it all. Isolated on a beautiful coastline and surrounded by lush hills and valleys, once you've arrived here you'll not be in a hurry to leave. What it lacks in size it more than makes up for with spirit. It's the perfect place to retreat to for a few days when you want to escape the hustle and bustle of Havana. Stay in one of the many Casa Particulares, feast of seafood straight from the ocean and hike through a lush teeming green landscape.

GETTING THERE
Flying is the easiest way to get to Baracoa, but booking ahead is essential unless you're schedule is very flexible. Cubana currently flies from Habana to Baracoa on Thursdays and Sundays, and on Sunday there is also a flight from Santiago de Cuba. If you'd rather travel by bus, Viazul have a daily afternoon service to Baracoa from Guantánamo and Santiago de Cuba.

ACCOMODATION
Hotels in Baracoa include Hotel El Castillo and Villa Gaviota Baracoa. There are also a wide selection of Casa Particulares, which are a perfect way to get to see the place through the eyes of a local. Recommended Casa Particulares include Casa Azul Baracoa, Casa Colonial Ykira and Casa Colonial Yalina y Gustavo.

FOOD
Many Casa Particulares will cook food to order, but there's plenty of places around town to tempt you out. The old established Paladar el Colonial continues to deliver its unique Baracoan take on Carribean cuisine, but there are a growing range of great places to eat and drink like O Poeta and Al's.

WHAT TO DO
The Museo Municipal, found in the Fuetre Matachin fortress, explains the history of Cuba's oldest settlement, including exhibits on Che Guevara and the local chocolate factory. The Museo Arqueológico is worth seeing for its location alone. Found in Las Cuevas del Paraíso, the archeological exhibits are displayed in caves that were once used as burial chambers. The 19th century church of Nuestra Señora de la Asunción contains the Cruz de la Parra, a wooden cross said to been erected by Columbus in 1492.

HIKING
In his journal, Christopher Columbus wrote about El Yunque, the hill across the bay from Baracoa. It's an 8km hike from the town, and the sights from the top as well as the wildlife you'll see along the way make it a trip well worth making. Local travel agent Cubatur offer a guided trip most days. Another popular hike through the lush local wilderness is to the Cueva del Aguas, a cave that contains a freshwater swimming hole.

FOR MORE
For more information on Baracoa before you go, visit our website. Once there, local travel agencies Cubatur and Ecotur are the places to visit.

Visit Cuba ▶
visitcubatoday.org

32. The screenshot above shows roughly what the finished leaflet should look like. If yours doesn't look exactly the same it'll probably be because the size of the frame containing the text and/or the photograph is different*. Part of the reason it's challenging to get it to match is that you've not yet learned some key features that will make this process much easier, such as the use of margin guides and text wrap, which you'll go on to learn about in the next exercise. So if you can't quite get it the same, my advice is to leave it now and come back to it later once you've learned a bit more. Once you're ready to move on, choose **File>Save** to save the document in an appropriate place and with an appropriate name so that you can return to it later if you wish.

* *You can adjust these by dragging their handles, as you did after you created the text frame at the top.*

Summary of Menu commands

File>New>Document *[Command+N]*
File>Place *[Command+D]*
File>Save *[Command+S]*
Edit>Select All *[Command+A]*
Edit >Undo *[Command+Z]*
View>Screen Mode>Presentation
Object>Text Frame Options *[Command+B]*

Summary of Tools used

Rectangle Frame Tool
Selection Tool
Type Tool

Summary of shortcuts used

Command+2: view at 200% size
Command+0 (zero): Fit Page to Window
Esc: leave Presentation Mode

Summary of Panels used

Swatches (to apply a colour to the text)
Control Panel (to change font and type size)

2) A more complex leaflet for Visit Cuba

Whilst this second leaflet does not look that different to the first, it will be put together in a much more robust way, making use of InDesign's column guides and margin guides. You'll also learn how to work with text in multiple frames, flowing it from one frame to another, and how to make it automatically wrap around pictures.

1. Choose **File>New** to create a new document. In the *New Document* dialogue box, *uncheck* **Facing Pages,** for number of **Columns** choose 3, and insert the following values for the Margins (click on the padlock in the middle of the values to unlock it, so that you can apply different values to each margin): **Top:** *40mm;* **Bottom, Left** and **Right:** *15mm.*

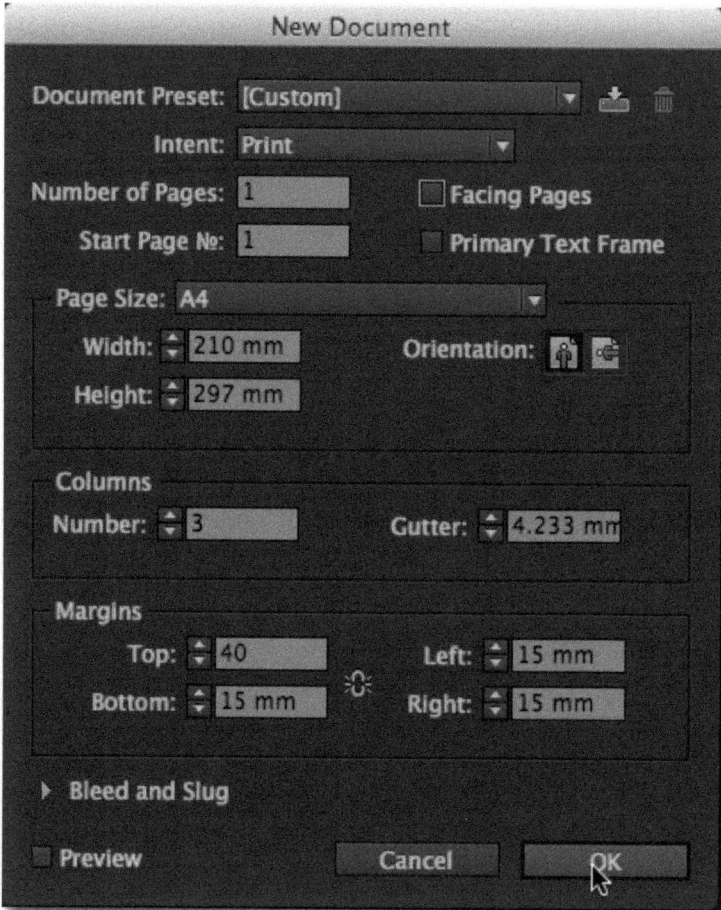

New Document

Document Preset:	[Custom]
Intent:	Print
Number of Pages:	1
	☐ Facing Pages
Start Page №:	1
	☐ Primary Text Frame
Page Size:	A4
Width:	210 mm
Orientation:	
Height:	297 mm

Columns

Number:	3	Gutter:	4.233 mm

Margins

Top:	40	Left:	15 mm
Bottom:	15 mm	Right:	15 mm

▶ Bleed and Slug

☐ Preview   Cancel   OK

2.   Once you've pressed the **OK** button you'll see the structure
     of margins and columns shown below. This is a more robust
     approach to setting up a document than you used in the
     previous exercise in that using margin and column guides you've
     deliberately specified the area into which the text will flow.

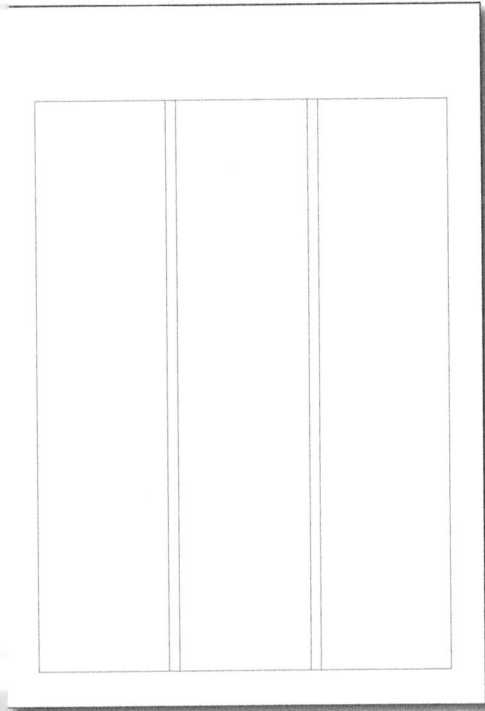

3. There are two broad approaches you can use when working with a large
    amount of text. One is the approach used previously, which is to create
    a frame, import the text, then specify the number of columns the frame
    will have. The alternative approach, which you'll use now, is to allow
    InDesign to create separate frames, based on the margin and column
    guides settings, and link them together so that the text flows from one to
    the next. To use this approach make sure you're using the **Selection Tool.**

4. In the same way that you imported the logo by attaching it
    to your cursor, you're going to do the same now with some
    text. Choose the **File>Place** command, select the *visit-
    cuba-essentials.txt* file and press the **Open button.**

5. Notice how the text has become attached to your cursor.

6. Place it at the top of the leftmost column and simply click. As you can see, InDesign creates a text frame that automatically snaps to the column guides.

7. Notice the little red '+' that you can see at the bottom right of the text frame. This is located in the area known as the *Out Port,* which shows whether or not the text continues once it's reached the bottom of the frame.

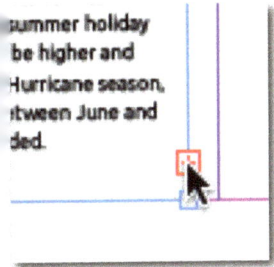

8. The little red '+' that you can see in the Out Port is known as an *overset mark,* and it signifies that there isn't room for all of the text in the frame. In the earlier example, to fix it you merely made the text smaller. However, this time, as you have no idea how much text there is, that's unlikely to work. Instead, you're going to create a second frame for the text to flow into.

9. Ensuring you're still using the **Selection Tool,** click on the overset mark.

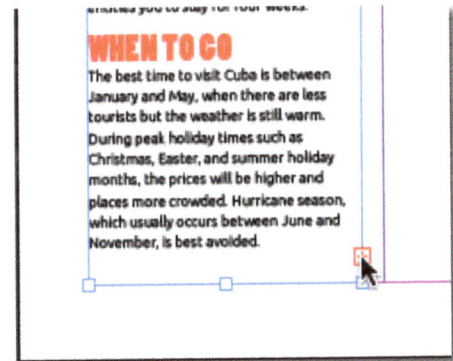

10. As you can see, your cursor becomes *Loaded* again. Click on the margin guide at the top of the middle column, and InDesign creates another text frame that automatically snaps to the column guides. This linkage of text frames is known as a *Story.*

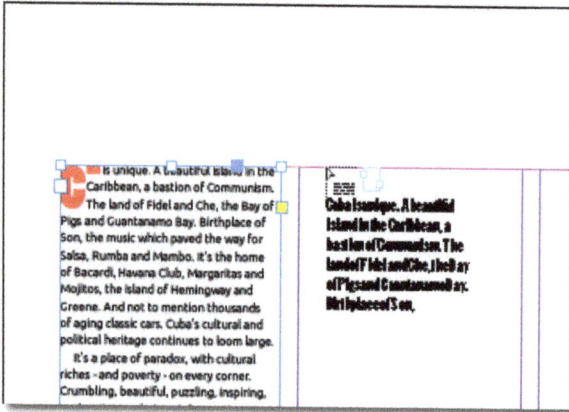

11. Notice that in the second frame the overset mark has disappeared and that the out port is now empty. This indicates that the story ends here.

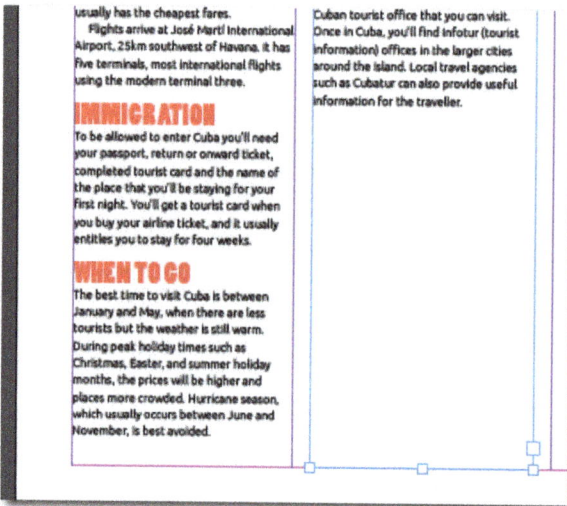

12. Even though there is currently enough room in the two columns to accommodate all of the text, shortly there won't be, and a third column will be needed. So in the same way you've just done, click on the second column's out port, reload the cursor again and click at the top of the third column to create a final frame for the text to flow into when needed.

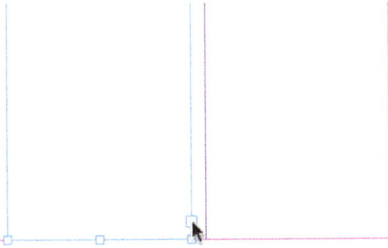

13. Next you're going to place a picture onto the page. But unlike the picture in the previous leaflet, this one will occupy the same space as the text. With the **Rectangle Frame Tool** create an empty frame that snaps across the second and third columns, as shown in the screenshot below.

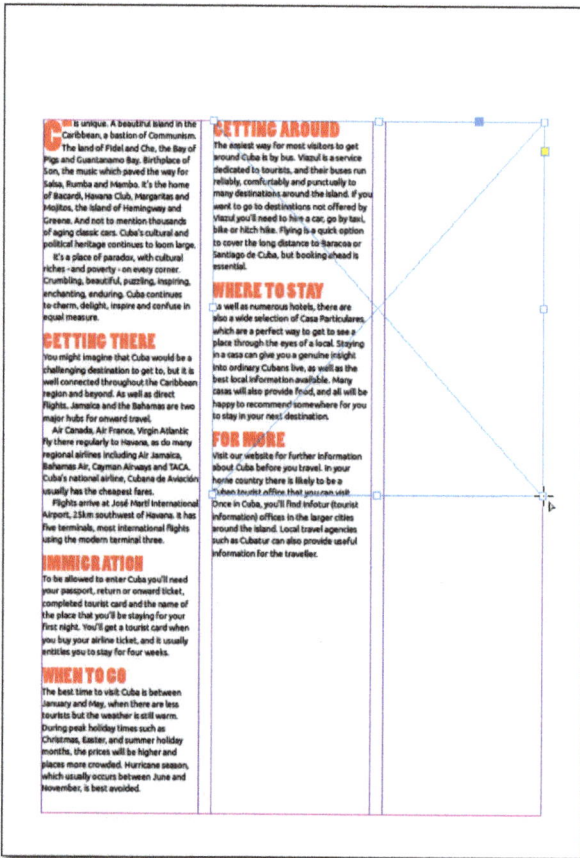

14. Import the *visit-cuba-havana-sidecar.jpg* image. As you can see, the picture is sitting on top of the text and obscuring it from view. However, you can make the Frame push the text away so that the text can only be seen where the picture frame is not. This feature is known as *Text Wrap*.

15. To access the text wrap command you'll need the *Text Wrap Panel.* This is one of the many panels that is not out on the screen by default, so you'll have to locate it. Like all of the panels, it can be found in the **Window menu,** where the panels are listed alphabetically. Choose **Window>Text Wrap** to display it.

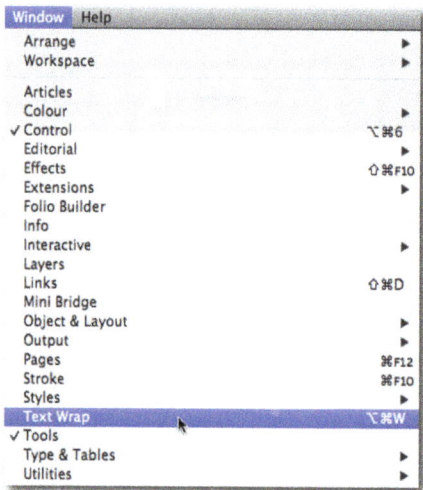

16. Choose the **Selection Tool** and ensure the frame containing the picture is selected. Notice that at the top of the Text Wrap Panel are five buttons (at this point you're only going to explore the two on the left hand side). The one (that should be highlighted) on the left indicates that there is *no text wrap.* This is why the picture simply covers the text beneath it.

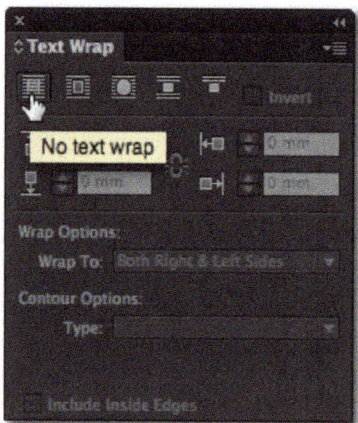

17. Click the **second button** in from the left, called *Wrap around bounding box.* As you can see, this pushes the text away from the picture, forcing it to wrap around the frame.

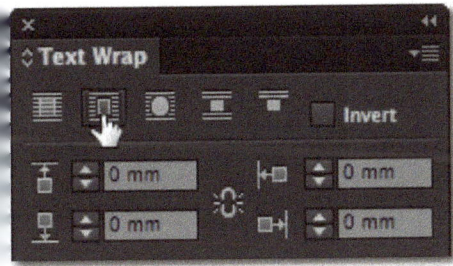

18. Whilst this is an improvement, you might notice that the text is sitting very close to the bottom of the picture. You're going to adjust the amount of space that will be created between the picture and the text.

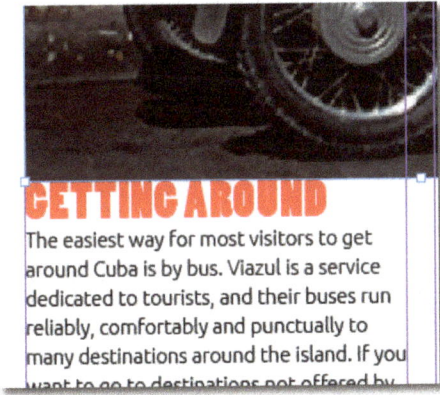

GETTING AROUND

The easiest way for most visitors to get around Cuba is by bus. Viazul is a service dedicated to tourists, and their buses run reliably, comfortably and punctually to many destinations around the island. If you want to go to destinations not offered by

19. Look in the **Text Wrap Panel** and notice the four *0* values. These show how near any text is allowed to come to the picture frame. Notice also the padlock symbol in the middle of those values. By default that padlock is locked, meaning that if you change one of the values, they will all change. As you want to only affect the text underneath the picture, ensure the padlock icon appears unlocked (click on it if it's not) so that the values no longer behave as one. Then change the bottom left value to about *4mm.*

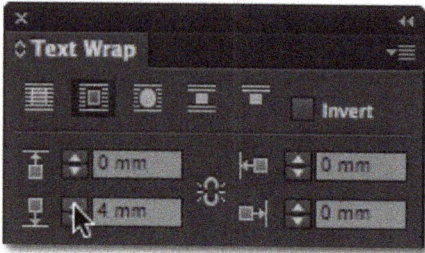

GETTING AROUND

The easiest way for most visitors to get around Cuba is by bus. Viazul is a service dedicated to tourists, and their buses run reliably, comfortably and punctually to many destinations around the island. If you

20. Most pages, whether in leaflets, newsletters, newspapers, brochures or magazines are a mixture of text and pictures. There's always a balance to be struck between the amount of text and the size of the pictures*. This is where Text Wrap comes in. By making a picture bigger, extra space can be filled and the text pushed down to the end of the column, page or frame. Or by making a picture smaller, text that previously couldn't fit may be able to.

* *In the world of magazines and newspapers, writers, editors and sub-editors can be protective of the words, just as designers and art directors can be of pictures. But the reality of most publications is there is a finite amount of space to be filled, a certain amount copy written, and a certain number of usable pictures.*

21. Next you're going to create a frame at the top of the page that will contain its title. However you have a problem in that there are no guides to snap your frame to. To fix this, you'll create some extra guides. If you look carefully at your screen you should see little rulers above and to the left of your page*.

* *If you don't see the little rulers above and to the left of the page, from the View menu choose Show Rulers.*

22. Using your **Selection Tool,** click on the ruler to the left of your page. Drag your mouse to the right, and you should see that you're dragging a light blue guide from the ruler. When you reach the pink margin guide, notice that the arrows that form your cursor change from *black* to *white* – this shows that you are lined up with the pink guide – so let go to place the guide here.

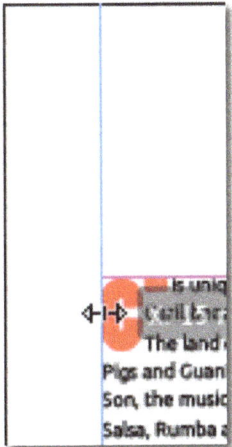

23. Drag another guide from the left ruler to line up with the right hand pink margin guide.

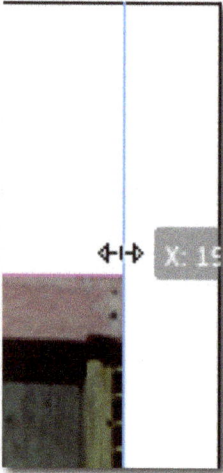

24. Now drag a guide from the ruler at the top of the page. Drag it roughly into position as shown below, and then click on it with the **Selection Tool.** It will change colour from light blue to dark to indicate that it is selected.

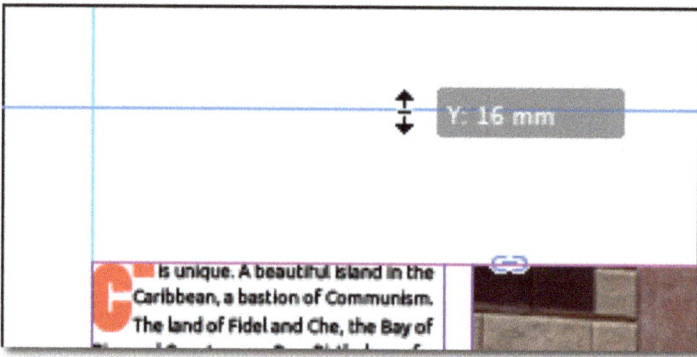

25. Look at the bottom left of the **Control Panel** and notice that there is a "Y" value for this guide. This indicates how far something is positioned down the page. Change the value so that it is exactly *15mm*.

26. Now use the **Rectangle Frame Tool** to create a frame that aligns to the three guides that you've just placed, with the bottom of the frame stopping just above the pink margin guide that denotes the start of the text.

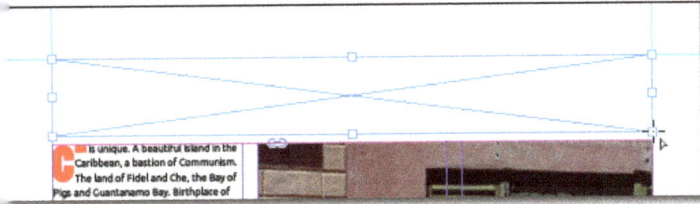

27. Change to the **Type Tool,** click in the empty frame and type "Cuba: Essential Info" in the new text frame. Then select all of the text and change the **Font** to *Poplar Std,* **Tracking** to around *10* and the **Size** to about *65pt.* Press the ***All Caps*** button and change the text colour to *Red* using the **Swatches Panel.** Try to get the text to fill the width of the frame by adjusting a combination of its size and tracking.

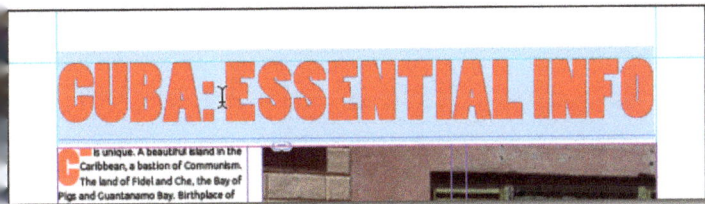

28. As with the previous leaflet you're going to place the *Visit Cuba* logo in the bottom right corner of the page. Change to the **Selection Tool** and ensure nothing is selected (by clicking somewhere off the edge of the page). Then choose **File>Place** and import the *visit_cuba_indesign_red* file. Click and drag near the bottom right corner of the page to place it, trying to make it the width of the second and third columns. Adjust its location with the **Selection Tool** if need be.

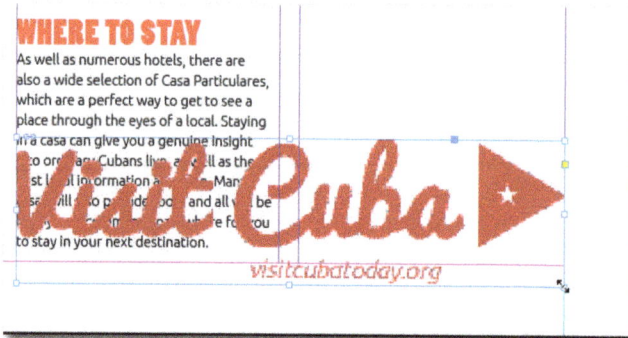

WHERE TO STAY

As well as numerous hotels, there are also a wide selection of Casa Particulares, which are a perfect way to get to see a place through the eyes of a local. Staying in a casa can give you a genuine insight to ordinary Cubans live, as well as the best local information around. Many casas will also provide food and all you need, it won't be hard to find somewhere for you to stay in your next destination.

visitcubatoday.org

29. So that the text doesn't overlap the logo, select the logo you've just imported and apply **text wrap** as you did before, only this time with an amount of about *2mm* at the top of the image.

WHERE TO STAY

As well as numerous hotels, there are also a wide selection of Casa Particulares, which are a perfect way to get to see a

Cuban tourist office that you can visit. Once in Cuba, you'll find Infotur (tourist information) offices in the larger cities around the island. Local travel agencies such as Cubatur can also provide useful information for the traveller.

visitcubatoday.org

30. Look towards the bottom right of your page. If you see an overset mark, you have made your picture frame too big. If you feel there is too much white space (empty space) at the bottom of the right hand column, you might want to make your picture frame bigger. Using the **Selection Tool,** drag the middle handle on the bottom of the picture frame either up or down.

31. If you've adjusted the frame, the picture inside it might need adjusting. You'll learn in great detail how to adjust images in the fourth exercise, but for now, a quick way to resize an image is to choose *Object>Fitting>Fill Frame Proportionally.* Once you're happy with the balance of the picture and the text, deselect everything and change to **Presentation Mode.** Notice how your use of margins, columns and guides has made it straightforward to create a complex yet flexible document. As before choose **File>Save** to save the document in an appropriate place and with an appropriate name so that you can return to it later if you wish.

Summary of new Menu commands

File>Place (for text instead of a picture) *[Command+D]*

Window>Text Wrap*[Command+Alt+W]*

Object>Fitting>Fill Frame Proportionally

Summary of new Panels used

Text Wrap Panel

3) A double-sided leaflet for Discover Cultural Tours

In this next lengthy exercise the document you'll create will be the first one you've looked at to use more than one page. It will also be where you learn to create Paragraph Styles, which is the most reliable and flexible way to format text with InDesign.

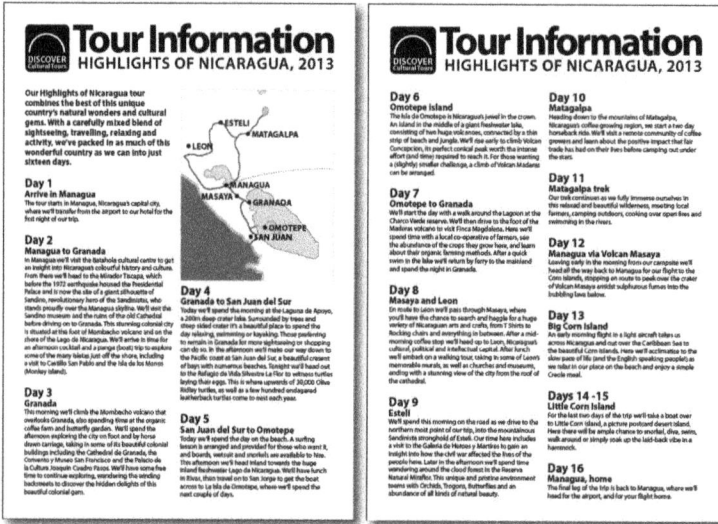

1. Choose **File>New** to create a new document. In the *New Document* dialogue box, change the **Number of Pages** to *2, uncheck* **Facing Pages,** and for number of **Columns** choose *2.* **Uncheck** the padlock in the middle of all the *Margins* values, then retype the **Top** value to make it *50mm,* but leave the other sides at their default values (12.7mm).

New Document

Document Preset: [Custom] ▾ ⬆ 🗑

Intent: Print ▾

Number of Pages: 1   ☐ Facing Pages

Start Page №: 1   ☐ Primary Text Frame

Page Size: A4 ▾

Width: ⬍ 210 mm   Orientation: 📄 📄

Height: ⬍ 297 mm

Columns

Number: ⬍ 2   Gutter: ⬍ 4.233 mm

Margins

Top: ⬍ 50 mm   Left: ⬍ 12.7 mm

Bottom: ⬍ 12.7 mm ⊗ Right: ⬍ 12.7 mm

▸ Bleed and Slug

✓ Preview   Cancel   OK

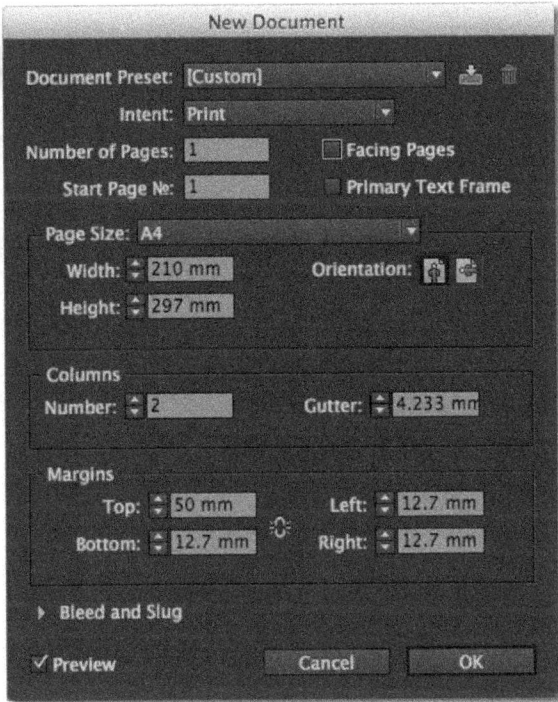

2. The margin guides that you've defined are the same on both of the pages of the document. They will define the edges of where the *body copy** goes, which as you can see leaves a little room for the logo and heading at the top of the page. In the two documents you've already created you've used two different approaches to import text. Here you'll combine the two, firstly by creating an initial frame, but later on by linking it to another. With your **Rectangle Frame Tool,** click and drag from where the margins intersect at the top left of the page, down and across to where they intersect at the page's bottom right.

* *This term is used to describe the main bulk of the text in a document.*

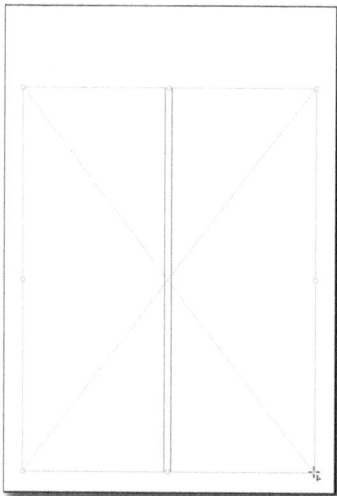

3. Change to the **Type Tool,** click on the empty frame, then choose **Object>Text Frame Options,** and change the number of columns to *2.*

4. Choose **Place** from the **File menu** and import the *discover-nicaragua-highlights.txt* file

5. This time the text has come in without any formatting applied to it. The previous documents you've created have all featured pre-formatted text, but it's much more typical to import plain text and then apply formatting within InDesign. If you're going to apply formatting you have several choices. For example, you could apply it to each paragraph of text manually, you could select all of the text and apply it all at once, or you could format one paragraph and then use InDesign's *Eyedropper Tool* to copy the formatting across. All of these approaches would work, but in practice you would be likely to find that if you wanted to change the style of your text later, or repeat it exactly in a subsequent document, it could be quite a complex procedure. A far more robust, flexible and creative approach is to use *Paragraph Styles*.

6. To see how Paragraph Styles work in practice, open either of the documents you've previously created. When you imported the body copy text it came in using paragraph styles that had already been created. To see them, firstly choose **Show Hidden Characters** from the **Type menu.** If you can't see the text very clearly, change to the **Type Tool,** place your cursor in the text and zoom in to 200% by pressing **Command+2.** The *show hidden characters* command shows you characters that, whilst they will not print, are nevertheless an essential component of text. Spaces are indicated by a simple dot (this is a useful way to find double spaces in text) and a paragraph symbol is one of these: ¶. This shows you where a paragraph ends (one appears every time you hit the **Return key** whilst typing).

GETTING AROUND¶

The easiest way for most visitors to get around Cuba is by bus. Viazul is a service dedicated to tourists, and their buses run reliably, comfortably and punctually to many destinations around the island. If you want to go to destinations not offered by Viazul you'll need to hire a car, go by taxi, bike or hitch hike. Flying is a quick option to cover the long distance to Baracoa or Santiago de Cuba, but booking ahead is essential.¶

7. To see how this relates to paragraph styles you'll need to look at the *Paragraph Styles Panel*, which may not be showing on your screen. If you can't see it amongst the panels on the right hand side of your screen, from the **Window menu** choose *Styles>Paragraph Styles.*

8. Look carefully at your text. Everything that's between two of these paragraph symbols is a paragraph. Place your cursor in any paragraph, look at your **Paragraph Styles Panel,** and notice that each paragraph uses one of the styles. To change a paragraph to a different style, simply click on a different style name in the panel.

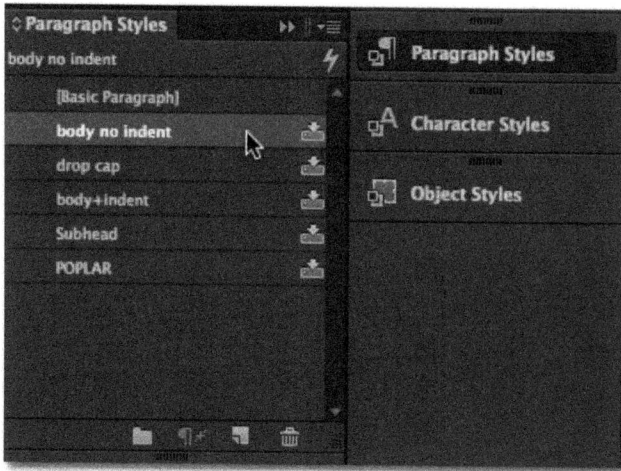

9. In this document the styles were imported with the text, but the usual procedure within InDesign is for someone to create the styles, which can be used in the document, or copied to a different document. You'll now look at how to create the paragraph styles you need for the Discover Tour Information Sheet, so return to that document. Once you're back in the document, choose **Type>Show Hidden Characters** so that you can clearly see the different paragraphs.

10. This is an outline of the steps you'll to use to create a Paragraph Style:
    i) Select a Paragraph.
    ii) Apply Character Formatting.
    iii) Apply Paragraph Formatting.
    iv) Turn the above formatting into a Style and apply it to the paragraph.

11. Select the first paragraph of text in your newly created document (that begins *"Our highlights..."*). The easiest way to do this is to click on it four times in quick succession*

* *Along the way, you may have realised that two clicks selects a word; three clicks selects a line; five clicks selects the whole story (all the text in a Frame, or any sequence of linked frames).*

12. Click on the **Character Formatting button** on the top left of the **Control Panel,** if it's not already selected. Change the **Font** to *Myriad Pro, Bold* **Weight,** *14pt* **Size,** *16pt* **Leading** and *-5* **Tracking.**

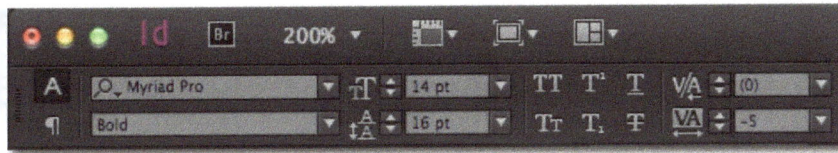

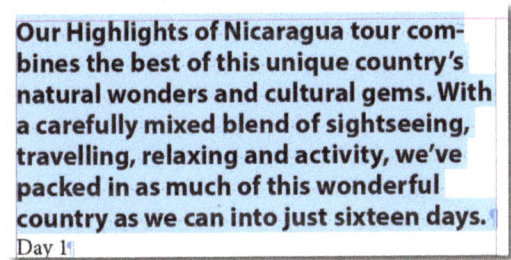

13. Click on the *Paragraph Formatting button* on the left of the Control Panel. *Uncheck* Hyphenate.

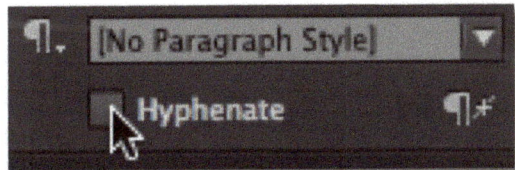

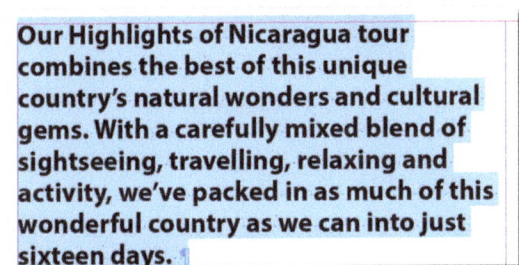

14. To capture the character and paragraph formatting you've just applied and turn them into a paragraph style, click on the **dropdown menu** at the top right corner of the **Paragraph Styles Panel** and choose *New Paragraph Style.*

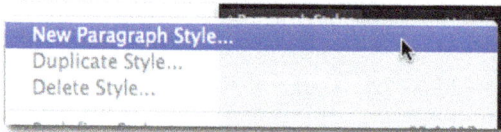

Paragraph Styles

(No Styles)

[Basic Paragraph]

New Paragraph Style...
Duplicate Style...
Delete Style...

15. The *New Paragraph Style* dialogue box opens. At the bottom under *Style Settings* you can see a description of the formatting that you've just applied, and that the style will capture. The highlighted text at the top of the dialogue box is the name of the Style. By default, it's called it *Paragraph Style 1.*

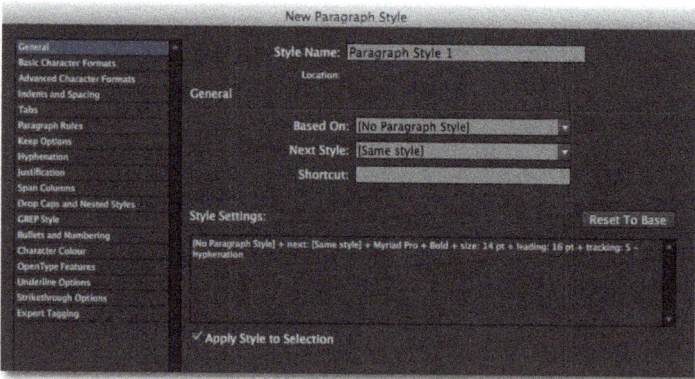

New Paragraph Style

General
Basic Character Formats
Advanced Character Formats
Indents and Spacing
Tabs
Paragraph Rules
Keep Options
Hyphenation
Justification
Span Columns
Drop Caps and Nested Styles
GREP Style
Bullets and Numbering
Character Colour
OpenType Features
Underline Options
Strikethrough Options
Export Tagging

Style Name: Paragraph Style 1
Location:

General

Based On: [No Paragraph Style]
Next Style: [Same style]
Shortcut:

Style Settings: Reset To Base

[No Paragraph Style] + next: [Same style] + Myriad Pro + Bold + size: 14 pt + leading: 16 pt + tracking: 5 + hyphenation

✓ Apply Style to Selection

16. Change the name of the style to *Introduction.* Before you leave this dialogue box, make sure that *Apply Style to Selection* is checked, then press the **OK button.**

17. If you look at the Paragraph Styles Panel now you should see that there is a new style there – *Introduction* – that you've just created. The subtle highlight on it shows that it's applied to the currently selected text.

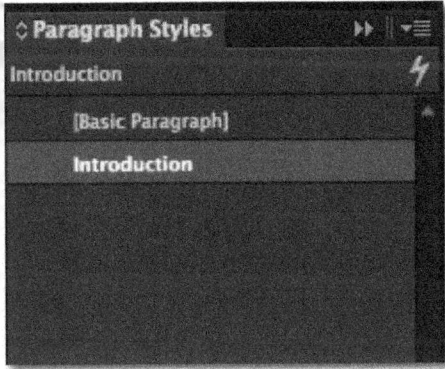

18. You'll repeat this four stage process described above to create a second style, this one for the paragraphs that specify each day of the tour. Select the second paragraph in the document *(Day One)* and apply the following Character formats: *Myriad Pro, Bold, 20pt* **Size,** *23pt* **Leading.**

19. Apply the following Paragraph format: ***Space Before*** *5mm.*

20. Using the Paragraph Styes Panel's **dropdown menu** again, create a new Paragraph Style called *Days.*

21. Apply the *Days* Paragraph Style to the *"Day 2"* paragraph by placing your cursor in it and then by clicking on the *Days* Paragraph Style in the Paragraph Styles Panel.

Day 1¶
Arrive in Managua¶
The tour starts in Managua, Nicaragua's capital city,
where we'll transfer from the airport to our hotel for
our first night. ¶

Day 2¶
Managua to Granada¶

22. Select the third paragraph in the document *(Arrive in Managua)* and apply the following character formats: *Myriad Pro, Bold, 15pt* **Size,** *16pt* **Leading.** In the same way you did before, create a new paragraph style called Places, then apply it to the *Managua to Granada* paragraph.

Day 1¶
Arrive in Managua¶

The tour starts in Managua, Nicaragua's capital city,
where we'll transfer from the airport to our hotel for
our first night. ¶

Day 2¶
Managua to Granada¶

In Managua we'll visit the Batahola cultural centre
to get an insight into Nicaragua's colourful history

23. The final style you'll create is the style you'll use for the *body text**. Select the whole of the paragraph that begins *"The tours starts..."* and use the following settings: *Myriad Pro, Regular, 11pt* **Size,** *13pt* **Leading.** Click on the **Paragraph Formatting button** on the left of the Control Panel and *Uncheck* Hyphenate. Create a paragraph style called *Body*.

* *The term body is often used to describe the main body of the text, as opposed to headings, subheads etc.*

Day 1¶
Arrive in Managua¶
The tour starts in Managua, Nicaragua's capital city,
where we'll transfer from the airport to our hotel for our
first night.¶

24. Apply the *Body* style to the paragraph that begins *"In Managua we'll visit..."*, and then continue through the document, applying the appropriate styles to each paragraph.

Day 1
Arrive in Managua
The tour starts in Managua, Nicaragua's capital city, where we'll transfer from the airport to our hotel for our first night.

Day 2
Managua to Granada
In Managua we'll visit the Batahola cultural centre to get an insight into Nicaragua's colourful history and culture. From there we'll head to the Mirador Tiscapa, which before the 1972 earthquake housed the Presidential Palace and is now the site of a giant silhouette of Sandino, revolutionary hero of the Sandinistas, who stands over the Managua skyline. We'll visit the Sandino museum and the ruins of the old Cathedral before driving on to Granada.

Our Highlights of Nicaragua tour combines the best of this unique country's natural wonders and cultural gems. With a carefully mixed blend of sightseeing, travelling, relaxing and activity, we've packed in as much of this wonderful country as we can into just sixteen days.

Day 1
Arrive in Managua
The tour starts in Managua, Nicaragua's capital city, where we'll transfer from the airport to our hotel for our first night.

Day 2
Managua to Granada
In Managua we'll visit the Batahola cultural centre to get an insight into Nicaragua's colourful history and culture. From there we'll head to the Mirador Tiscapa, which before the 1972 earthquake housed the Presidential Palace and is now the site of a giant silhouette of Sandino, revolutionary hero of the Sandinistas, who stands over the Managua skyline. We'll visit the Sandino museum and the ruins of the old Cathedral before driving on to Granada. Granada is a stunning colonial city, set at the foot of Mombacho volcano and on the shore of the Lago de Nicaragua. We'll arrive in time for an afternoon cocktail and a panga trip to explore some of the many isletas just off the shore, including a visit to Castillo San Pablo and the Isla de los Monos (Monkey Island).

Day 3
Granada
This morning we'll climb the Mombacho volcano that overlooks Granada, also spending time at the organic coffee farm and butterfly garden.
We'll spend the afternoon exploring the city on foot and by horse drawn carriage, taking in some of its beautiful colonial buildings including the Cathedral de Granada, the Convento y Museo San Francisco and the Palacio de la Cultura Joaquin Cuadro Pasos. We'll have some free time to continue exploring, wandering the backstreets to discover the hidden delights of this beautiful colonial gem.

Day 4
Granada to San Juan del Sur
Today we'll spend the morning at the Laguna de Apoyo, a 200m deep crater lake. Surrounded by trees and steep sided crater it's a beautiful place to spend the day relaxing, swimming or kayaking. Those preferring to remain in Granada for more sightseeing or shopping can do so.
In the afternoon we'll make our way down to the Pacific coast at San Juan del Sur, a beautiful cresent of bays with numerous beaches. Tonight we'll head out to the Refugio de Vida Silvestre La Flor to witness turtles laying their eggs. This refuge is where upwards of 30,000 Olive Ridley turtles, as well as a few hundred endagered leatherback turtles come to nest each year.

Day 5
San Juan del Sur to Omotepe
Today we'll spend the day on the beach. A surfing lesson is arranged and available for those who want it, and boards, wetsuit and snorkels are free to hire.
This afternoon we'll head inland towards the huge inland Lago de Nicaragua. We'll have lunch in Rivas, then travel on to San Jorge to get the boat across to La Isla de Omotepe, where we'll spend the night.

Day 6
Omotepe Island
The Isla de Omotepe is Nicaragua's jewel in the crown. An island in the middle of a giant freshwater lake, consisting of two huge volcanoes, connected by a thin strip of beach and jungle.
We'll rise early to climb Volcan Concepcion, its perfect conical peak worth the intense effort (and time) required to reach it. For those wanting a (slightly) smaller challenge, a climb of Volcan Maderas can be arranged.

Day 7
Omotepe to Granada
We'll start the day with a walk around the Lagoon at the Charco Verde reserve. We'll then drive to the foot of the Maderas volcano to visit Finca Magdalena. Here we'll spend time with a local co-operative of farmers, see the abundance of the crops they grow here, and learn about their organic farming methods.

25. When you reach the end of the first page you might notice that you've run out of text. You'll shortly make the story continue on the second page of the document. To begin this process, ensure that you're using the **Selection Tool** and click on the overset mark at the bottom right of the text frame. As you discovered previously, this loads your cursor with any text that remains in the story that there isn't currently room for.

26. Click on the *Pages Panel* to open it up, and double-click on the *Page 2* icon to view page 2. If you can't see the whole page press **Command+0 (zero)** to zoom out.

27. With your loaded cursor, click and drag from the top left intersection of the margin guides down to the bottom right intersection to create a large text frame.

28. Choose **Object>Text Frame Options** to change this frame to a *2* column frame, like the one on page 1. Continue applying the paragraph styles through to the end of the document.

29. Once you've reached the end of the text you'll see there is still some room underneath it. This is because some room has been left for a map, which will be placed on the front page of the leaflet. Open up the **Pages Panel** again and double click on the *Page 1* icon to return to the first page.

30. Using the **Rectangle Frame Tool,** create a frame that's aligned to the width of the right hand column, and comes down to cover nearly half of the text.

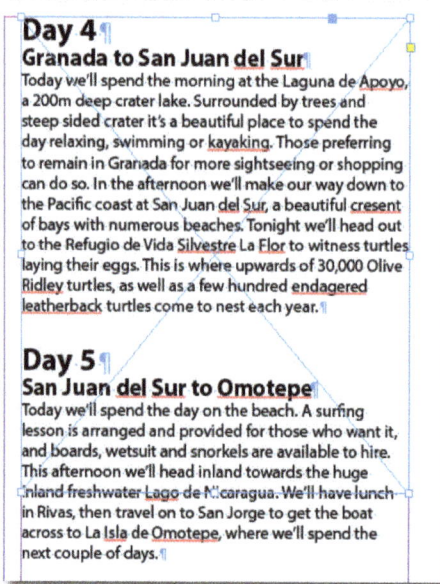

Day 4
Granada to San Juan del Sur
Today we'll spend the morning at the Laguna de Apoyo, a 200m deep crater lake. Surrounded by trees and steep sided crater it's a beautiful place to spend the day relaxing, swimming or kayaking. Those preferring to remain in Granada for more sightseeing or shopping can do so. In the afternoon we'll make our way down to the Pacific coast at San Juan del Sur, a beautiful cresent of bays with numerous beaches. Tonight we'll head out to the Refugio de Vida Silvestre La Flor to witness turtles laying their eggs. This is where upwards of 30,000 Olive Ridley turtles, as well as a few hundred endagered leatherback turtles come to nest each year.

Day 5
San Juan del Sur to Omotepe
Today we'll spend the day on the beach. A surfing lesson is arranged and provided for those who want it, and boards, wetsuit and snorkels are available to hire. This afternoon we'll head inland towards the huge inland freshwater Lago de Nicaragua. We'll have lunch in Rivas, then travel on to San Jorge to get the boat across to La Isla de Omotepe, where we'll spend the next couple of days.

31. Use the **Text Wrap Panel** to push the text away from the frame, leaving a gap of approximately *3mm* underneath.

Day 4
Granada to San Juan del Sur
Today we'll spend the morning at the Laguna de Apoyo,

32. Adjust the depth of the frame to make it either deeper or
shallower (by dragging the bottom centre handle with the
Selection Tool) so that all of the *body* paragraph that follows
Day 5 remains together at the foot of the first page.

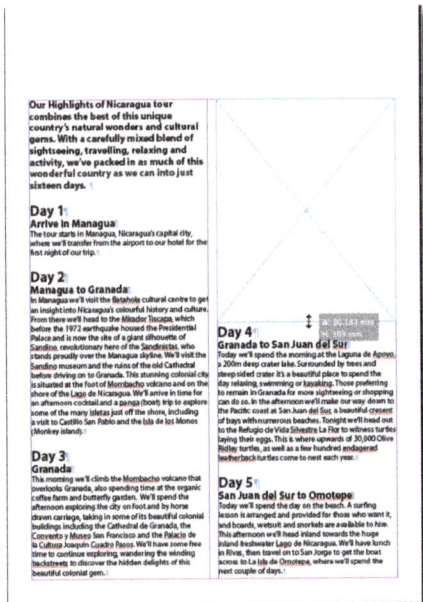

33. Place the *discover-nicaragua-map-bw.ai* image into the frame.

34. To emphasise the edge of the map you'll place a thin stroke (border) around the edge of its frame. To do this, make sure the frame is selected, press the **Stroke button** in the Control Panel and apply the black swatch.

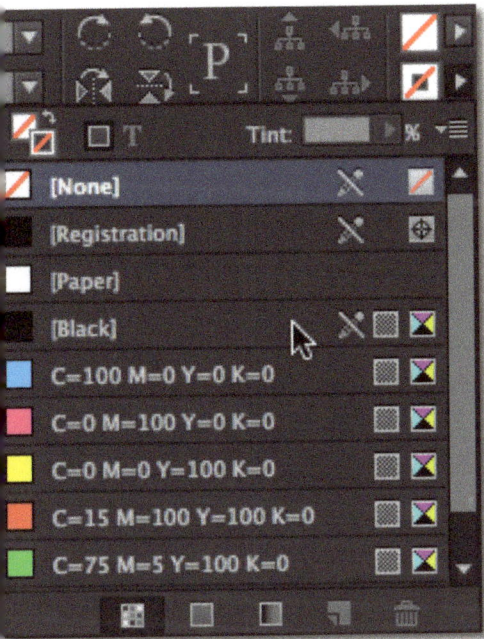

35. If you want to adjust the thickness of the stroke, press on
the dropdown menu to the right of the stroke weight.

36. To finish the leaflet you'll import the *Discover* logo and create the
heading at the top of the first page. As you've done in previous leaflets,
you'll drag some guides from the rulers to give you something to
align to. Drag a guide from the ruler at the left of the screen and
align it to the margin guide at the left of the page. Repeat to create
another guide aligned to the right margin guide. From the ruler at
the top of the screen drag down two guides, and adjust them so that
one is 12.7mm from the top of the page and the other is 40mm.

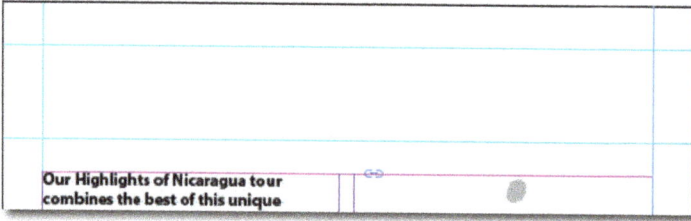

Our Highlights of Nicaragua tour
combines the best of this unique

37. Choose **File>Place** to attach the *discover-logo-wob-round.ai* logo to your cursor. Line up your loaded cursor with the top left intersection of the guides you've just drawn, then drag carefully diagonally down and to the right until your cursor aligns to the bottom blue guide. If you don't get it right the first time, choose **Edit>Undo** and try again.

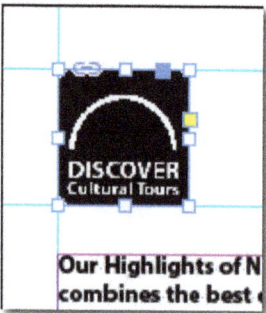

38. To create the remainder of the header you'll create two text frames, one for the words *Tour Information* and one for the title of the tour. You already know how to create text frames and to adjust the font, size and tracking of the text. What you'll try and do here is a little more challenging in that you'll try and make the heading as large as possible, while also trying to align it to the logo in a way that makes it look as if these two elements should belong together. Look below at a finished version and notice how the baseline of the text (the line on which it all sits) aligns with the bottom of the semicircle in the logo. Aligning disparate elements like this helps gives the impression that they belong together. You might find it useful to drag another guide down from the top ruler that aligns to the bottom of the semicircle in the logo.

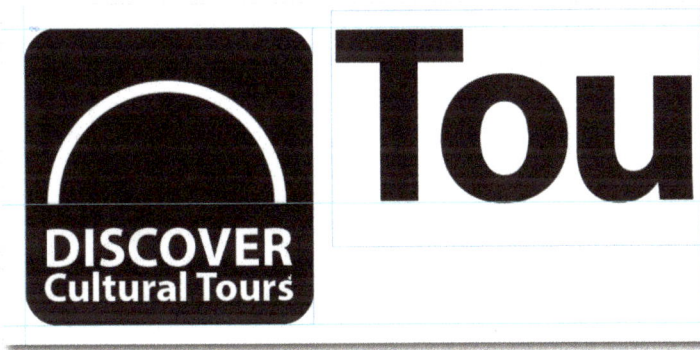

39. The finished version was created deliberately using a text frame that was larger than the finished text. This gave not only more room to experiment with the size and tracking of the text but also in the positioning of it, which can be done by moving it with the Selection Tool or nudging it with the arrow keys. The finished version uses Myriad Pro bold at a **Font Size** of *66pt,* and **Tracking** of *-55*. Once you've finished adjusting the heading, change back to the Selection Tool and make the text frame no smaller than it needs to be – this will make it clearer as you add some more text in a separate frame.

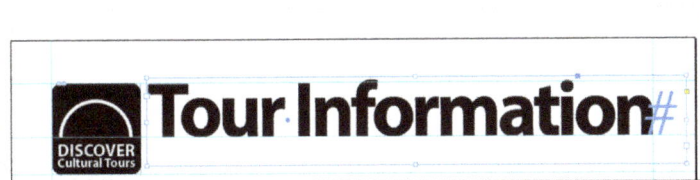

40. The name of the tour should be placed in a separate text frame, again sized a little larger than necessary, lined up with the baseline of the text at the bottom of logo, using upper case text, a **Font Size** of *27pt* and 24 **Tracking.**

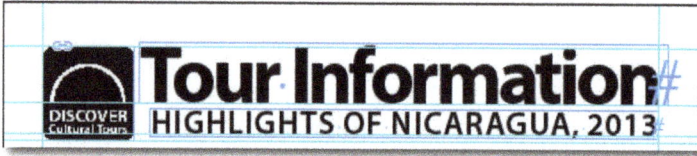

41. Rather than recreate the same elements again on the second page you'll instead copy and paste them from the first page. Firstly, using your **Selection Tool,** click outside of the page to deselect everything, then click and drag around all of the elements of the heading at once to select them. Then from the **Edit menu** choose *Copy.*

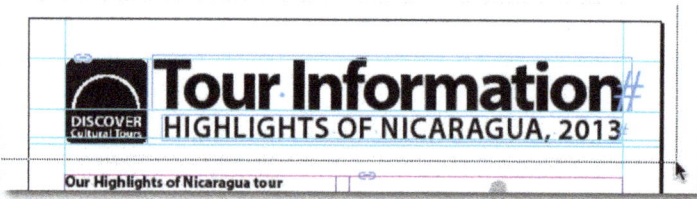

42. Double-click on *page 2* in the **Pages Panel** to view page 2. Then from the **Edit menu** choose *Paste in Place* to duplicate all of the header elements in the correct place, to finish the document.

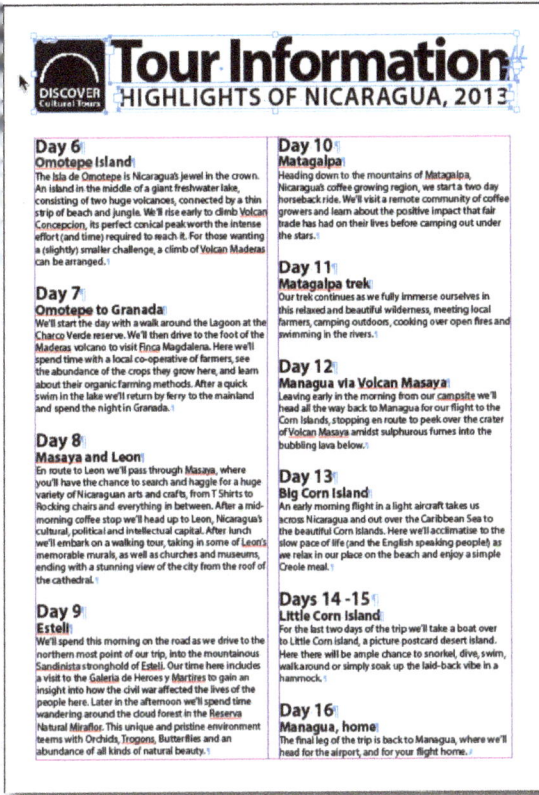

Tour Information
HIGHLIGHTS OF NICARAGUA, 2013

Day 6
Omotepe Island
The Isla de Omotepe is Nicaragua's jewel in the crown. An island in the middle of a giant freshwater lake, consisting of two huge volcanoes, connected by a thin strip of beach and jungle. We'll rise early to climb Volcan Concepcion, its perfect conical peak worth the intense effort (and time) required to reach it. For those wanting a (slightly) smaller challenge, a climb of Volcan Maderas can be arranged.

Day 7
Omotepe to Granada
We'll start the day with a walk around the Lagoon at the Charco Verde reserve. We'll then drive to the foot of the Maderas volcano to visit Finca Magdalena. Here we'll spend time with a local co-operative of farmers, see the abundance of the crops they grow here, and learn about their organic farming methods. After a quick swim in the lake we'll return by ferry to the mainland and spend the night in Granada.

Day 8
Masaya and Leon
En route to Leon we'll pass through Masaya, where you'll have the chance to search and haggle for a huge variety of Nicaraguan arts and crafts, from T Shirts to Rocking chairs and everything in between. After a mid-morning coffee stop we'll head up to Leon, Nicaragua's cultural, political and intellectual capital. After lunch we'll embark on a walking tour, taking in some of Leon's memorable murals, as well as churches and museums, ending with a stunning view of the city from the roof of the cathedral.

Day 9
Esteli
We'll spend this morning on the road as we drive to the northern most point of our trip, into the mountainous Sandinista stronghold of Esteli. Our time here includes a visit to the Galeria de Heroes y Martires to gain an insight into how the civil war affected the lives of the people here. Later in the afternoon we'll spend time wandering around the cloud forest in the Reserva Natural Miraflor. This unique and pristine environment teems with Orchids, Trogons, Butterflies and an abundance of all kinds of natural beauty.

Day 10
Matagalpa
Heading down to the mountains of Matagalpa, Nicaragua's coffee growing region, we start a two day horseback ride. We'll visit a remote community of coffee growers and learn about the positive impact that fair trade has had on their lives before camping out under the stars.

Day 11
Matagalpa trek
Our trek continues as we fully immerse ourselves in this relaxed and beautiful wilderness, meeting local farmers, camping outdoors, cooking over open fires and swimming in the rivers.

Day 12
Managua via Volcan Masaya
Leaving early in the morning from our campsite we'll head all the way back to Managua for our flight to the Corn Islands, stopping en route to peek over the crater of Volcan Masaya amidst sulphurous fumes into the bubbling lava below.

Day 13
Big Corn Island
An early morning flight in a light aircraft takes us across Nicaragua and out over the Caribbean Sea to the beautiful Corn Islands. Here we'll acclimatise to the slow pace of life (and the English speaking people) as we relax in our place on the beach and enjoy a simple Creole meal.

Days 14 -15
Little Corn Island
For the last two days of the trip we'll take a boat over to Little Corn Island, a picture postcard desert island. Here there will be ample chance to snorkel, dive, swim, walk around or simply soak up the laid-back vibe in a hammock.

Day 16
Managua, home
The final leg of the trip is back to Managua, where we'll head for the airport, and for your flight home.

Summary of new Menu commands

Edit>Copy
Edit>Paste in Place
Type>Show Hidden Characters
Window>Styles>Paragraph Styles

Summary of Panels used

Control Panel (to change Leading)
Control Panel (to change paragraph formats: hyphenate, space before)
Text Wrap Panel
Pages Panel

4) An A5 four page leaflet for Visit Cuba

This document will feature text that flows over several pages and around images. It will have a cover that includes a montage of several images. This document will take a fair amount of time to put together, and you should be aware before starting it that to create the montage for the front page according to the instructions you'll need to be using *InDesign CS4* or later.

- Choose **File>New** to create a new document. In the *New Document* dialogue box, change the **Number of Pages** to *4, check* **Facing Pages,** and change the **Page Size** to *A5*. For number of **Columns** choose *3*, choose a *Gutter* value of *3mm*, and change the **Margins** so that all sides are *9mm.* Towards the bottom left of the *New Document dialogue box* is a toggle enabling you to show or hide the values for *Bleed and Slug.* Press on it to reveal the values and enter 3mm for all of the *Bleed* values. Then press the **OK button.**

In CS versions of InDesign you'll reveal the Bleed and Slug *values by pressing the* **More Options** *button that you'll find towards the top right of the New Document dialogue box.*

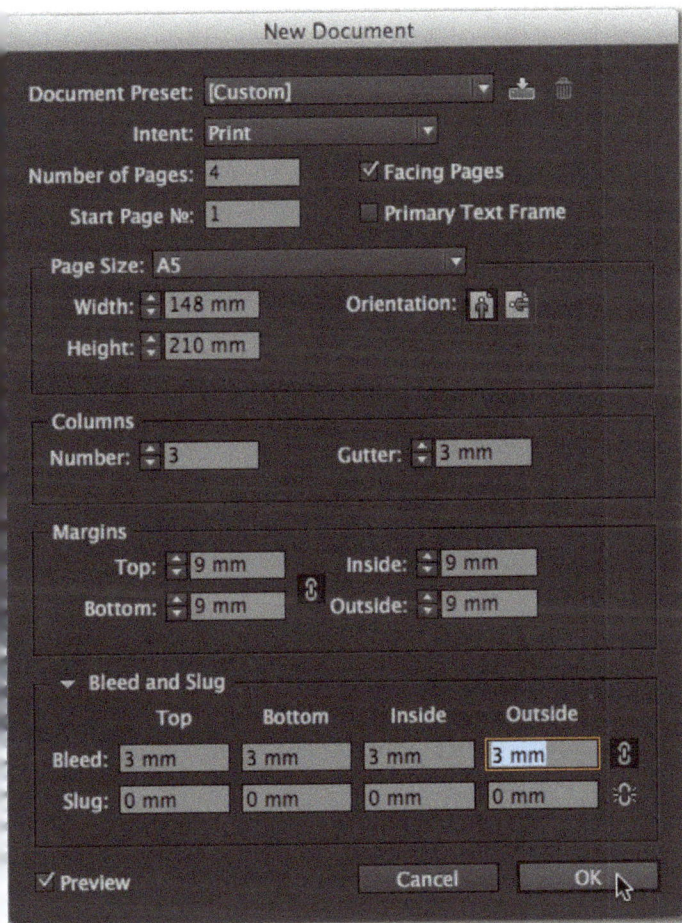

2. If you look at the edge of this document you'll see a red border outside the black border that you've seen on the previous document you created. As you know, the black border indicates the edge of your document, but that's not the full story. When you send your InDesign document to a commercial printer they are often printed on sheets or rolls of paper that are larger than the document size. They are then trimmed down to size on a guillotine, whose blade is lined up with *Trim Marks* (see the diagram below).

3. The black border represents where the trimming *should* occur. However, as the guillotine blade runs through a stack of paper its blade may bend slightly, and your document may be trimmed slightly inside or outside the black line. To allow for this, any elements that need to appear right at the edge of a page need to continue, or 'bleed' over the edge. The Bleed Guide makes it straightforward to create bleeds, as objects snap to the guide. 3mm is generally accepted as a suitable bleed amount for most work.

4. Click on the **Pages Panel** to open it. If you look carefully at the icons that represent the pages, notice the thin black line to the left of the first page, to the right of the final page and in between the second and third pages. This thin line represents the *spine* of the document. If you pick up any printed book and close it, you'll see that its spine is on the left hand side of the cover. Open the cover, and notice that the spine is now in the middle of the two pages. Two pages together like this are known as a *double page spread,* or simply, a *spread.*

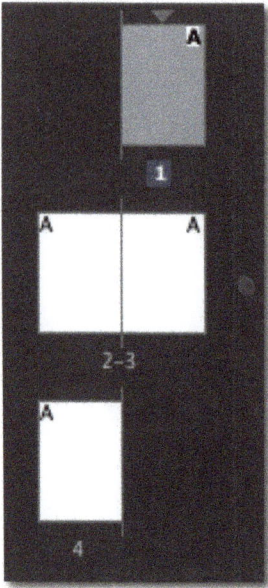

5. Page 1 of this document will be the front, page 4 will be the back, and pages 2-3 will be the inside of the leaflet, with a fold in between them. **Double click** on page 2. Using the **Rectangle Frame Tool,** draw a frame that starts from the intersection of the margins at the top left of the page and down to the intersection at the bottom right of the page.

6. Click on the frame with the **Type Tool** then choose **Object>Text Frame Options** to make it a *3* **Column** frame with a *3mm* **Gutter.**

7. Choose **File>Place** to import the *visit-cuba-highlights.txt* file. This text is going to fill the final three pages of the leaflet, and it'll do that by flowing from a frame on page 2 to one on page 3, then finishing on page 4. To do this, change to the **Selection Tool,** click on the *overset mark* at the bottom right of the text frame to reload the cursor, drag with it to create an identical frame on page *3*

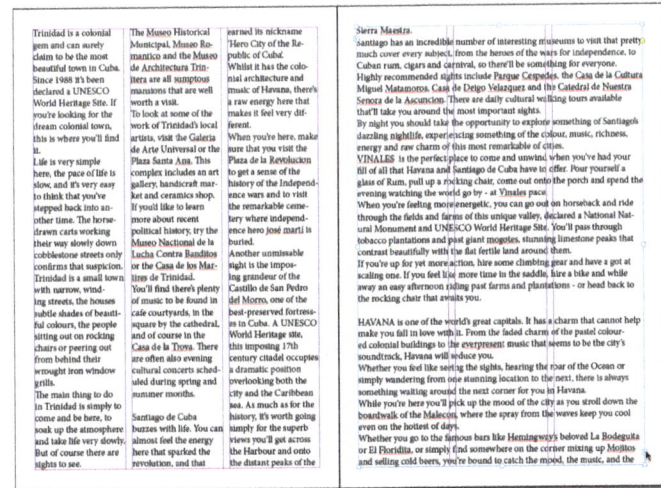

8. Now reload the cursor again and create a frame that finishes roughly two-thirds of the way down the final page.

9. Using the **Selection Tool,** select the frame on page
   4 and use **Object>Text Frame Options** to make it the
   same as the frame on page 2. Repeat for page 3.

10. Next you'll create a paragraph style for the majority of the text in
    the same way as you did previously. Following the steps you learned
    when creating the previous document, make sure that the hidden
    characters are showing, then select the second paragraph in your text.
    Apply the following character formats: **Font:** *Ubuntu* Regular, 8pt*
    Size, *12pt* **Leading.** Apply the following paragraph formats: *Uncheck*
    the **Hyphenate** button and click the ***Align to Baseline Grid*** button
    that's to the right of it (see screenshot below). You'll learn about what
    the baseline grid is shortly. Using the same method you used in the
    previous document, create a new **Paragraph Style** called *Body.*

* *You can of course use any font you wish, but I've created the branding for
this company using this font. One of the reasons I've used it is because it's
available for anyone to use. If you want to download the font, go to www.
fontsquirrel.com For instructions on how to install fonts, visit www.fontsquirrel.
com/help If you'd rather not install this font, a reasonable alternative
you can use that comes pre-installed with InDesign is Myriad Pro.*

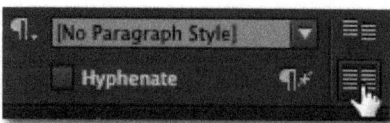

11. You're going to create the second paragraph style for this leaflet using a different approach. This new style is going to be called *Body +indent,* so called because it's going to be identical to Body, except that it will have an indent on the paragraph's first line. Whilst you could go through the same process as before to create the style, a commonly used practice for designers is to *base one style on another.* This is useful in that if you base your new style on the Body style, then if you change the Body style later, the new style changes as well. To use this new approach, make sure your cursor is in a *Body* paragraph (make sure you can see *Body* highlighted in the Paragraph Styles Panel).

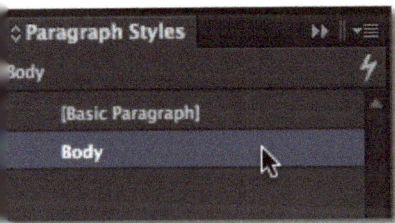

12. Click on the Paragraph Styles Panel's **dropdown menu** and choose **New Paragraph Style.** Inside the *New Paragraph Style* dialogue box, notice there is a section towards the top that states *Based On: Body.* This means that the new style will be based on the Body style (because the *Body* style was highlighted when you created the new Style). All you need to do now is change the name, and specify how this style is different from the *Body* Style.

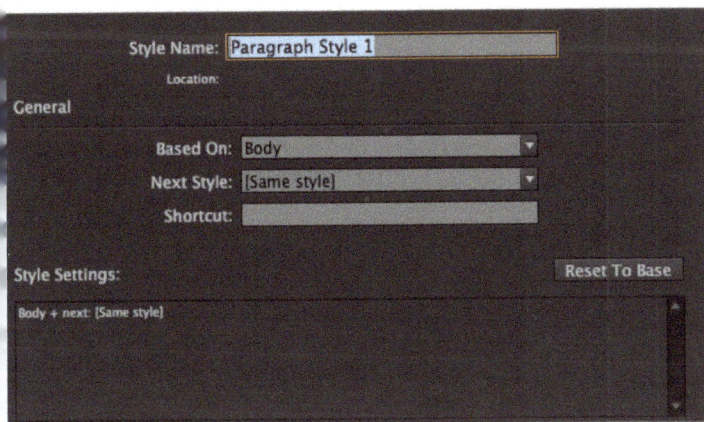

13. Look to the left of the dialogue box and you'll see lots of different attributes that can be applied as part of a Style. Click on *Indents and Spacing.* Insert a *12pt* value into **First Line Indent.** Click on *General* at the top of the dialogue box, change the name of the style to *Body + indent** and press the **OK button.**

* *This naming convention is often used as it's a reminder that this style is based on the Body style.*

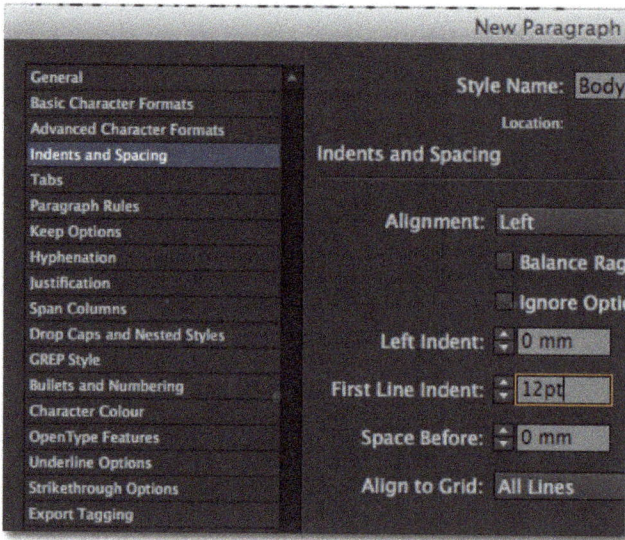

14. Click five times in quick succession to select all of the text and apply the *Body+Indent* style to all of it. Then click on the first paragraph and apply the *Body* style.

TRINIDAD is a colonial gem and can surely claim to be the most beautiful town in Cuba. Since 1988 it's been declared a UNESCO World Heritage Site. If you're looking for the dream colonial town, this is where you'll find it.

15. Read through the document to find the other three paragraphs that start with an uppercase place name: SANTIAGO, VINALES and HAVANA. Apply the *Body* style to these too.

16. The leaflet looks fairly sparse at the moment, but once you start adding some images in it'll start to look better. The potential difficulty here is to get the images and the text to work together, and not just use the images to fill space. Look at the image below to see how you're going to achieve this.

17. The text will flow around the images using the *Text Wrap* feature you've used before. The slight difference with this leaflet is that you'll make use of the *Baseline Grid*. A moment ago when you created the paragraph styles for this document you incorporated a paragraph format that hasn't been explained yet: *align text to the baseline grid*. To see what this feature does, from the **View Menu** choose ***Grids & Guides>Show Baseline Grid****.

* *If you don't see the grid appear, firstly check that you're not in Preview Mode by choosing* **View>Screen Mode>Normal.** *If the grid still hasn't appeared it'll likely be because its settings need to be adjusted for a small screen size. To adjust this, on a Mac go to the* **InDesign menu** *at the top left of your screen and from it choose* **Preferences** *(on a PC, choose* **Preferences** *from the* **Edit menu).** *Once in preferences, under* **Grids,** *change the View Threshold setting from 75% down to 50%.*

18. If you look closely at your text, notice how its *baseline* (the line on which the text sits) is aligned to the light blue grid. This means not only that the text is aligned across all the columns, but also that you can easily align the bottom of the images to the baseline of the text. This is quite different to all of the text you've worked with before, which will not have aligned across columns like this.

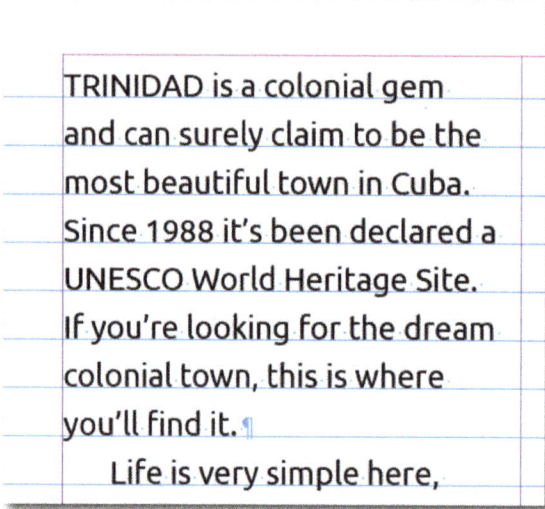

TRINIDAD is a colonial gem
and can surely claim to be the
most beautiful town in Cuba.
Since 1988 it's been declared a
UNESCO World Heritage Site.
If you're looking for the dream
colonial town, this is where
you'll find it.
    Life is very simple here,

19. Create a landscape shaped frame that's the width of the two columns at the right of page two, ensuring that it aligns to the *bleed guide* above the top of the leaflet, the *column guide* on the left, the *spine* at the right and one of the *baseline grid lines* on the bottom. Apply a small text wrap value to the bottom of the frame so that the text flows around it.

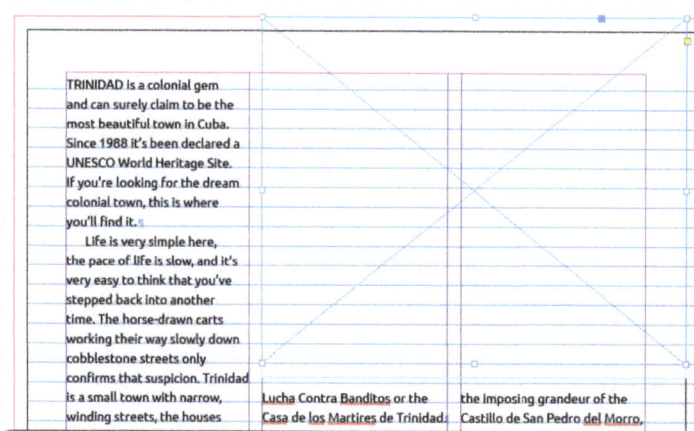

TRINIDAD is a colonial gem
and can surely claim to be the
most beautiful town in Cuba.
Since 1988 it's been declared a
UNESCO World Heritage Site.
If you're looking for the dream
colonial town, this is where
you'll find it.
    Life is very simple here,
the pace of life is slow, and it's
very easy to think that you've
stepped back into another
time. The horse-drawn carts
working their way slowly down
cobblestone streets only
confirms that suspicion. Trinidad
is a small town with narrow,
winding streets, the houses

Lucha Contra Banditos or the
Casa de los Martires de Trinidad;

the imposing grandeur of the
Castillo de San Pedro del Morro,

20. Create another landscape shaped frame at the bottom left of page two, this time adjusting the text wrap value *above* the frame if need be.

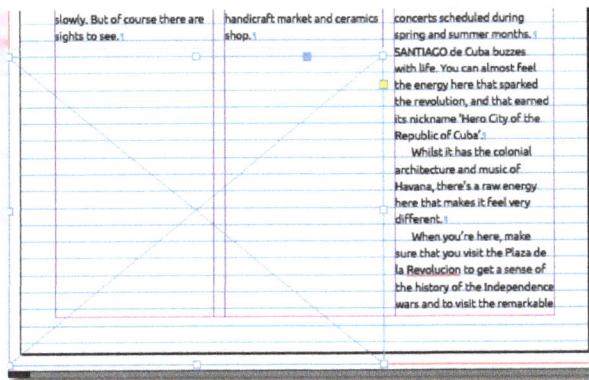

21. Repeat the same process with two portrait shaped frames, adding one at the top right of page three and one at the top right of page four.

22. Place the *visit-cuba-trinidad-house.jpg* image into the frame at the top of page two, the *visit-cuba-santiago-steps.jpg* image into the frame at the bottom of page two, the *visit-cuba-vinales-porch.jpg* on page three and the *visit-cuba-havana-sidecar.jpg* image on page four.

23. So far the images you've placed into InDesign have been carefully cropped so that you haven't had to get into repositioning or resizing them. But these images are more realistic in that they will need to be adjusted to fit properly. Click on the image at the top of page two to work with it first. Notice that at the moment the edge of the Frame is *blue*. This indicates that the *Frame itself* is selected. However, if you double-click on the image you will now see a brown frame*. This indicates that the *picture itself* is selected. The Brown frame is not exactly the same shape and size as the Blue frame because the picture has not been pre-sized to fit for you.

* *For users of InDesign older than CS5, change to the* **Direct Selection Tool** *(the white arrow) instead to adjust the picture, then revert back to the* **Selection Tool (the black arrow).**

24. If you press and hold down the mouse, any area of the picture that's outside the blue frame will be seen, but will be ghosted out. If you want to reposition the picture, drag your mouse and the picture will move within the frame.

25. If you want to resize your picture, drag one of the brown corner handles, but make sure you hold down the **Shift Key** as you drag to keep the shape of the picture in proportion.

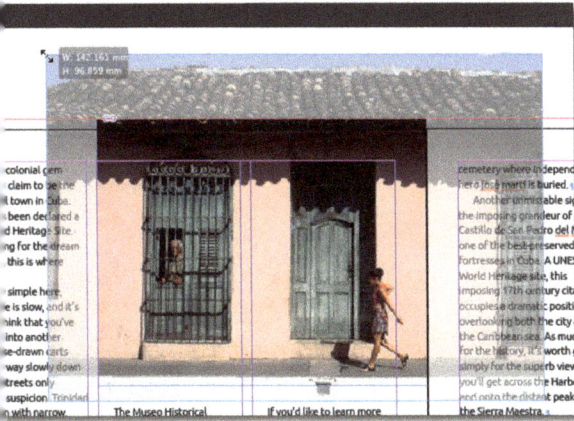

26. Often, a quicker way to crop images is to use the *Object>Fitting>Fill Frame proportionally* command. This automatically resizes the image, keeping it in proportion to the original dimensions, but ensuring that the whole frame is filled. Making use of **Object>Fitting>Fill Frame proportionally** and by double-clicking with the **Selection Tool,** to work directly with the brown frame, adjust all of the images so that they look good in the space that you've given them.

27. It is at this point that the work begins to try and make the text and the images work together. If you look at the screenshot below, the final version has the start of the text about each location aligning with the top of the appropriate picture. This is initially achieved by using a combination of the following techniques: making the image frames taller or shallower; re-writing the text to make it shorter or longer; using a small amount of tracking (usually no more than in the range of *-20* to *+20)* to make the text longer or shorter.*

* In this example you're given carte blanche to change anything you want, but in the real world that would depend on your role: designers would usually be free to adjust the pictures and possibly the tracking but not the words, and sub-editors or writers would be allowed to apply tracking or adjust the words, depending on the nature of the document.

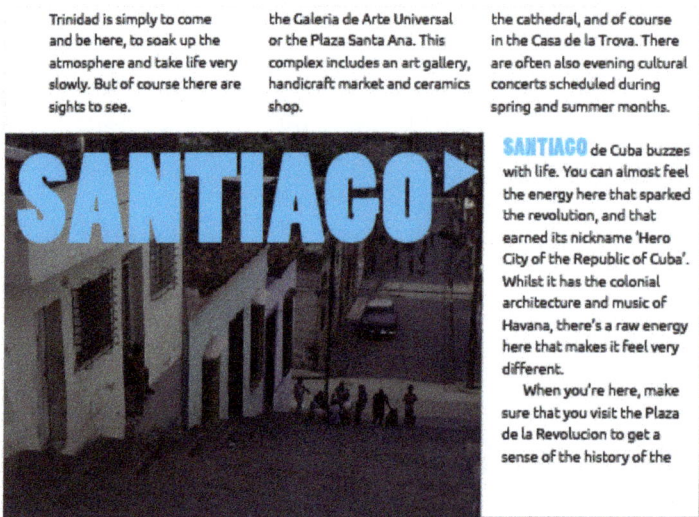

Trinidad is simply to come and be here, to soak up the atmosphere and take life very slowly. But of course there are sights to see.

the Galería de Arte Universal or the Plaza Santa Ana. This complex includes an art gallery, handicraft market and ceramics shop.

the cathedral, and of course in the Casa de la Trova. There are often also evening cultural concerts scheduled during spring and summer months.

SANTIAGO de Cuba buzzes with life. You can almost feel the energy here that sparked the revolution, and that earned its nickname 'Hero City of the Republic of Cuba'. Whilst it has the colonial architecture and music of Havana, there's a raw energy here that makes it feel very different.

When you're here, make sure that you visit the Plaza de la Revolucion to get a sense of the history of the

28. Try to make the text align as well as you can so that each location lines up with the top of the image associated with it. If need be use the **Return** key to move the text down a line or two, or the ***Enter*** key* to push all of the following text across to the start of the next column or frame.

** On a Mac Laptop, use the **Return** key in combination with the **fn** key at the bottom left of your keyboard.*

29. If you look at the final version of the leaflet you'll see that to strengthen the relationship between the images and the text, a visual element has been used repeatedly. The text at the start of each section deliberately uses a contrasting font and colour, and a larger version of the same text that starts each section has been placed on top of each image. In addition, a triangular arrow of the same colour points from the image to where the text associated with that section starts.

30. Select the word "Trinidad" and change it as follows: **Font:** *Poplar;* **Size:** *13pt;* **Tracking:** *10;* **Swatch:** *Red.* Use the same settings on the other uppercase words at the start of each section, using an appropriate colour for each one.

31. Off the edge of the page, use the **Rectangle Frame Tool** to create a landscape shaped frame roughly the same width as the picture at the top of page 2. Click inside the frame with the **Type Tool** and type in the word *Trinidad.* Give it exactly the same settings as you've just done, except for its **Size,** which should be about *60pt.* Then change back to the **Selection Tool** and resize the frame so it's not very much bigger than the text.

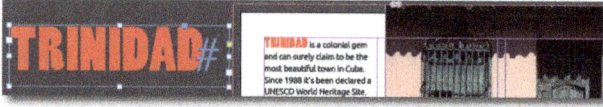

32. The reason you've created it off the edge of the page is that if you now drag the text frame on top of the image, the text will disappear. It will do that because the text wrap that you previously set up will affect *all* text, including the words that you'd like to appear on top of it. To prevent that happening, select your newly created text frame and choose **Object>Text Frame Options.** In the *Text Frame Options* dialogue box, check ***Ignore Text Wrap.***

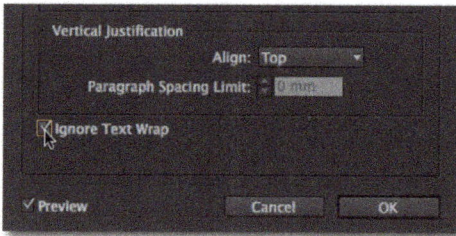

33. Rather than go through the same process again for all the other text frames, using the **Selection Tool,** hold down the *Alt key* as you drag the frame a little distance to quickly duplicate it.

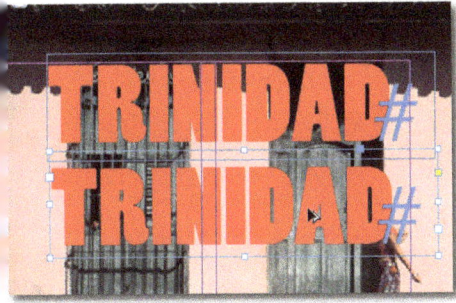

34. Do this twice more and drag each frame on top of its respective image, then retype its name with the **Type Tool.**

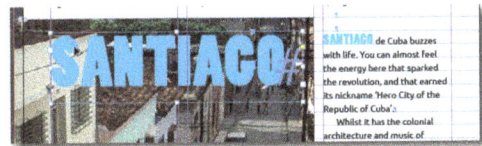

35. To create the triangular arrows press and hold down on the **Rectangle Frame Tool** in the **Tools Panel** until some other tools appear next to your cursor. Choose the *Polygon Frame Tool.*

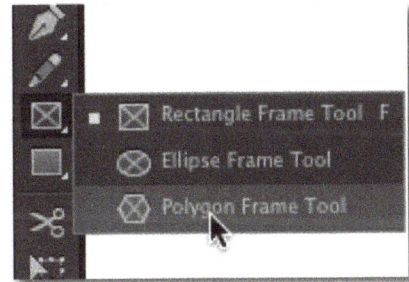

36. Click once on the page, and in the dialogue box that appears, type the following numbers: **Number of Sides:** 3; **Polygon Width:** *8mm;* **Polygon Height:** *8mm.*

37. Before you can apply a swatch to the triangle it's worth knowing about how InDesign applies *fills* and *strokes* to objects. To do this you'll need to see the area in the **Tools Panel** that shows this to you. Unfortunately in recent versions of InDesign this area is so small that it's hard to clearly see what it's for, so the first thing to do is make it larger. To do this, click on the tiny button (that resembles a Fast Forward button) at the very top left of the Tools Panel which makes the panel two columns wide.

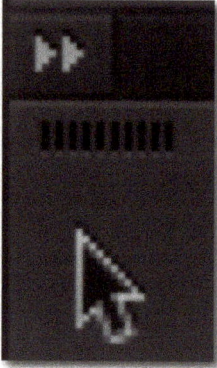

38. The area highlighted in the screenshot below describes the fill and stroke of the selected frame. The square on the top left describes its *fill* (the colour inside the frame) and the square on the bottom right describes its *stroke* (the colour around its edge). In this case, it's showing that both the fill and the stroke are *none* (or transparent).

39. When you click on the red swatch to change the colour of the triangle it'll either be applied to the fill or the stroke, depending on which of the two squares is in the front. For example, if the fill square is in the front, this will be the result:

40. If, however, the stroke square is in front, this will be the result:

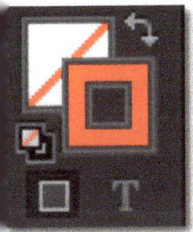

41. If you've inadvertently applied the red swatch to the stroke, apply the *none* swatch to the stroke by clicking in the area shown below, then click once on the *fill square* to bring it to the front, before applying the red swatch again.

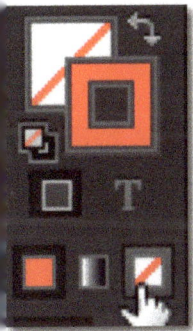

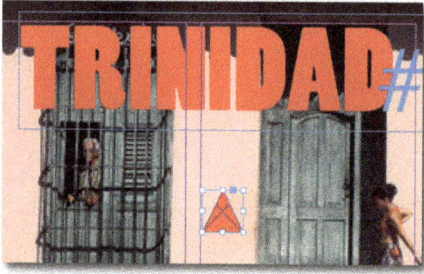

42. Once you've applied the Red swatch to the triangle, rotate it if need be using either of the *rotate icons* in the **Control Panel.**

43. In the same way you duplicated the text frames, make three copies of the triangle and align each one with the text it belongs with. Change each triangle's colour to match the text and rotate it to point towards the text at the start of each section. You may need to adjust the size and / or position of the text for best results.

44. For the final paragraph of text on the back cover of the leaflet you'll need to create a new frame. As you did earlier with the **Polygon Frame Tool,** press and hold down on it until the **Rectangle Frame Tool** appears before choosing it. Create a frame, click in it with the **Type Tool** and place in the *visit-cuba-highlights-end.txt* file. Change it all to use the *Poplar* font in a suitable colour and size to signify that it's different to the rest of the text.

For more information about any of the destinations mentioned here, and a complete guide to visiting Cuba, visit our website, www.visitcubatoday.org.

45. Place the *visit_cuba_indesign_red.eps* logo at a suitable size and position at the bottom of the leaflet.

46. You're about to create the cover of the leaflet. Before you continue it might help to know what it will look like. As you can see below, several images will combine to create a montage that resembles a stack of Polaroids. To make it easier to see what you're doing, choose *View>Grids & Guides>Hide Baseline Grid.*

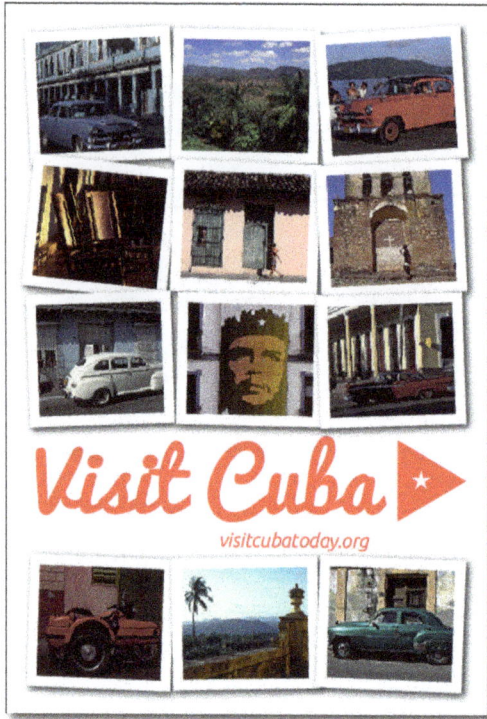

47. To create the cover you'll import several images at once to create a montage. How you'll do this will depend on which version of InDesign you're using. If you're using InDesign CS5 or later you can skip on to the next step. If you're using version CS4 you'll need to skip to *step 56*. If you're using a version of InDesign prior to CS4 you'll need to create the frames manually. One feature you can use to help you do this is **Create Guides,** found in the **Layout menu.** You'll find some guidance on how to use this in the final exercise at *step 24*.

48. Creating a grid has become a lot easier to do in recent versions of InDesign by means of the *Gridify* feature, which appeared in version CS5. You can use this feature in different ways to create a grid arrangement of frames. To do this, firstly double click on the *1* icon in the **Pages Panel** to make sure you're on page 1. Then choose the **Rectangle Frame Tool** from the **Tools Panel.**

49. Using the **Rectangle Frame Tool,** click and drag from the top left bleed guide all the way down to the bottom left bleed guide, *but when you get there don't release your mouse button.* Instead, press the **right arrow** key twice (to create 3 columns) and the **down arrow** key four times (to create 5 rows). When you release the mouse button you'll have created a total of fifteen frames, all ready to receive images.

50. The first thing you'll need to do is delete the row of frames second from the bottom. Do this by choosing the **Selection Tool,** clicking off the edge of the page to ensure that nothing is selected, then dragging carefully as shown below so that you only select those frames.

51. When the three frames are selected, press the **Backspace** or **Delete key** to remove them all. Later you'll fill the space with the red *Visit Cuba* logo.

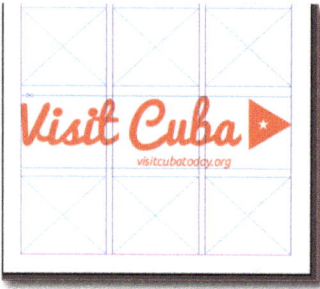

52. To import the pictures into the empty frames, firstly ensure that nothing is selected, then choose **File>Place** and choose all of the pictures in the *Leaflet 4 montage images* folder.*

*Make sure you're viewing the images as a list, then click on the first one, and press the Shift key whilst clicking on the last

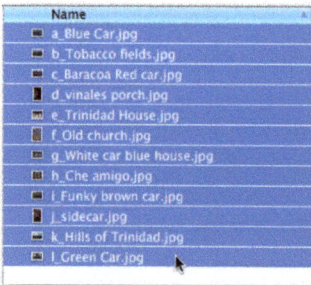

53. All of the images become attached to your cursor. Shortly you'll click on each frame in turn to place all the images quickly into them. Note the number next to it, telling you how many you have left.

54. I've ordered the images so that they should appear in the same order as the finished version, but if you want to change which image you're going to place next, simply press the **Up** or **Down** **arrow key** to cycle through the images, and when you want to place an image into an empty frame, simply click on it.

55. Once you've filled all of the frames with images, if you have any images still attached to your cursor, press the **Esc** key repeatedly to remove any leftover images.

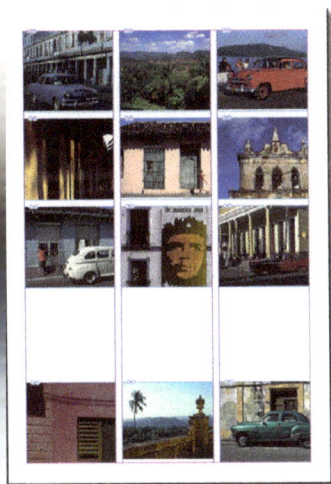

56. If you're using InDesign CS4 there is an alternative way to create a grid of images (if you're using CS5 or later, skip to the next step). It requires the use of several consecutive keyboard shortcuts, so I would recommend that you read the instructions through before starting. Making sure you're using the **Selection Tool** and that no frames are selected, choose **File>Place.** Within the *Leaflet 4 montage images* folder click on the first image to select it, then hold down the **Shift key** and click on the last image to select all of the images at once. The images will appear attached to your cursor, with the number *12* next to it, indicating that you have 12 images loaded on your cursor. Hold down the **Command** and **Shift** keys and notice that your cursor changes to something that resembles a grid. Click and drag from the top left intersection of the margin guides all the way down to the bottom right. When you have drawn one large frame, let go of the Command and Shift keys, but *keep the mouse button held down.* Press the ***Right Arrow key*** twice (to create 3 columns) and the ***Down Arrow key*** four times (to create five rows), then finally release the mouse button. You'll that the images are all in position, all in equally sized frames, but as you only had enough images attached to your cursor to fill four rows you'll only have created that many (but they'll be sized in the correct proportion so that you can move them to leave space for the *Visit Cuba* logo). To do that, drag around the bottom 3 images with the **Selection Tool** to select them all, then move them so that they all align to the bottom margin.

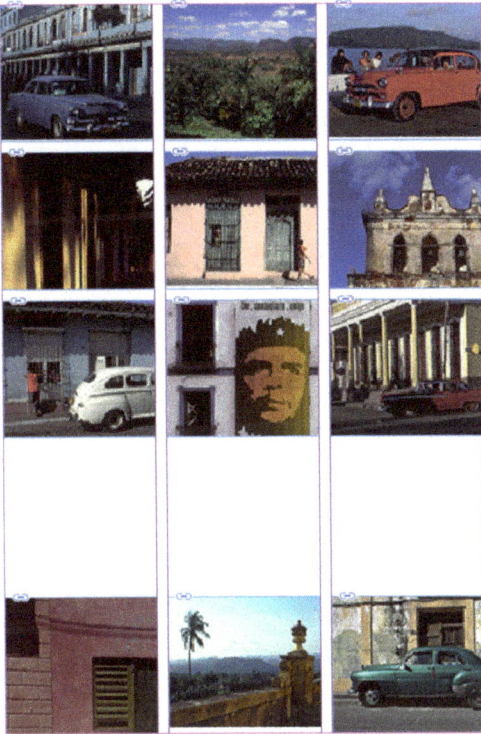

57. Now that all the images are in place you'll resize them all to fit their frames. Using your **Selection Tool,** click and drag over all of the frames at once to select them all, and choose **Object>Fitting>Fill Frame proportionally.** Whilst all of the frames are still selected and before you start to adjust the pictures individually, give all of the frames a *white* **stroke** of roughly *10pt*.

58. **Object>Fitting>Fill Frame proportionally** was a good first step to start to get the best from the images, but you'll want to examine each one in turn* by double-clicking on it, and either re-positioning or resizing it if need be.

* *To zoom in closer to an image press the **+** key whilst holding down the* **Command key,** *as many times as needed. To zoom back out to see the whole page again, press the **0 (zero) key** whilst holding down the* **Command key.**

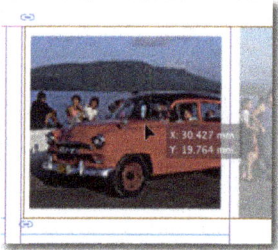

59. With all of the images adjusted, select them all again by dragging around them all with the **Selection Tool** and then press the *Fx button* in the *Control Panel,* and from the dropdown menu that appears, choose *Drop Shadow.*

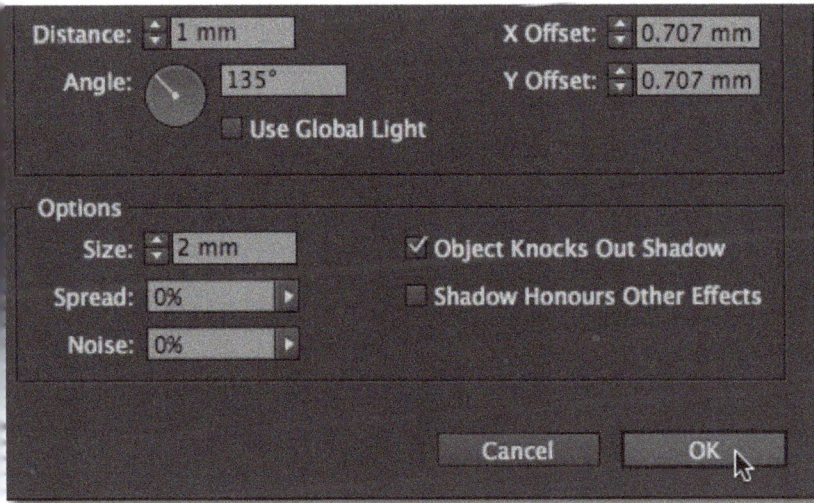

60. In the Drop Shadow dialogue box apply a **Distance** of *1mm,* a **Size** of *2mm* and press the **OK button.**

61. The images will start to resemble a montage of Polaroids once each has been subtly rotated and possibly repositioned. To rotate an image firstly make sure its frame is selected (the *blue* frame, not the brown) and press either of the arrows to the left of the *Rotation Angle* area of the Control Panel.

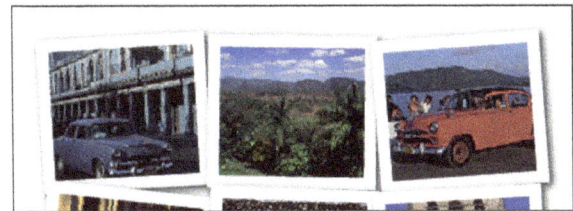

62. Keep adjusting the order, angle and positioning of the images until you're happy with the final result. To finish, fill the space near the bottom of the cover with the red *Visit Cuba* logo.

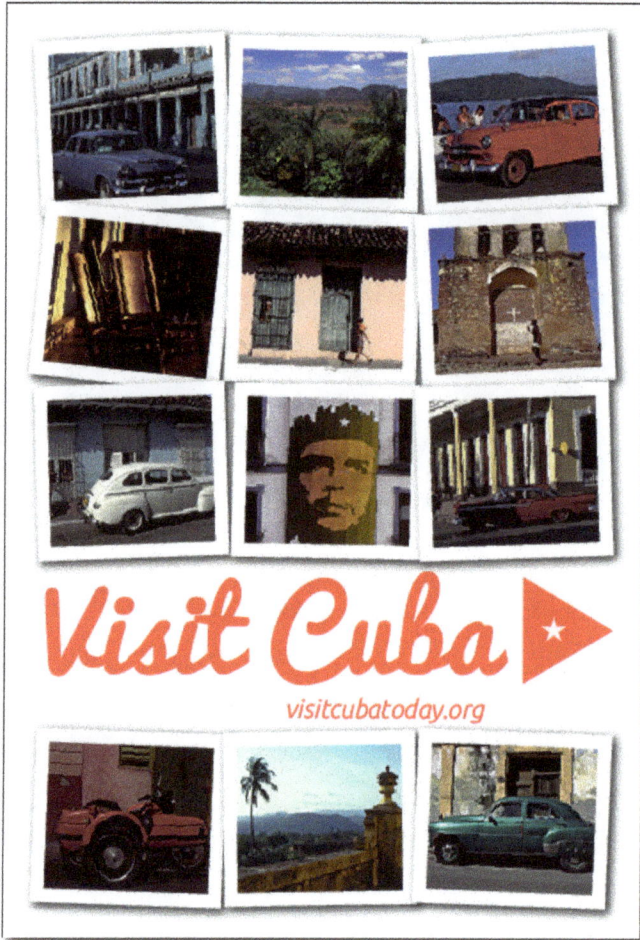

5) An eight page DL concertina fold leaflet

This final leaflet has eight pages, but unlike anything you've created previously, these eight pages are folded down using what's called a *concertina*, or *Z* fold. As you already have learned much of what you need to know in order to create this document, the instructions are written more sparingly, except to describe the new skills you'll need.

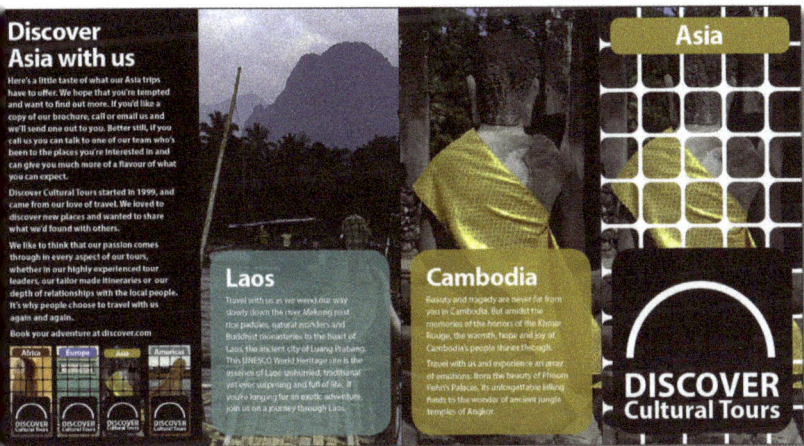

1. Choose **File>New** to create a new document. In the *New Document* dialogue box, change the **Number of Pages** to *8,* uncheck **Facing Pages,** change the page **Width** to 99mm and the **Height** to 210mm. Change the **Margins** so that all sides are *5mm* and enter 3mm for all of the *Bleed* values. Then press the **OK button.**

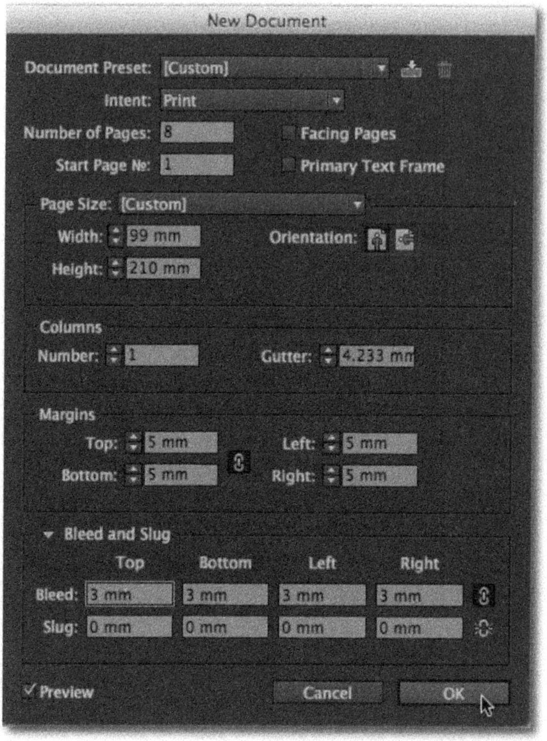
New Document
Document Preset: [Custom]
Intent: Print
Number of Pages: 8
Facing Pages
Start Page №: 1
Primary Text Frame
Page Size: [Custom]
Width: 99 mm
Orientation:
Height: 210 mm
Columns
Number: 1
Gutter: 4.233 mm
Margins
Top: 5 mm
Left: 5 mm
Bottom: 5 mm
Right: 5 mm
Bleed and Slug
Top
Bottom
Left
Right
Bleed: 3 mm 3 mm 3 mm 3 mm
Slug: 0 mm 0 mm 0 mm 0 mm
Preview
Cancel
OK

2. Once you've pressed **OK,** click on the **Pages Panel** to open it. Unlike in the previous document you will not see a black line (that represents a spine) next to any of these pages, because this is a *non-facing pages* document. Like the double sided leaflet you created earlier, these pages are independent of each other.

3. However, this concertina fold leaflet is going to be made of two *spreads,* each of which is to be made of 4 pages. So pages 1-4 will be connected together as one spread, and pages 5-8 will be connected as another. The images below show you how the final spreads will look.

4. Once this document has been printed it will be folded down to
   DL size (*99mm* wide x *210mm* high – or a third of A4). Page 4
   (with the large logo) will be the front, and the other pages are
   folded away beneath it, resembling a concertina, as the image
   below attempts to show: the diagram on the left shows how the
   leaflet will start to fold, and continues until it's almost flat.

5. If you look at your own document's pages in the **Pages Panel** you'll notice that the eight pages are not kept together, and if you try to drag any of those pages together in the Pages Panel you'll quickly discover that they won't stay together. To enable pages to stay together, go to the *dropdown menu* at the top right of the **Pages Panel** and uncheck *Allow Document Pages to Shuffle.*

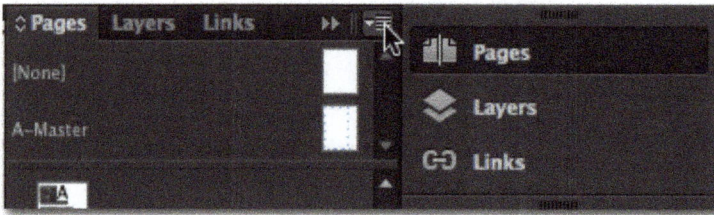

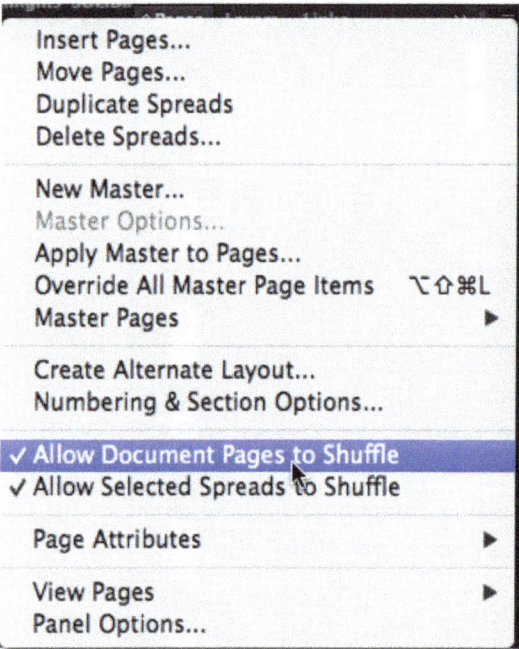

6. Now if you drag the *Page 2* icon near to the right of *Page 1* icon you will see a thin black line appear, indicating that you're about to turn these pages into a spread. When you release your mouse button page 1 and 2 are now a spread, as shown by the *1-2* text underneath them.

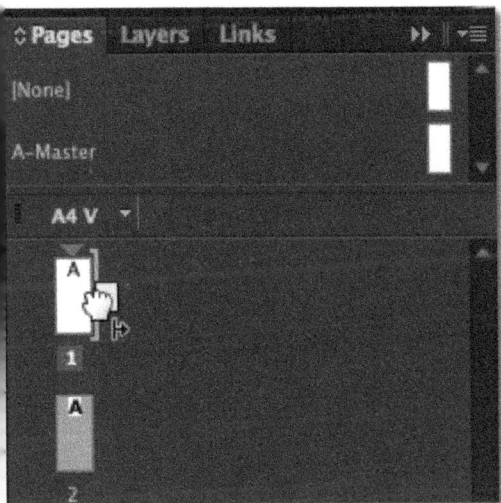

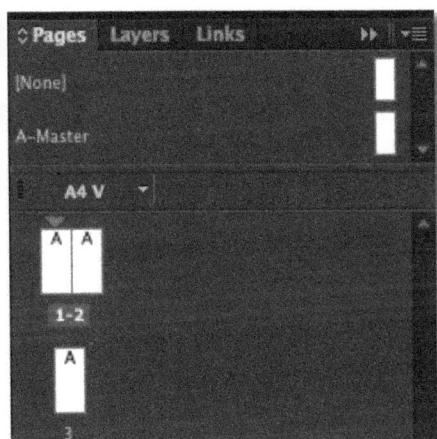

7. Drag pages 3 and 4 across to make a 4 page spread, then create a second spread of pages 5-8 in the same way. Now that you're working with spreads, a very useful command to know is **Fit Spread in Window** from the **View menu.** This zooms out your view of the screen so you can see all of the pages in the spread at once.

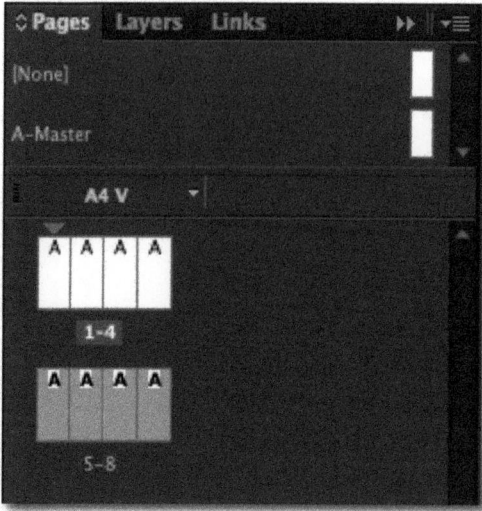

8. If you've created all of the previous leaflets so far, you'll know most of what you need to create the finished leaflet. So instead of giving you complete instructions I'll briefly outline the steps you'll need to finish it. Pages 2, 3, 5, 6, 7 and 8 all have the same formatting. For these pages create a frame and **place** the appropriate image (from the *Leaflets 5 images* folder) for each, using the skills you know to get the most from each image.

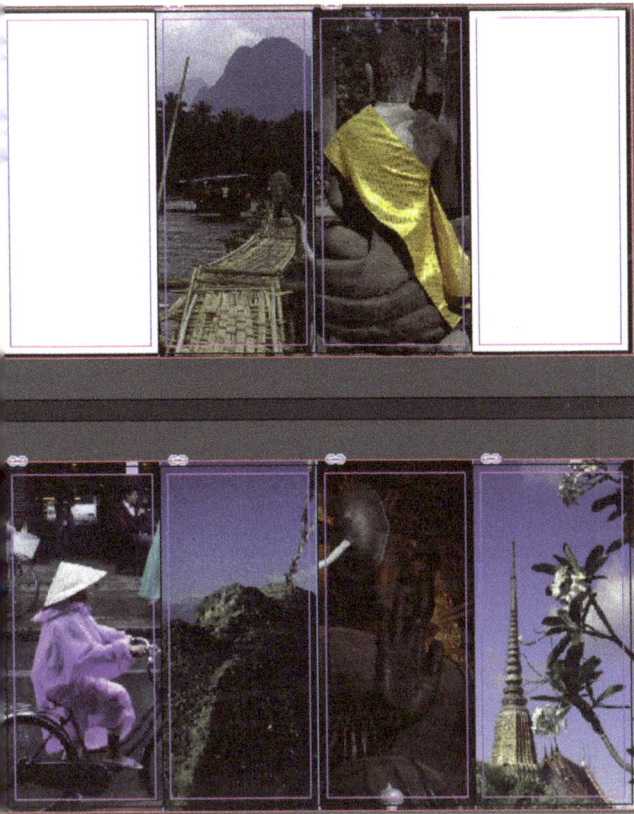

9. On page 3, using the **Rectangle Frame Tool** and keeping the **Shift key** held down, draw a perfectly square frame that snaps to the bottom, left and right margins.

10. To apply rounded corners to the empty frame, from the **Object menu** choose *Corner Options.* In the dialogue box that appears ensure that the padlock icons appear locked, then click on any of the icons to the right of the numbers to apply a rounded effect.* Adjust the numbers to somewhere around *10mm* (to match the roundedness of the Discover logo that you'll bring in shortly).

* *Prior to InDesign CS5 the dialogue box was simpler, but will still enable you to achieve the same effect.*

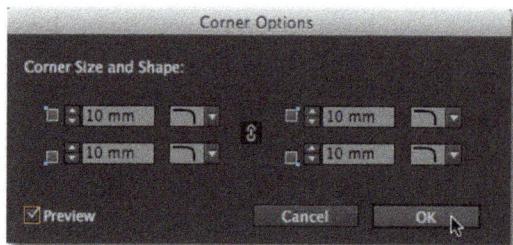

11. So far the only colours that you've used have been provided for you. Very often you'll want to use a colour that works well with the image, and a good way to do that is to sample a colour directly from an image on the page. To do this, ensure the new frame you've just created is selected, and ensure that at the bottom of the Tools Panel that the colour you'll sample will be applied to the fill and not the stroke.

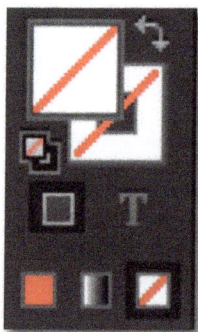

12. Choose the *Eyedropper Tool* from the **Tools Panel.**

13. Notice that the eyedropper's pipette is currently *white*. Click with the eyedropper on an area of colour in the image that you think you might want to use. Notice when you do it, that firstly the frame colour changes to match, and that secondly the pipette becomes *black,* as if it's sucked the colour up from the picture.

14. If you don't like the colour you've sampled and want to try again, hold down the **Alt key** and notice that the eyedropper's pipette becomes white again, enabling you to sample a different area of colour. Once you've found a colour you want to use, click with the **Eyedropper Tool** onto the *new swatch button* near the bottom right of the **Swatches Panel** (shown below) thereby keeping it for future use. Then change back to the **Selection Tool.**

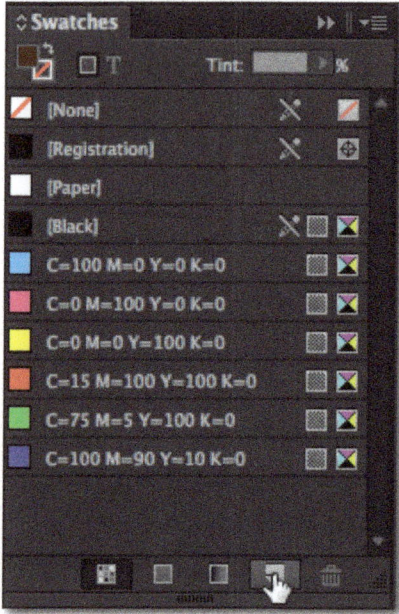

15. Use the **Selection Tool** in combination with the **Alt key** to drag copies of the rounded coloured frames into position on top of the remaining pictures. Then use the **Eyedropper** to apply a suitable colour to each one.

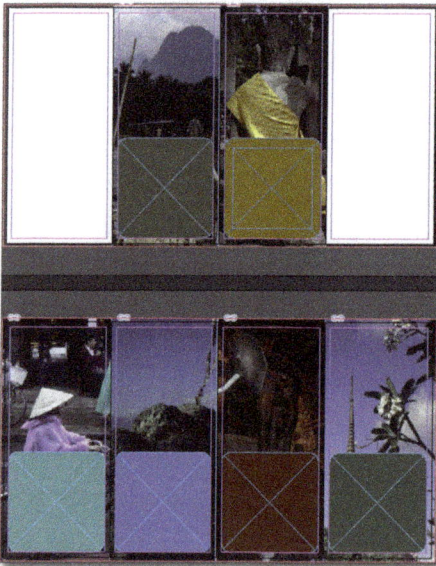

16. On one of the pages create a frame for the advert's text on top of the coloured panel you've just created.* Keep the frame square by holding down the **Shift key** as you drag, and try and align its centre "X" to that of the frame underneath. Duplicate this frame on top of all the other coloured frames.

* *Having a separate text frame can make it easier to control and adjust the position of the text.*

17. Previously the text you've imported has remained in the same story and has flowed from one column or frame to another. Whilst that approach could be used here, in reality it would be unnecessarily complex. Instead it will be much simpler to open the text in a text editor like *Textedit* or *Word* and copy and paste the appropriate text into the relevant frame. To do this, go to your preferred text editor and from there open the *discover-asia.txt* file.

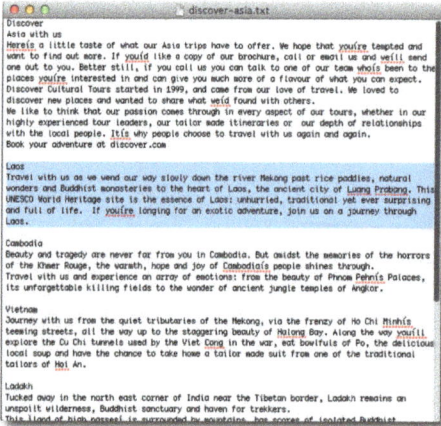

18. Carefully copy and paste the appropriate text for each page*.

* *If you want some guidance as to which image comes from which location, click on an image and open the **Links Panel** from the top right of your screen, where you'll see the name of the image, which includes its location.*

19. Making use of **Type>Show Hidden Characters*,** create and apply paragraph styles (using *Myriad Pro* if you want to stick to the brand guidelines), at appropriate sizes so that the text fits and reads well. Edit the text or use a small amount of tracking if need be to fit it to each page.

* *You might notice a couple of frequent issues that commonly arise when copying or importing text: 1)The text has been typed with multiple return to increase space between paragraphs (depending on how you want to format the text you may or may not want to get rid of them). 2)Some characters such as apostrophes can become corrupted when transferring from PC to Mac or vice-versa (if this happens, re-type them).*

Cambodia

Beauty and tragedy are never far from you in Cambodia. But amidst the memories of the horrors of the Khmer Rouge, the warmth, hope and joy of Cambodia's people shines through.

Travel with us and experience an array of emotions: from the beauty of Phnom Pehn's Palaces, its unforgettable killing fields to the wonder of ancient jungle temples of Angkor.

20. Once you've pasted and applied paragraph styles to all of the text for the pages you've worked on so far, go to page *1,* create a frame that covers the whole page and give it a *black* fill. Then create a separate frame for the text on top of it. Paste the introductory text in *(Discover Asia with us)*, then create and apply paragraph styles for it too.

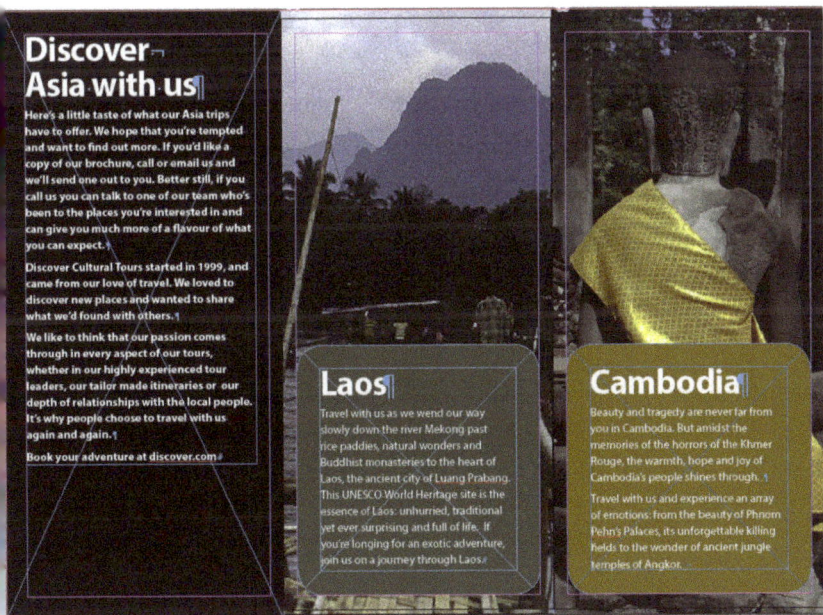

21. Whilst still on page *1,* import the four pdfs of the *Discover* leaflets' covers from the *Leaflets 5 Covers* folder. You can either place them one at a time (using the method you've already used to bring in logos) or by using whichever method you used to place multiple images for the cover of the previous leaflet.

22. If you want to make the coloured frames (that sit behind the text) subtly blend in to their backgrounds, choose **Effects** from the **Window menu.** If you make the *Opacity* lower than *100%* they will become semi-transparent. To ensure that the type can still be read over the top of the backgrounds, don't lower their opacity too much, and change the colour of the frames if need be. You might find **Presentation mode** can help you determine how legible the text is once you've made the backgrounds transparent.

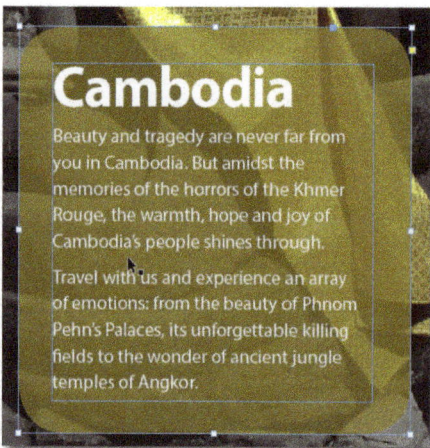

23. The cover page is simpler to create than it might appear. How you create it will depend on which version of InDesign you have. If you have version CS5 or later, use InDesign's *gridify* feature* to break a frame covering the whole page up into several small ones. If you have a version of InDesign prior to CS5, skip to the step below.

* *Press the up, down, left and right keys as you draw the frame*

24. If you have a version of InDesign prior to CS5 you'll have to create the individual frames manually. To do this you'll firstly create some guides to help you, using **Create Guides** from the **Layout menu.** In the dialogue box that appears, specify *8* rows, *4* columns with a *5mm* gutter between each, as shown in the screenshot below. With the guides in place, create a single small frame that snaps to one of the squares the guides have made, then duplicate it repeatedly (using the **Selection Tool** in combination with the **Alt** key) until one appears in every square.

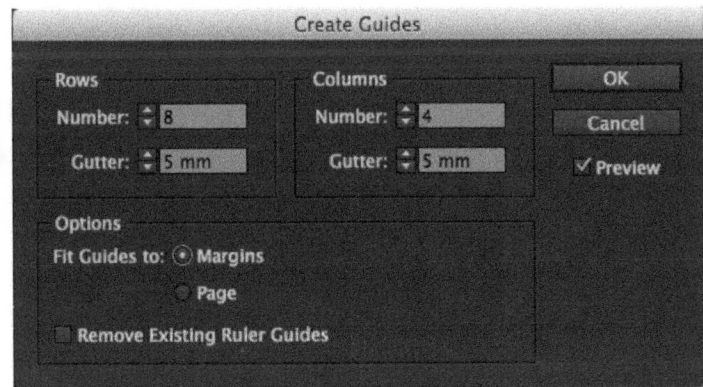

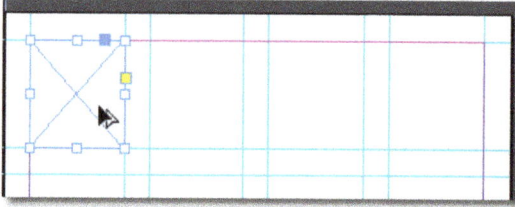

25. Once all of the frames are in place, make sure they are all selected and then apply round corners as you've previously done in this exercise. Finally to make all of these separate frames become one, choose **Object>Pathfinder>Add.** Then you can place the cover picture into this complex frame.

26. For the finishing touches of this final leaflet, import the *Discover* logo and create the leaflet's title (with a coloured rounded background) at the top.

Discover Asia with us

Here's a little taste of what our Asia trips have to offer. We hope that you're tempted and want to find out more. If you'd like a copy of our brochure, call or email us and we'll send one out to you. Better still, if you call us you can talk to one of our team who's been to the places you're interested in and can give you much more of a flavour of what you can expect.

Discover Cultural Tours started in 1999, and came from our love of travel. We loved to discover new places and wanted to share what we'd found with others.

We like to think that our passion comes through in every aspect of our tours, whether in our highly experienced tour leaders, our tailor made itineraries or our depth of relationships with the local people. It's why people choose to travel with us again and again.

Book your adventure at discover.com

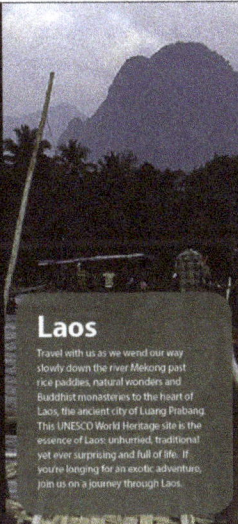

Africa	Americas	Asia	Europe
DISCOVER Cultural Tours	DISCOVER Cultural Tours	DISCOVER Cultural Tours	DISCOVER Cultural Tours

Asia

Laos

Travel with us as we wend our way slowly down the river Mekong past rice paddies, natural wonders and Buddhist monasteries to the heart of Laos, the ancient city of Luang Prabang. This UNESCO World Heritage site is the essence of Laos: unhurried, traditional, yet ever surprising and full of life. If you're longing for an exotic adventure, join us on a journey through Laos.

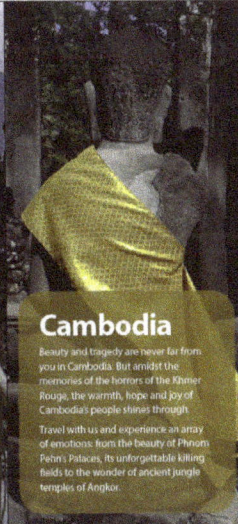

Cambodia

Beauty and tragedy are never far from you in Cambodia. But amidst the memories of the horrors of the Khmer Rouge, the warmth, hope and joy of Cambodia's people shines through.

Travel with us and experience an array of emotions: from the beauty of Phnom Pehn's Palaces, its unforgettable killing fields to the wonder of ancient jungle temples of Angkor.

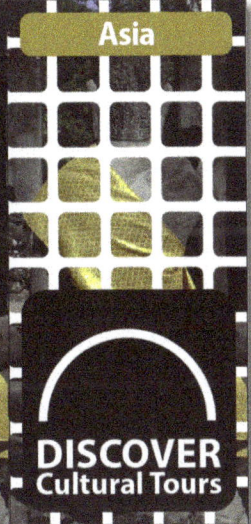

DISCOVER
Cultural Tours

DESIGN THEORY IN BRIEF FOR BEGINNERS

This chapter is an attempt to introduce key elements of design theory as briefly and simply as possible. The examples shown are all ones that are featured in the other chapters, so that you can look at work that you've either already created or that you have the opportunity to create. It's hoped that as you can understand some of these concepts and can name them, that you'll be able to use aspects of design theory, where appropriate, in your own work.

Elements of design theory
1) Contrast

The deliberate use of contrasting elements on a page can bring a design to life.

Notice how the white text and logos are in contrast to the black background.

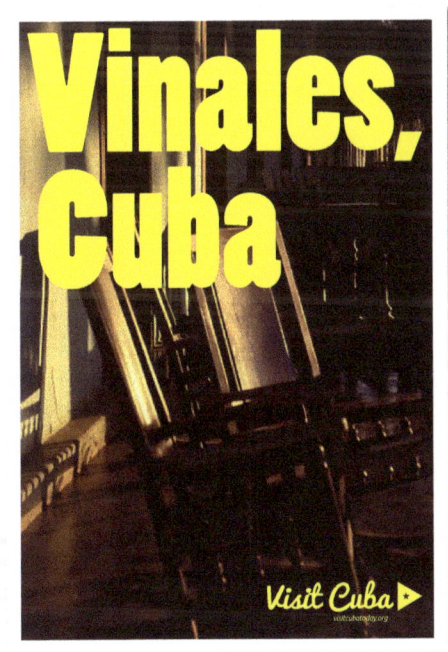

Notice how the large display text is in contrast to the small logo.

PERU

FROM ANDEAN PEAKS TO the roar of the Pacific Ocean, Peru has it all.

Experience the energy and diversity of what this country has to offer as we travel from the depths of the Amazon to the heights of Maccu Pichu.

For more information on our Highlights of Cuba tour, visit us at go-adventures.com or pick up our South America brochure from your local travel agent.

GO! ADVENTURES.COM

START YOUR ADVENTURE

The large headline and logo are in contrast with the small text, and the white text and logo are in contrast to the blue background.

2) Repetition

Contrast is tempered by repetition, which is the deliberate repeated use of particular elements, to make things feel like they belong together. This is particularly important when strong contrast is used.

All of the examples shown previously to demonstrate contrast feature repetition. For example, this *Ocean Hotels* advert repeatedly uses the following things: black backgrounds, white text, the same typeface, the same large size of the typeface, the same gap used consistently (both around the edge of the document and in between the logo and the background of the text). If you want to, go back and look for the use of repetition in the other two *contrast* examples before reading on.

As well as the repeat of the white colour and the typeface in both the text and the logo, the brown background to the text has been deliberately chosen from the image beneath it. The round corners of the brown background deliberately mirror those in the logo.

Discover Europe with us

From deserted Greek islands to street markets in Turkey, we'll show you the very best that Europe can offer even the most seasoned traveller. Leave it all to us, and discover it with us.

To receive our Europe brochure call **02344 3456123** or visit **www.discover-tours.com**

DISCOVER
Cultural Tours

As well as the repeat of the black colour and the typeface in both the text and the logo, the six images are the same size, are spaced equally, and also share the round corners of the logo.

CUBA: ESSENTIAL INFO

Cuba is unique. A beautiful island in the Caribbean, a bastion of Communism. The land of Fidel and Che, the Bay of Pigs and Guantanamo Bay. Birthplace of Son, the music which paved the way for Salsa, Rumba and Mambo. It's the home of Bacardi, Havana Club, Margaritas and Mojitos, the island of Hemingway and Greene. And not to mention thousands of aging classic cars. Cuba's cultural and political heritage continues to loom large.

It's a place of paradox, with cultural riches - and poverty - on every corner. Crumbling, beautiful, puzzling, inspiring, enchanting, enduring. Cuba continues to charm, delight, inspire and confuse in equal measure.

GETTING THERE

You might imagine that Cuba would be a challenging destination to get to, but it is well connected throughout the Caribbean region and beyond. As well as direct flights, Jamaica and the Bahamas are two major hubs for onward travel.

Air Canada, Air France, Virgin Atlantic fly there regularly to Havana, as do many regional airlines including Air Jamaica, Bahamas Air, Cayman Airways and TACA. Cuba's national airline, Cubana de Aviación usually has the cheapest fares.

Flights arrive at José Martí International Airport, 25km southwest of Havana. It has five terminals, most international flights using the modern terminal three.

IMMIGRATION

To be allowed to enter Cuba you'll need your passport, return or onward ticket, completed tourist card and the name of the place that you'll be staying for your first night. You'll get a tourist card when you buy your airline ticket, and it usually entitles you to stay for four weeks.

WHEN TO GO

The best time to visit Cuba is between January and May, when there are less tourists but the weather is still warm. During peak holiday times such as Christmas, Easter, and summer holiday months, the prices will be higher and places more crowded. Hurricane season, which usually occurs between June and November, is best avoided.

GETTING AROUND

The easiest way for most visitors to get around Cuba is by bus. Viazul is a service dedicated to tourists, and their buses run reliably, comfortably and punctually to many destinations around the island. If you want to go to destinations not offered by Viazul you'll need to hire a car, go by taxi, bike or hitch hike. Flying is a quick option to cover the long distance to Baracoa or Santiago de Cuba, but booking ahead is essential.

WHERE TO STAY

As well as numerous hotels, there are also a wide selection of Casa Particulares, which are a perfect way to get to see a place through the eyes of a local. Staying in a casa can give you a genuine insight into ordinary Cubans live, as well as the best local information available. Many casas will also provide food, and all will be happy to recommend somewhere for you to stay in your next destination.

FOR MORE

Visit our website for further information about Cuba before you travel. In your home country there is likely to be a Cuban tourist office that you can visit. Once in Cuba, you'll find Infotur (tourist information) offices in the larger cities around the island. Local travel agencies such as Cubatur can also provide useful information for the traveller.

Visit Cuba ▶

visitcubatoday.org

As well as repeating the red colour from the logo, notice how the (contrasting) font used in the headline is repeated for the crossheads and also in the drop cap (at the start of the article). Notice how the subtle space above the crossheads is applied consistently. You could argue that all of that, in addition the image of a red sidecar is pushing the repetition of red a bit too far.

If you want to, look back at the other examples to notice the balance of contrast and repetition, and consider whether you'd want to use more or less of either.

3) Alignment

Another way to make things feel like they belong together
on a page is to align them in some way.

CUBA: ESSENTIAL INFO

Cuba is unique. A beautiful island in the Caribbean, a bastion of Communism. The land of Fidel and Che, the Bay of Pigs and Guantanamo Bay. Birthplace of Son, the music which paved the way for Salsa, Rumba and Mambo. It's the home of Bacardi, Havana Club, Margaritas and Mojitos, the island of Hemingway and Greene. And not to mention thousands of aging classic cars. Cuba's cultural and political heritage continues to loom large.

It's a place of paradox, with cultural riches - and poverty - on every corner. Crumbling, beautiful, puzzling, inspiring, enchanting, enduring. Cuba continues to charm, delight, inspire and confuse in equal measure.

GETTING THERE

You might imagine that Cuba would be a challenging destination to get to, but it is well connected throughout the Caribbean region and beyond. As well as direct flights, Jamaica and the Bahamas are two major hubs for onward travel.

Air Canada, Air France, Virgin Atlantic fly there regularly to Havana, as do many regional airlines including Air Jamaica, Bahamas Air, Cayman Airways and TACA. Cuba's national airline, Cubana de Aviación usually has the cheapest fares.

Flights arrive at José Martí International Airport, 25km southwest of Havana. It has five terminals, most international flights using the modern terminal three.

IMMIGRATION

To be allowed to enter Cuba you'll need your passport, return or onward ticket, completed tourist card and the name of the place that you'll be staying for your first night. You'll get a tourist card when you buy your airline ticket, and it usually entitles you to stay for four weeks.

WHEN TO GO

The best time to visit Cuba is between January and May, when there are less tourists but the weather is still warm. During peak holiday times such as Christmas, Easter, and summer holiday months, the prices will be higher and places more crowded. Hurricane season, which usually occurs between June and November, is best avoided.

GETTING AROUND

The easiest way for most visitors to get around Cuba is by bus. Viazul is a service dedicated to tourists, and their buses run reliably, comfortably and punctually to many destinations around the island. If you want to go to destinations not offered by Viazul you'll need to hire a car, go by taxi, bike or hitch hike. Flying is a quick option to cover the long distance to Baracoa or Santiago de Cuba, but booking ahead is essential.

WHERE TO STAY

As well as numerous hotels, there are also a wide selection of Casa Particulares, which are a perfect way to get to see a place through the eyes of a local. Staying in a casa can give you a genuine insight into ordinary Cubans live, as well as the best local information available. Many casas will also provide food, and all will be happy to recommend somewhere for you to stay in your next destination.

FOR MORE

Visit our website for further information about Cuba before you travel. In your home country there is likely to be a Cuban tourist office that you can visit. Once in Cuba, you'll find Infotur (tourist information) offices in the larger cities around the island. Local travel agencies such as Cubatur can also provide useful information for the traveller.

Visit Cuba ▶

visitcubatoday.org

Notice here how everything aligns to something else in some
way, for example, the photograph and logo aligning not only to
the edges of the columns of text, but also to eachother.

Discover Europe with us

From deserted Greek islands to street markets in Turkey, we'll show you the very best that Europe can offer even the most seasoned traveller. Leave it all to us, and discover it with us.

To receive our Europe brochure call **02344 3456123**
or visit **www.discover-tours.com**

It is especially important to use alignment when one element is distant from other elements, as is the case with this headline.

Subtlety is often required when trying to align type, as shown here in the Ocean Hotels advert. The *x-height* of the upper line of text is being aligned to the top of the upper circle in the logo. The *baseline* of the middle line is being aligned to the bottom of the lower circle in the logo. The baseline of the lowest line of type is aligned to the baseline of the text in the logo.

4) Proximity

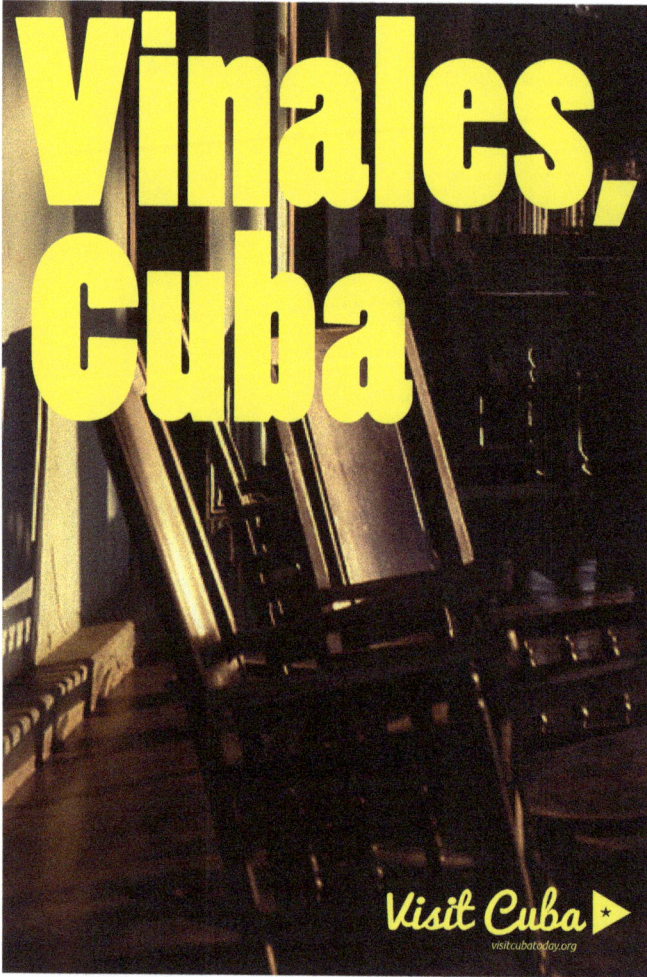

If you look at the whole page you're likely to see two elements on top of the background: the text at the top of the page, and the logo at the bottom. You'll likely see the logo as one thing, even though it contains the name of the organisation, the triangular element and the website address. This is an example of *proximity*, where, because these things are placed closely together, we perceive them as one thing. It's another example, then, of making things feel like they belong together, but this time due to their closeness to eachother.

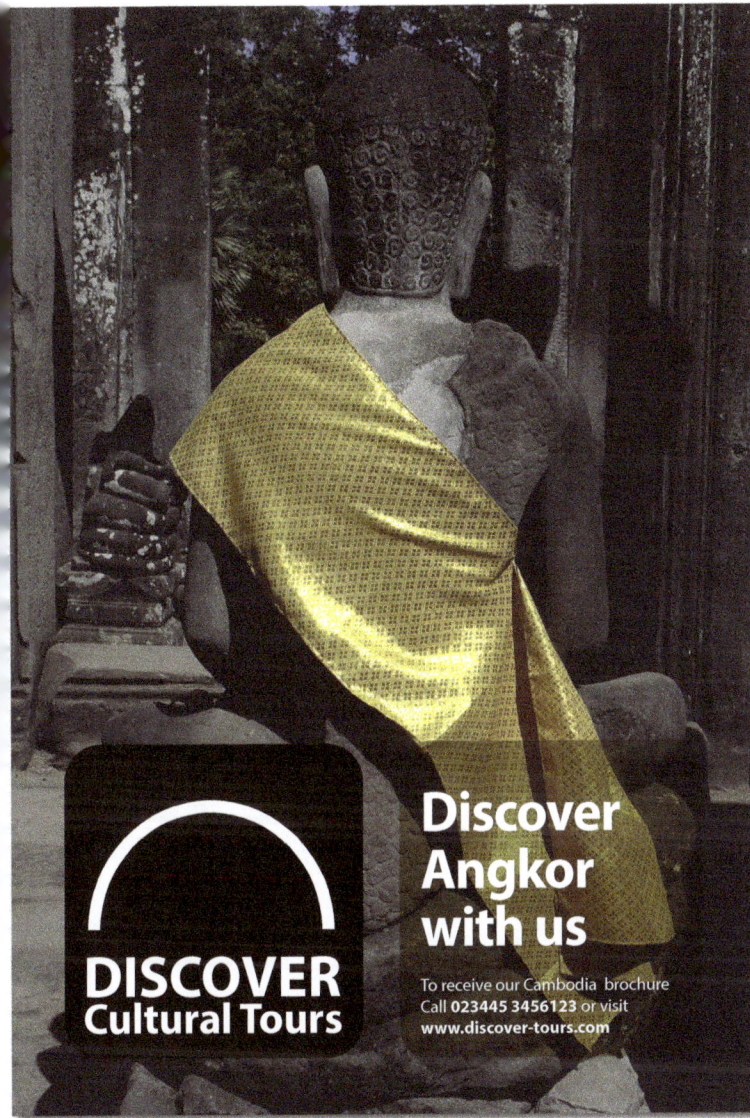

The above advert uses proximity in a couple of ways. The relationship between the large and small text is implied because they are both on the same background, but the distance between them, as well as their relative size means that a reader will nevertheless perceive them as different, and will only be likely read the small text if already intrigued by the larger text.

Tour Information

DISCOVER Cultural Tours

HIGHLIGHTS OF NICARAGUA, 2013

Our Highlights of Nicaragua tour combines the best of this unique country's natural wonders and cultural gems. With a carefully mixed blend of sightseeing, travelling, relaxing and activity, we've packed in as much of this wonderful country as we can into just sixteen days.

ESTELI
MATAGALPA
LEON
MANAGUA
MASAYA
GRANADA
OMOTEPE
SAN JUAN

Day 1
Arrive in Managua
The tour starts in Managua, Nicaragua's capital city, where we'll transfer from the airport to our hotel for the first night of our trip.

Day 2
Managua to Granada
In Managua we'll visit the Batahola cultural centre to get an insight into Nicaragua's colourful history and culture. From there we'll head to the Mirador Tiscapa, which before the 1972 earthquake housed the Presidential Palace and is now the site of a giant silhouette of Sandino, revolutionary hero of the Sandinistas, who stands proudly over the Managua skyline. We'll visit the Sandino museum and the ruins of the old Cathedral before driving on to Granada. This stunning colonial city is situated at the foot of Mombacho volcano and on the shore of the Lago de Nicaragua. We'll arrive in time for an afternoon cocktail and a panga (boat) trip to explore some of the many isletas just off the shore, including a visit to Castillo San Pablo and the Isla de los Monos (Monkey island).

Day 3
Granada
This morning we'll climb the Mombacho volcano that overlooks Granada, also spending time at the organic coffee farm and butterfly garden. We'll spend the afternoon exploring the city on foot and by horse drawn carriage, taking in some of its beautiful colonial buildings including the Cathedral de Granada, the Convento y Museo San Francisco and the Palacio de la Cultura Joaquin Cuadro Pasos. We'll have some free time to continue exploring, wandering the winding backstreets to discover the hidden delights of this beautiful colonial gem.

Day 4
Granada to San Juan del Sur
Today we'll spend the morning at the Laguna de Apoyo, a 200m deep crater lake. Surrounded by trees and steep sided crater it's a beautiful place to spend the day relaxing, swimming or kayaking. Those preferring to remain in Granada for more sightseeing or shopping can do so. In the afternoon we'll make our way down to the Pacific coast at San Juan del Sur, a beautiful cresent of bays with numerous beaches. Tonight we'll head out to the Refugio de Vida Silvestre La Flor to witness turtles laying their eggs. This is where upwards of 30,000 Olive Ridley turtles, as well as a few hundred endagered leatherback turtles come to nest each year.

Day 5
San Juan del Sur to Omotepe
Today we'll spend the day on the beach. A surfing lesson is arranged and provided for those who want it, and boards, wetsuit and snorkels are available to hire. This afternoon we'll head inland towards the huge inland freshwater Lago de Nicaragua. We'll have lunch in Rivas, then travel on to San Jorge to get the boat across to La Isla de Omotepe, where we'll spend the next couple of days.

This is taken even further in above example, where the logo, headline and name of the tour are designed to be seen as one; the introductory text is designed to be distinct from the rest of the text; and within the body text, each day is designed to be clearly separated from the rest, by use of a consistent space before each "Day" paragraph.

5) Balance

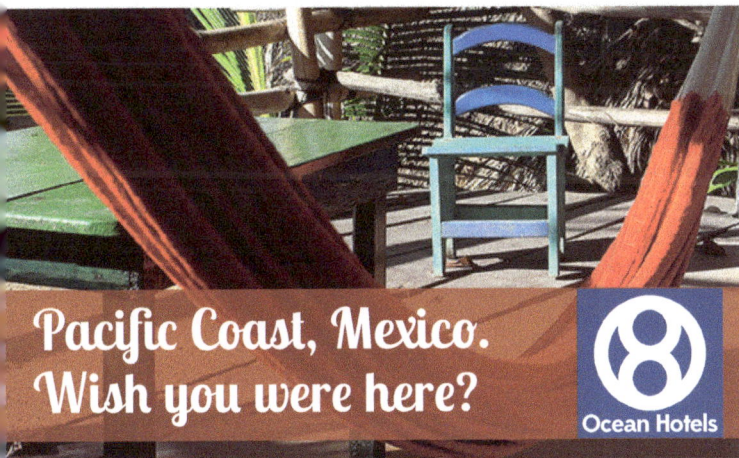

The two adverts above are roughly symmetrical. The elements on the left are roughly balanced on the right.

This gets more complicated, however, with designs that
are asymmetrical, as is this example below:

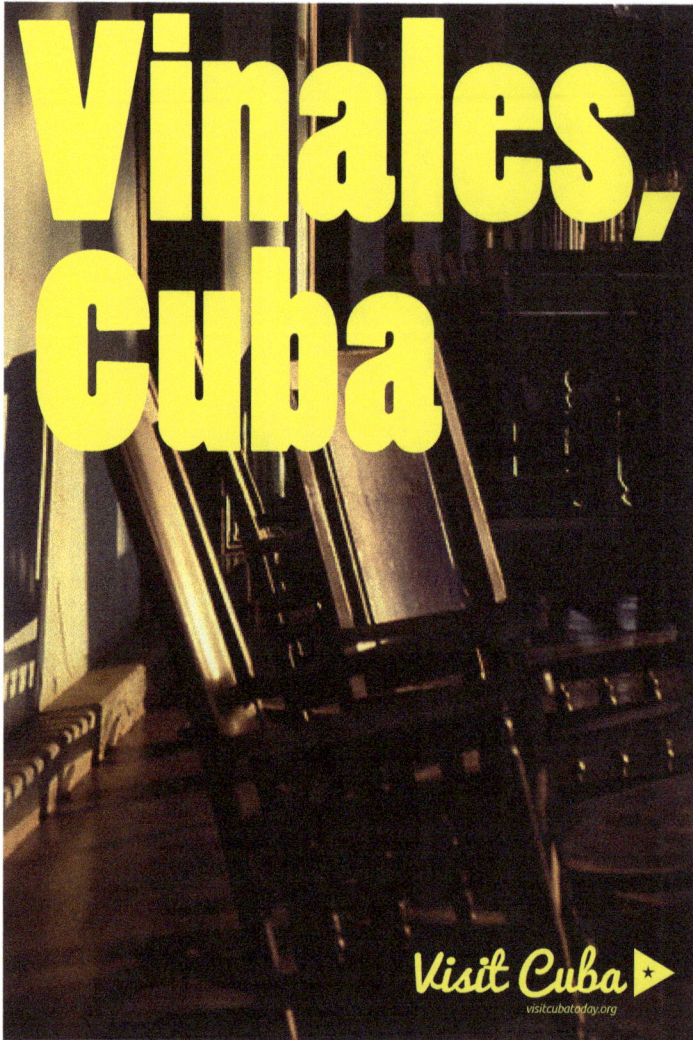

The large yellow text is predominantly on the left of the page, so
the logo is on the bottom right of the page to help balance it.

PERU

FROM ANDEAN PEAKS TO the roar of the Pacific Ocean, Peru has it all.

Experience the energy and diversity of what this country has to offer as we travel from the depths of the Amazon to the heights of Maccu Pichu.

For more information on our Highlights of Cuba tour, visit us at go-adventures.com or pick up our South America brochure from your local travel agent.

GO! ADVENTURES .COM

START YOUR ADVENTURE

The large Llama on the left of the page is balanced by the logo and text on the right.

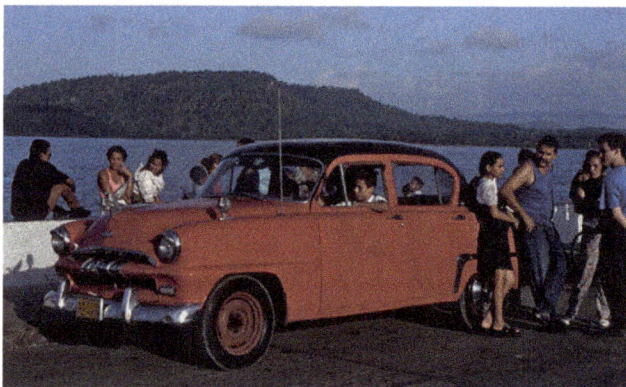

Baracoa: Essential Info

WHY GO?

Beautiful, green, quirky, funky, Baracoa has it all. Isolated on a beautiful coastline and surrounded by lush hills and valleys, once you've arrived here you'll not be in a hurry to leave. What it lacks in size it more than makes up for with spirit. It's the perfect place to retreat to for a few days when you want to escape the hustle and bustle of Havana. Stay in one of the many Casa Particulares, feast of seafood straight from the ocean and hike through a lush teeming green landscape.

GETTING THERE

Flying is the easiest way to get to Baracoa, but booking ahead is essential unless you're shedule is very flexible. Cubana currently flies from Habana to Baracoa on Thursdays and Sundays, and on Sunday there is also a flight from Santiago de Cuba. If you'd rather travel by bus, Viazul have a daily afternoon service to Baracoa from Guantánamo and Santiago de Cuba.

ACCOMODATION

Hotels in Baracoa include Hotel El Castillo and Villa Gaviota Baracoa. There are also a wide selection of Casa Particulares, which are a perfect way to get to see the place through the eyes of a local. Recommended Casa Particulares include Casa Azul Baracoa, Casa Colonial Ykira and Casa Colonial Yalina y Gustavo.

FOOD

Many Casa Particulares will cook food to order, but there's plenty of places around town to tempt you out. The old established Paladar el Colonial continues to deliver its unique Baracoan take on Carribean cuisine, but there are a growing range of great places to eat and drink like O Poeta and Al's.

WHAT TO DO

The Museo Municipal, found in the Fuetre Matachin fortress, explains the history of Cuba's oldest settlement, including exhibits on Che Guevara and the local chocolate factory. The Museo Arqueológico is worth seeing for its location alone. Found in Las Cuevas del Paraíso, the archeological exhibits are displayed in caves that were once used as burial chambers. The 19th century church of Nuestra Señora de la Asunción contains the Cruz de la Parra, a wooden cross said to been erected by Columbus in 1492.

HIKING

In his journal, Christopher Columbus wrote about El Yunque, the hill across the bay from Baracoa. It's an 8km hike from the town, and the sights from the top as well as the wildlife you'll see along the way make it a trip well worth making. Local travel agent Cubatur offer a guided trip most days. Another popular hike through the lush local wilderness is to the Cueva del Aguas, a cave that contains a freshwater swimming hole.

FOR MORE

For more information on Baracoa before you go, visit our website. Once there, local travel agencies Cubatur and Ecotur are the places to visit.

Visit Cuba ▶
visitcubatoday.org

When attempting to balance things out you'll find that some things seem to have more 'weight' than others. One of the reasons why the small yellow logo on the Visit Cuba poster could balance out the much larger text is that the triangle in the logo pointed to the right. Viewers eyes tend to follow such visual clues, adding to the impact they can have to shift the balance of a page.

For that reason, in the above example, the arrow in the Visit Cuba needs to be subtly counterbalanced. So it's no accident that in the image, the car is facing in the opposite direction.

6) Focal point

The logos in the previous section were able to counterbalance other elements on the page because they carried more "weight." Another way of saying this is that they were good at drawing the viewers eye towards them, or that they had become the focal point of the page. Look back at the three preceding examples and notice where your eye naturally falls, and try the same thing with these next three as well.

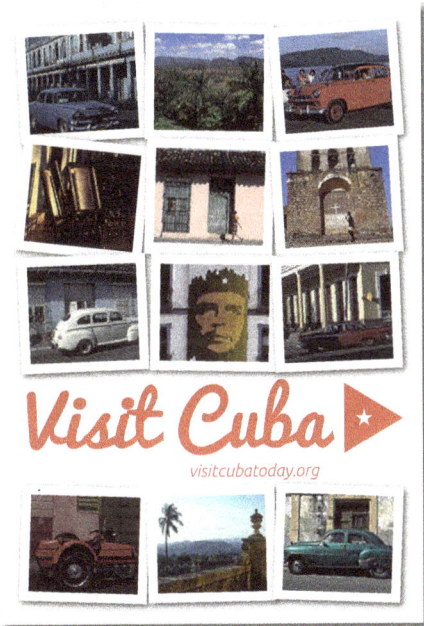

7) Colour

A little understanding of colour theory will help you choose how to combine colours. Here you'll look at three examples that demonstrate different ways to select colours.

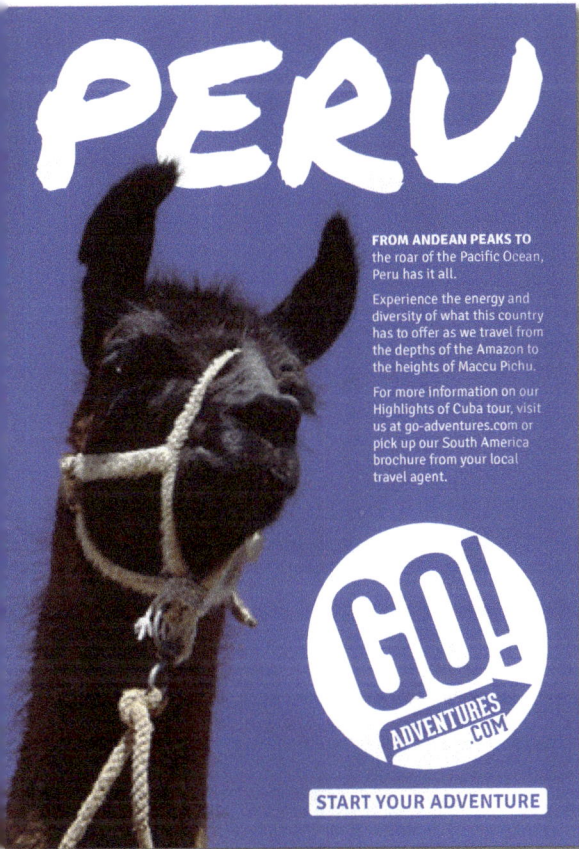

PERU

FROM ANDEAN PEAKS TO the roar of the Pacific Ocean, Peru has it all.

Experience the energy and diversity of what this country has to offer as we travel from the depths of the Amazon to the heights of Maccu Pichu.

For more information on our Highlights of Cuba tour, visit us at go-adventures.com or pick up our South America brochure from your local travel agent.

GO!
ADVENTURES
.COM

START YOUR ADVENTURE

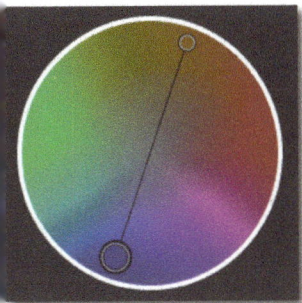

The blue colour was chosen for the background because it's a *complementary* colour of the brown – opposite it on the colour wheel.

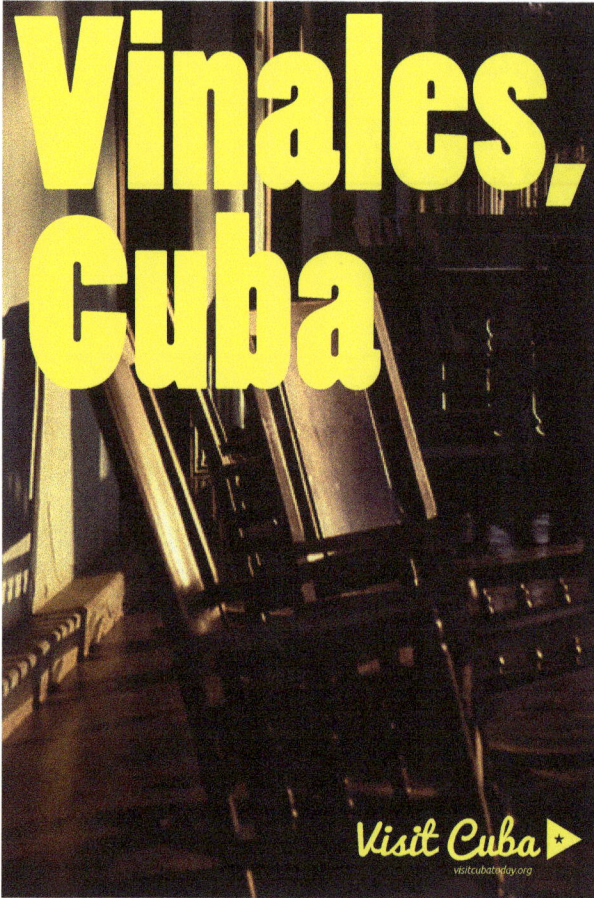

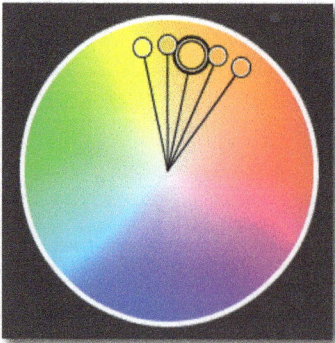

These colours go well together because they are *analogous* colours – close together on the colour wheel.

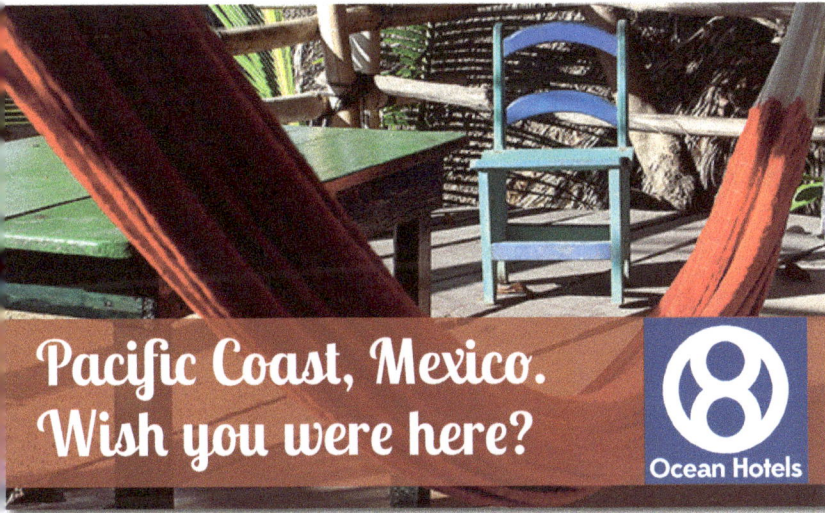

Pacific Coast, Mexico.
Wish you were here?

Ocean Hotels

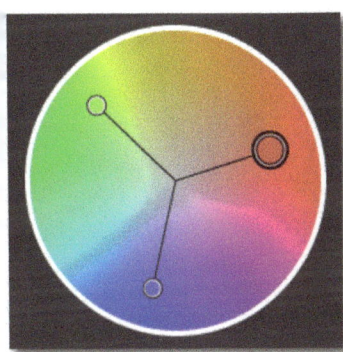

These colours go well together, and give a more energetic feel because they are *triadic* colours – spaced apart equally on the colour wheel.

8) Ratios

Certain ratios are known to be more appealing to us when we look at things. You can deliberately use these ratios when placing different elements on a page. Here are a couple of examples to help you start to notice them.

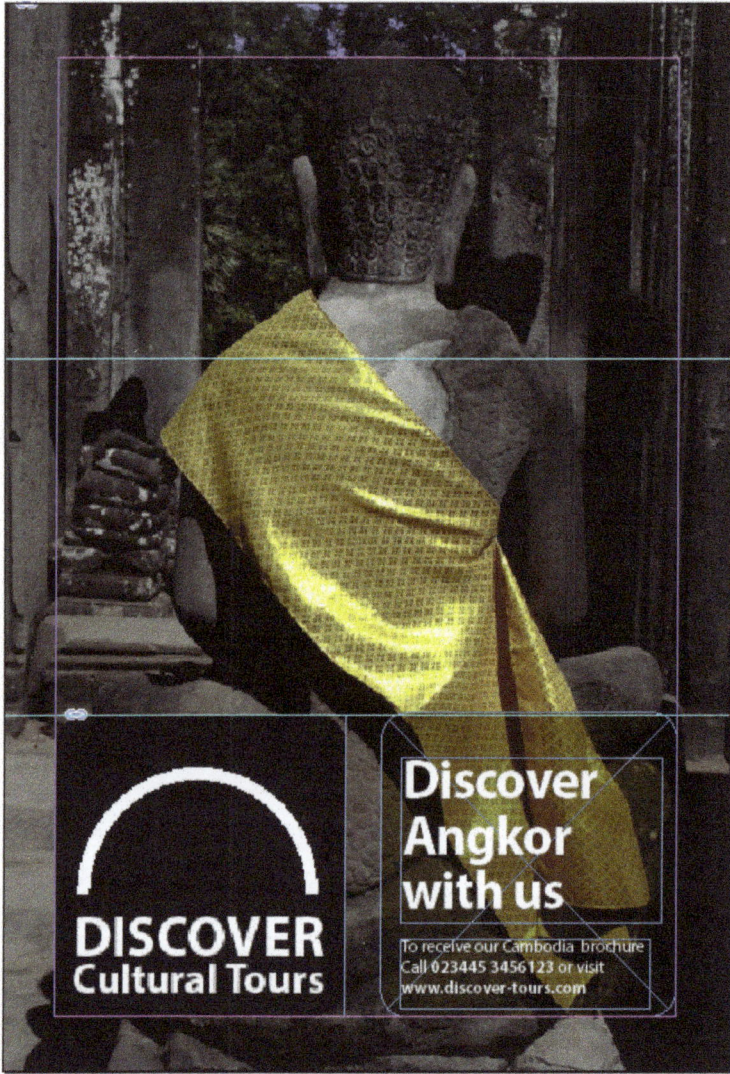

You can see from the blue guides (applied using InDesign's *Layout>Create Guides* command) that this page is divided into thirds, giving a ratio of 1:3.

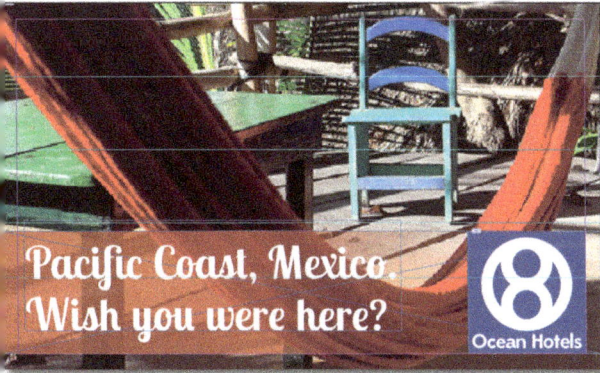

This page is divided into five and the logo and banner occupy roughly 2 sections, giving a very appealing ratio of 2:3.

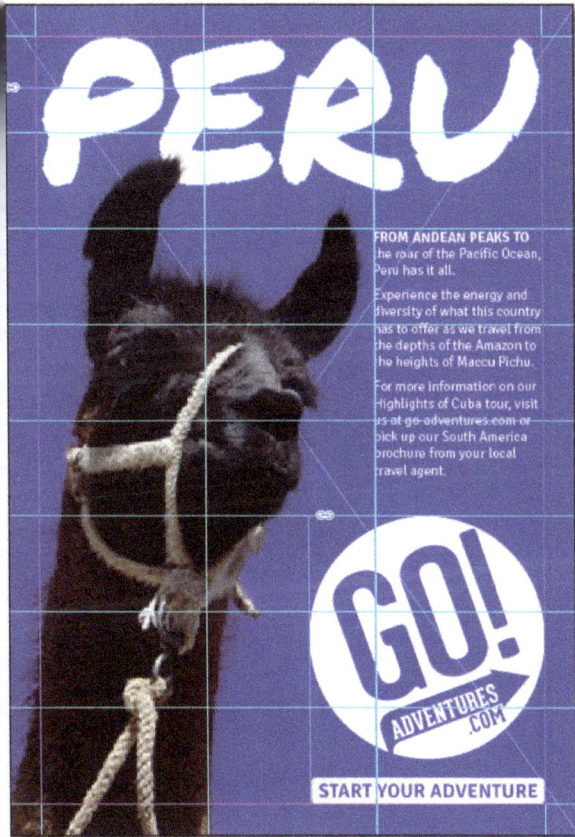

This page is divided into eight; the logo and body text occupy 3 sections, and the headline occupies 2, again utilising the ratio of 2:3.

9) Rhythm

Rhythm describes the mood of a design. Here are two
examples of rhythms conveyed by different things.

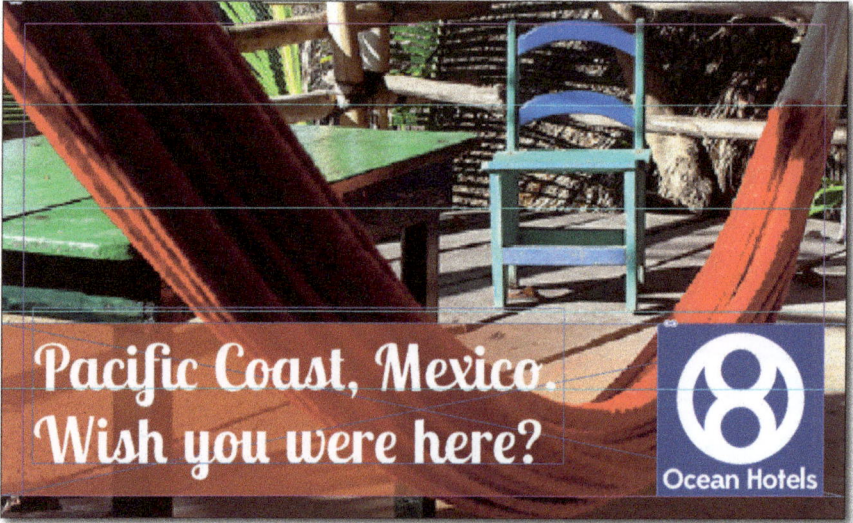

The wide, landscape shape of this advert, and the wide
stripe across it give a suggestion of calm.

PERU

FROM ANDEAN PEAKS TO the roar of the Pacific Ocean, Peru has it all.

Experience the energy and diversity of what this country has to offer as we travel from the depths of the Amazon to the heights of Maccu Pichu.

For more information on our Highlights of Cuba tour, visit us at go-adventures.com or pick up our South America brochure from your local travel agent.

GO!
ADVENTURES
.COM

START YOUR ADVENTURE

In contrast, the logo at an angle implies a sense of excitement.

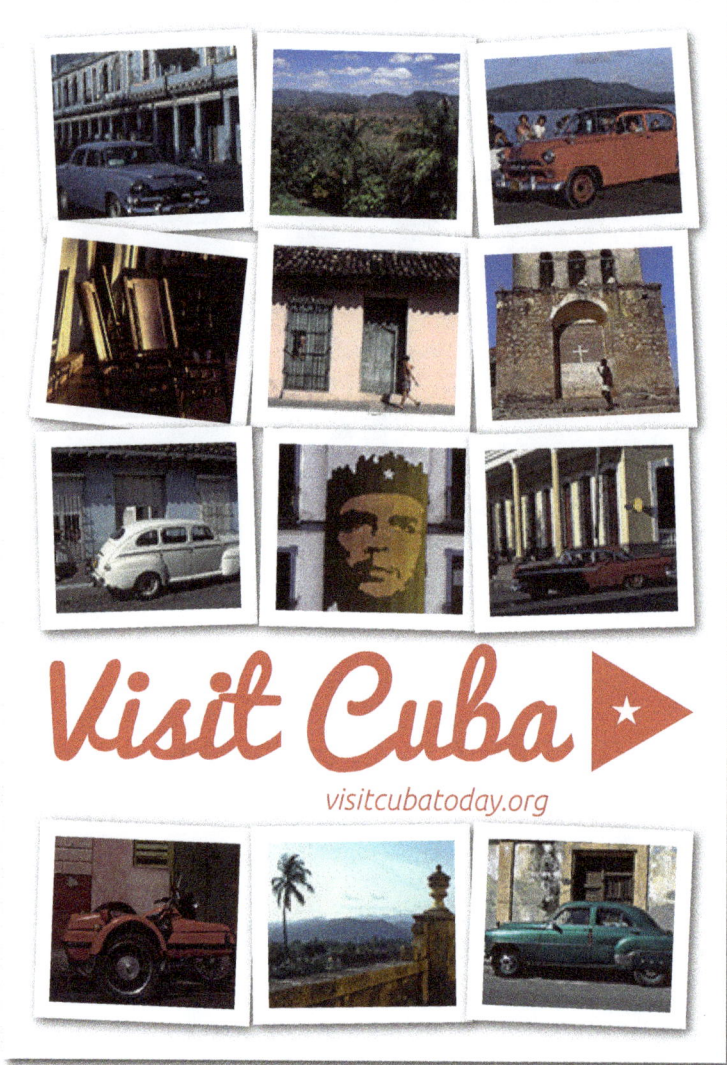

Here, these images at differing angles imply a sense of excitement.

10) Type: tracking and leading

The more you know about working with type the more your design work will improve. It's a vast subject, but here are a couple of typographical terms to get you started.

Compare the two versions of the larger text above, and notice how much tighter the lower version is. Negative *tracking* has been applied, bringing the letters closer together (horizontally), making it look more punchy and less generic.

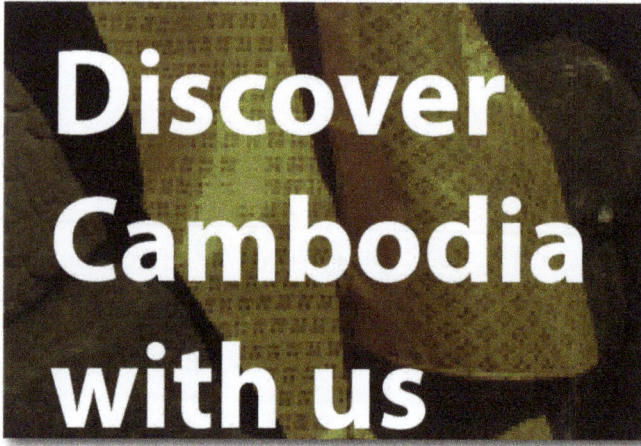

Compare the two versions of the text above. As well as having negative tracking applied, the lower one has had it's *leading* reduced, bringing the lines closer together vertically, making it appear less generic and more of a unit.

PREPARING INDESIGN FILES FOR PRINTING

This chapter is about preparing documents to be printed. If you've read the preceding chapters you'll know that they contain some brief guidance on this subject, but this section is for those that would like to have a greater understanding. As with the other chapters, you'll work through a series of documents, each of which will help demonstrate some different things to be aware of when you're sending a document to be printed.

1) An overview of the preflight process

The first document you'll prepare for print has essentially no problems with it, but you'll work through it to get used to some of the different concepts, terminology and areas of InDesign that you'll need to become familiar with.

Discover Europe with us

From deserted Greek islands to street markets in Turkey, we'll show you the very best that Europe can offer even the most seasoned traveller. Leave it all to us, and discover it with us.

To receive our Europe brochure call **02344 3456123** or visit **www.discover-tours.com**

DISCOVER Cultural Tours

1. From the *File menu* choose *Open* to open the a *1-Introduction* document. This advert is deliberately straightforward and will cause no problems when it's sent to print*, so you'll use it largely to compare with the documents that will present problems. All you're going to do here is take a close look at the images used within it, then create a pdf that's ready to send to a printer.

* *As you work through these documents you're going to learn how to check these possible areas of concern before sending a document to a printer: bleed, swatches, fonts, images and transparency. This first document does not require bleed, it uses only the default black swatch, it uses fonts that come installed with InDesign and it features no transparency.*

2. Open the *Links Panel* by clicking on it at the top right of your screen.

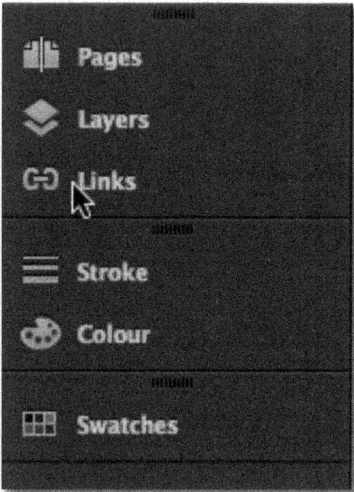

3. The Links Panel contains list of all the images that have been imported into the document (using the *File>Place* command). When you place an image into InDesign it is not strictly imported into the document; instead a lower quality version of it is brought in which is linked to the original file on your computer. It's important that these links are maintained, so that when you either create a pdf or a package to send to a printer (more about these later) InDesign can retrieve the full quality image from the original file.

4. If InDesign is not able to locate the original file because it's been moved or renamed, you'll see a red question mark next to the image in the Links Panel's *status column* (underneath the triangular icon with the exclamation mark). In the case of these images the column should be empty because they are properly linked.

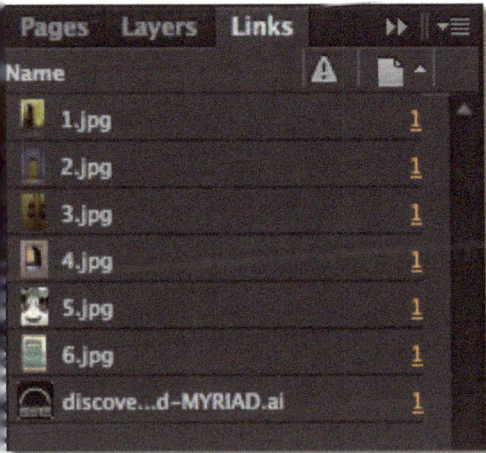

5. The other preliminary thing to check with the links is to make sure that they haven't been modified since they were placed into InDesign. Later on you'll learn how to modify images in a way that ensures InDesign can keep track of them, but for now, all you need to know is that if an image has been modified without InDesign knowing, there will be a yellow exclamation mark icon in the status column next to it. As before, this should not be the case for these images.

About CMYK

The majority of all commercially printed work is printed using *Four Colour Process* (alternatively called Four Colour, CMYK, Full Colour, Process Colour). This works by printing the four process colours, Cyan, Magenta, Yellow and blacK (hence CMYK) in a close arrangement of tiny dots in combinations that can simulate millions of different colours. If you look on the spine of a newspaper you'll probably see the letters CMYK, or possibly little squares or circles printed of those colours. As a general guide, anything you produce that has a colour photograph on it will be produced in Four Colour Process. If you are creating a document which will be printed in Process Colour, any image you place into InDesign should ideally be defined using CMYK*. This means that every one of the thousands or millions of pixels** that make up the image contains four pieces of information: how much Cyan, Magenta, Yellow and blacK. As digital cameras and most scanners work in RGB (like monitors, they work with light rather than ink), the majority of the images you will come across will probably be made up of RGB pixels.

* *I say ideally because even if the images are not in CMYK, it's possible for InDesign to convert them when creating a pdf, as you'll discover later.*

** *You're probably familiar with the term pixels – if not, it means the tiny squares of colour that make up a digital image. That is essentially all a digital photograph is – many thousands of tiny squares, each one capable of having its own unique colour or shade.*

6. To see more information about the *1.jpg* image, click on its name in the **Links Panel.**

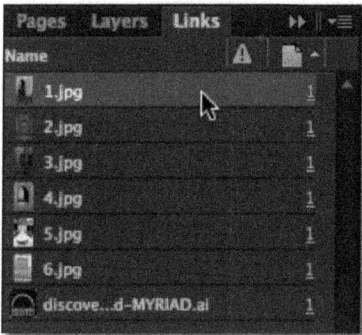

7. Information about the image appears in the *Link Info* section at the bottom of the panel.

8. As you should be able to see from the screenshot above, the *Colour Space* of this image is *CMYK*. Click on all of the other jpg images in turn to check that they all are too. The final image listed (with the *.ai* suffix) is an Illustrator file. Leave this for now, but later you'll explore a specific issue that can arise with this type of image.

About resolution

As well as checking images to ensure that they are not missing, not modified and have a CMYK colour space, you will also need to check their *Resolution*. Resolution essentially determines whether an image is of suitable quality to print. It is measured in *ppi*, the number of *pixels per inch*. For an image to be suitable quality for on screen work, it needs to have around *72*ppi. But for printed work, a resolution of around *300*ppi is advised. Printers often talk of dpi, rather than ppi, but it refers to the same thing. They also will refer to "High res" and "Low res" images, meaning high and low resolution, again high res normally meaning around 300ppi.

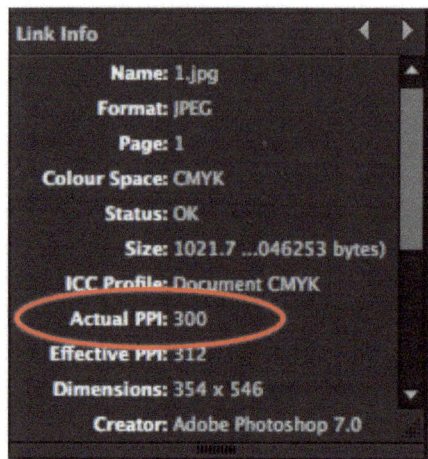

9. The Link Info for the *1.jpg* image is shown above. Its resolution is shown as *Actual ppi* and *Effective ppi*. The Actual ppi is resolution of the image at its original size (300) and the Effective ppi is the resolution at the sized that it's used on the page (312)*.

* *The reason they are different is because the image has been made slightly smaller within InDesign, and as it's measured by the number of pixels per inch of the image, if the image is made smaller the resolution will consequently go up. This is what is meant by the Effective ppi.*

10. Click on each link in turn and you should see that for each one the *Effective ppi* is around *300*, which is what you should ideally be aiming for. If they are not, you'll be taking a risk that they will look poor quality.

Creating a print-ready pdf

As mentioned previously, whilst there are several other checks you'd normally make before sending your document to be printed, in this case you've made all the appropriate ones, so now you'll export the advert as a pdf.

11. To create a pdf choose **Export** from the **File menu.** In the dialogue box that appears you'll need to choose the *Adobe PDF (Print)* format, give it an appropriate name and save it in a suitable location. Once you've done that, a dialogue box appears that contains a choice of pdf export options. Whole books have been written on the best settings to use here – I'm going to simply suggest two options.

2. The first is to ask your printer to supply you with a *Preset** of the settings they would recommend. They can either talk the setting through to you for you to type in, or send you a *job options* file. For the purpose of this exercise you'll continue to the next step, but the footnote below gives you instructions to follow if you are sent settings by your printer.

*If they were to supply you with a file, you'd choose **File>Adobe PDF presets>Define,** then press the **Load** button, locate the file they'd sent, then press the **Done** button. When you next use the File>Export command, the options they sent will be in the list of **Adobe PDF Presets** at the top of the dialogue box.*

3. In your case (and generally in the absence of advice or a preset given by your printer), choose the *[PDF/X-1a:2001]* preset from the options at the top of the *Export Adobe PDF* dialogue box. This preset's settings were created to be used in advertising, and are generally agreed to work amongst print professionals, so you're unlikely to get any nasty surprises. Press the **Export** button to finish creating the pdf, and if you want to look at it, locate it where you saved it and double-click on it to open it.

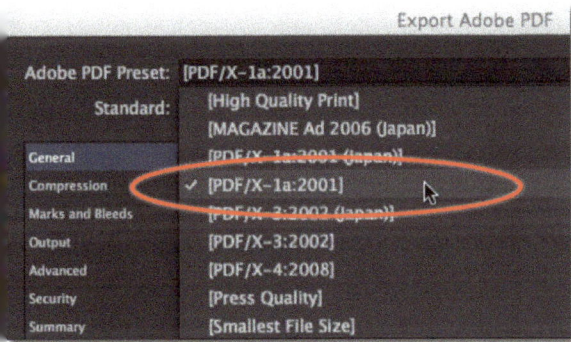

Summary of checks you made

Checked for missing images (Links Panel: Status column)
Checked for modified images (Links Panel: Status column)
Checked that images were CMYK (Links Panel: Link Info)
Checked the resolution of images (Links Panel: Link Info)

Summary of commands used

File>Open
File>Export (to create a pdf)

2) Essential checks: bleeds, fonts, links, resolution

The previous document was setup ready to go to print, but this one is not. Here you'll discover how to work with images that are missing, images with a low resolution, fonts that are missing and learn about bleeds.

1. From the **File menu** choose **Open** to open the a *2-Essential-checks* document. Before the document has even opened you should be presented with a dialogue box warning you that one of the links is missing.

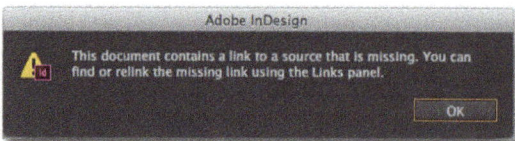

2. Once you've pressed the **OK button** you'll probably* be presented with another dialogue box, this time telling you that this document uses a font that you don't have installed on your computer.

* *If you've previously installed this font on your computer you won't see this dialogue box appear.*

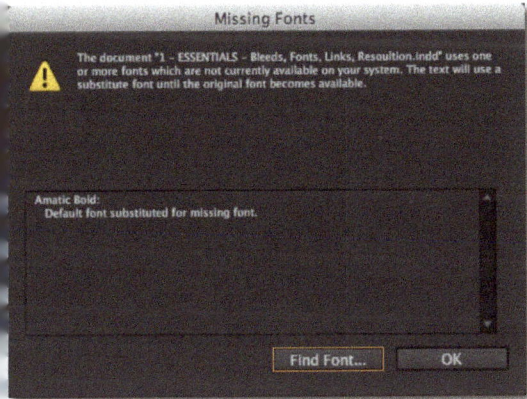

3. The dialogue box invites you to use the *Find Font* command to fix the problem, but ignore it for now by pressing the **OK button**.

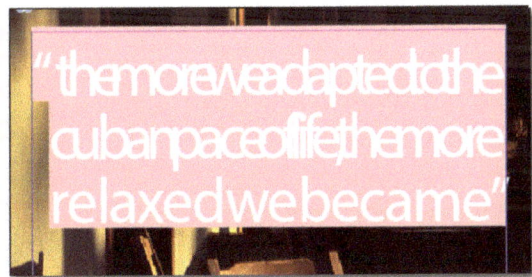

4. Once the document is opened, if you don't have the *Amatic Bold* font installed, the text will appear highlighted in pink to alert you that the missing font has been substituted with one that you do have on your computer. You could also consider it a none too subtle reminder that you need to fix this – which you will shortly.

5. Before you fix the font problem you'll address the missing link. Click once on the **Links Panel** to open it, and notice the red question mark icon in the link status column next to the *visit_cuba_white.eps* file.

6. Double click on the **question mark icon** to relink the file*, which is another way of saying that you'll tell InDesign where it can locate the missing image.

   * *If you have InDesign CS6 or later you might have noticed there is also a missing link icon on the logo itself. You can alternatively relink by double-clicking directly on that.*

7. To finish the process of relinking you now have to locate the original image. In this case I'm going to tell you where it is, but in everyday work you'd possibly need to search on your computer, ask a colleague, client, photographer or designer to send it to you. Look in the *Logos* folder (inside the *Preparing InDesign documents for print* folder) and click on the *visit_cuba_white.eps* logo to relink it. When you return to the document you'll notice the red icon has disappeared.

8. Whilst in the **Links Panel** click on the *visit-cuba-vinales-a3.jpg* image and look at its resolution in the *Link Info Panel*. Notice that the Effective ppi of this image is *72*. This means that it's a low resolution image, suitable for viewing on screen, but not for being commercially printed.

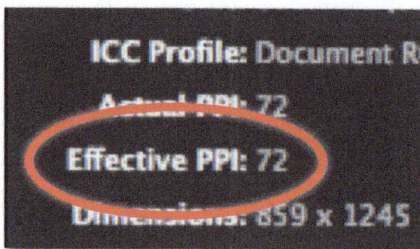

9. For the purposes of these exercises it doesn't make any difference what the image's resolution is, but on a real project it's important that the images are of sufficient quality. As mentioned previously they should ideally be around *300ppi*. If they are not, you'll be taking a risk that they will look poor quality. If this happens to you, your options are to source higher resolution images from the photographer, use different images, use them at smaller sizes, or as a last resort resample the image using Photoshop's *Image Size* command (which is beyond the remit of this book).

10. Notice also in the Link Info that this image's *Colour Space* is *RGB* and not CMYK. Whilst this is something that can't be adjusted in InDesign, the program makes it easy for you to open the image in Photoshop and change it there. Before you learn how to do this I should mention that whilst it's commonplace for designers to use Photoshop to convert images from RGB to CMYK, it's not strictly essential to do this, because if you create a pdf from InDesign using a setting such as *[PDF/X-1a:2001]* it will convert any RGB images and swatches to CMYK as it does it.

Link Info

Name: visit-cuba-
Format: JPEG
Colour Space: RGB
Size: 611.7 KB (6

11. To open the image in Photoshop make sure the image is selected at the top of the Links Panel, press on the dropdown menu at the top right of the panel and choose **Edit With** from the list of commands that appear. A list of suitable programs will appear – if you have Photoshop installed on your computer, choose that.

Pages   Layers   **Links**

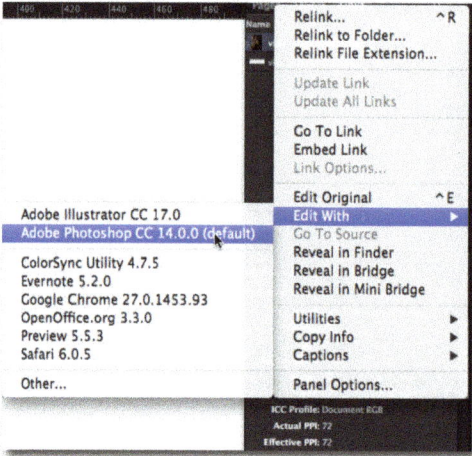

12. In Photoshop, choose **Image>Mode>CMYK.** Then save and close
the file, and return to InDesign. When you click on the image
the Info Panel should now indicate that it is a CMYK image.

About missing fonts

13. In the same way that InDesign needs access to the original images
that have been placed in a document before creating a pdf, it also
needs access to any fonts that were used when creating it. As you've
already seen, you will be altered by means of a dialogue box and the
pink highlighting of text that you need to deal with missing fonts. To
have a closer look at this, from the *Type menu* choose *Find Font.*

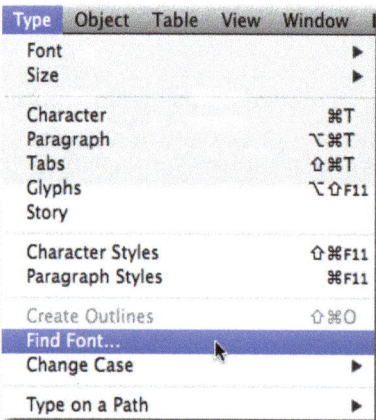

4. The *Find Font* command lists all of the fonts used in the document and highlights ones that are missing by means of a yellow exclamation mark icon. In this document only one font is used, *Amatic Bold,* and it is missing.

5. How you'll handle missing fonts will be depend on the circumstances. In some cases the font that is missing might not be critical for the design or branding and can be easily substituted for another one you do have. In that case you'd use the *Find First* and *Change* or *Change All* buttons on the right to search for the places where the font is used have InDesign replace it with a different one. But it's more likely that you'd fix the problem by installing that font on your computer. The font used here is one whose designer has made freely available. If you want to install it, press the *Done* button to leave the Find Font dialogue box*.

* *If you'd rather not install it, follow these instructions to replace it with a different font that you have on your computer. Click on the* **Amatic Bold** *font at the top of the dialogue box, choose a font from the list at the bottom of the dialogue box, then press the* **Change All** *button to replace every instance of Amatic Bold with the font of your choice.*

16. You can download the *Amatic Bold* font for free from
www.fontsquirrel.com. While you're there you might also want to
download the *Permanent Marker, Signika* and *Ubuntu* fonts that
you'll use in later exercises. Instructions on how to install them
can be found at *www.fontsquirrel.com/help* You might find this
Wiki How tutorial useful for installing on a PC: *www.wikihow.
com/Install-Fonts-on-Your-PC* and Mac users can find a similar
tutorial here: *www.youtube.com/watch?v=3AIR7_ch9No*

17. Once you've installed the font and returned to InDesign
you should notice the pink highlight has disappeared,
indicating that the font is no longer missing.

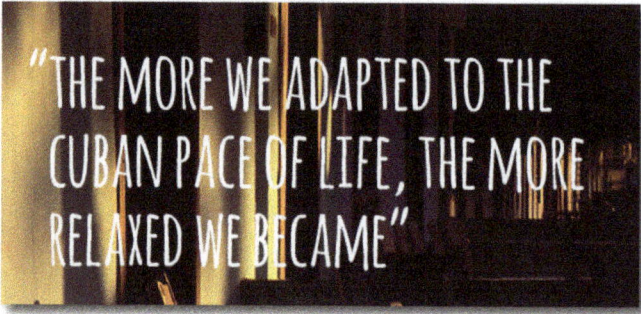

About Bleeds

As you know, the black border around every page edge indicates the edge of the document, but that's not the full story. When you send an InDesign document to a commercial printer they are often printed on sheets or rolls of paper that are larger than the document size. They are then trimmed down to size on a guillotine, whose blade is lined up with *Trim Marks* (see the diagram below).

The black border represents where the trimming should occur. However, as the guillotine blade runs through a stack of paper its blade may bend slightly, and your document may be trimmed slightly inside or outside the black line. To account for this, any elements that need to appear right at the edge of a page need to continue, or 'bleed' over the edge. A *bleed guide* makes it straightforward to create bleeds, as objects snap to the guide that sits just outside the edge of the page. The diagram below shows a close up of the top left corner of a document with a bleed guide.

18. As you can see from the screenshot below, this poster has a photograph that extends to the edge of the page on every side, and so it should have a bleed guide. However there is no bleed guide, and the image simply stops at the edge of the page. If the bleed guide wasn't set up when the document was created it can be added later. You'll do this now by choosing *Document Setup* from the **File menu.**

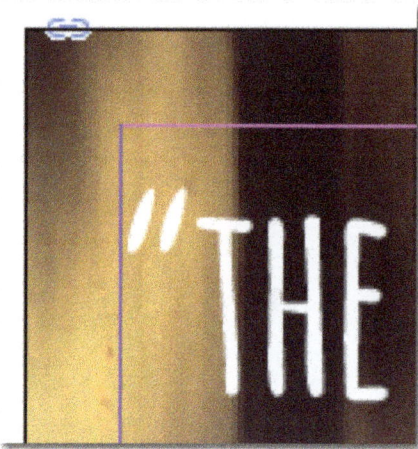

19. At the bottom of the *Document Setup* dialogue box you should see a dropdown button next to the words **Bleed and Slug*.**

* *If you're using a version of InDesign prior to CC (any of the CS versions) you'll instead press the* **More Options** *button towards the top right of the New Document dialogue box to reveal the Bleed and Slug values.*

20. Once you can see the Bleed and Slug values, enter *3mm* for one of the *Bleed* values and click on the padlock to apply the same value to all edges of the document. Then press the **OK button.**

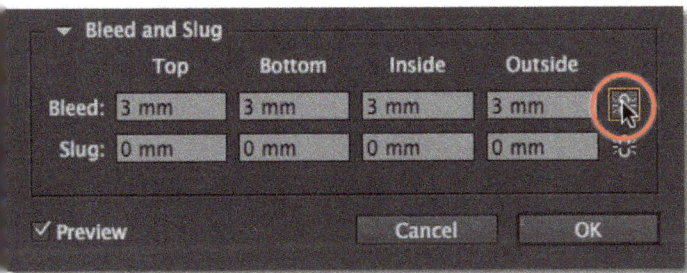

21. You'll now see a red *bleed guide* has appeared just outside the edge of the document.

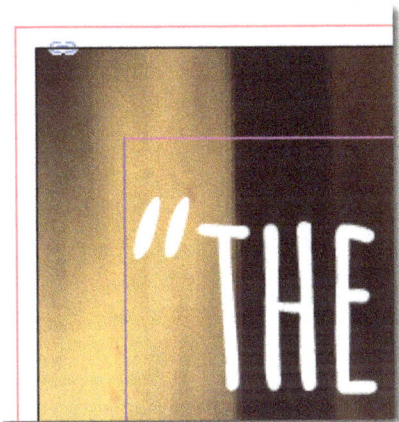

22. Choose the **Selection Tool** from the **Tools Panel** and click on the edge of the frame that contains the picture.

23. Using the **Selection Tool,** drag the square *handle* on the top left of the frame out to the bleed guide. Do the same thing with the handle on the bottom right of the page, creating a *3mm* bleed.

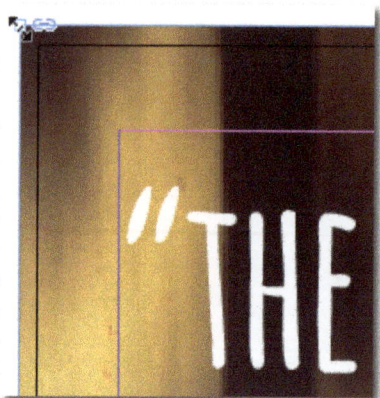

24. Finally you'll create a pdf. Use **File>Export** as you did previously and choose the *[PDF/X-1a:2001]* preset from the options at the top of the *Export Adobe PDF* dialogue box. The pdf you created previously was for an advert, and the assumption there was that the advert would be placed somewhere in the middle of a page in a magazine, alongside others. Because of that it would not be printed on its own, nor need to be trimmed down to size, nor need to allow for any bleed. This poster is different. As it's going to be printed conventionally it is advisable to add printers marks – things like trim marks they can use to trim the document once it's been printed. To do this, firstly click on *Marks and Bleeds* from the list on the left hand side of the dialogue box.

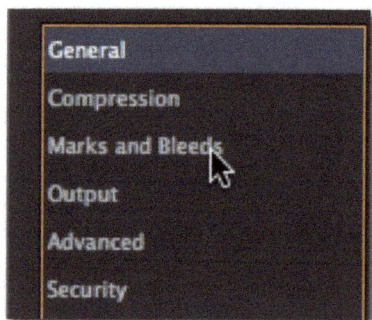

25. In the *Marks and Bleeds* section of the PDF Export Dialogue box, check both the *All Printer's Marks* checkbox and the *Use Document Bleed Settings* checkbox before pressing the **Export button.**

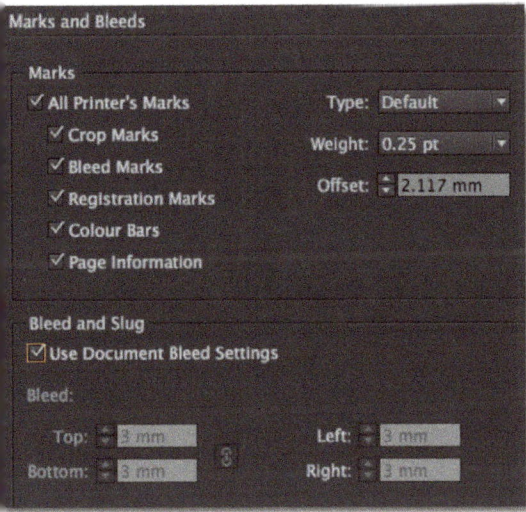

26. If you look at the finished pdf (by double clicking on it, outside of InDesign) you'll see the trim marks around the edge of the document, and also the area of the image outside the bleed guides that should be trimmed off once the document has been printed.

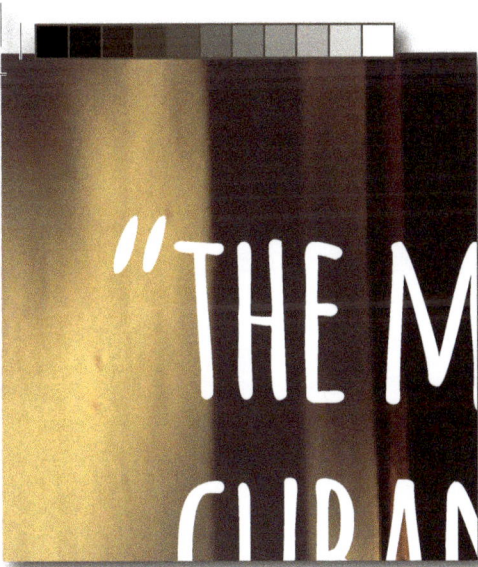

Summary of what you've learned

How to relink a missing image

How to change an RGB image to CMYK

How to recognise a low resolution image

How to notice / replace a missing font

How to add a bleed guide

How to export a pdf with bleeds and trim marks

Summary of new commands used

Links Panel>Relink (or double-click on missing link icon)

Links Panel>Edit With

Type>Find Font

File>Document Setup

Intermission

If you've been working through the exercises to try and understand what to do in order to send your own documents to print, at this point in the book you've already covered everything that's generally likely to arise. To gain an understanding of some other issues that are less likely to arise, please read on, but if you're in a hurry to get working on your own documents you can probably skip to the final chapter, *About Packages and Preflight*. Let me also mention again that whilst I'm going to continue to assume that you'll be converting images (and swatches, which you'll learn about) to CMYK manually, it's not strictly essential to do this, because if you create a pdf from InDesign using a setting such as *[PDF/X-1a:2001]* it will convert any RGB images and swatches to CMYK as it does it.

3) Checking for sampled colours, RGB colours and RGB images

As you continue working through issues might affect printing you'll take another look at RGB images and also have a brief look at the Swatches Panel.

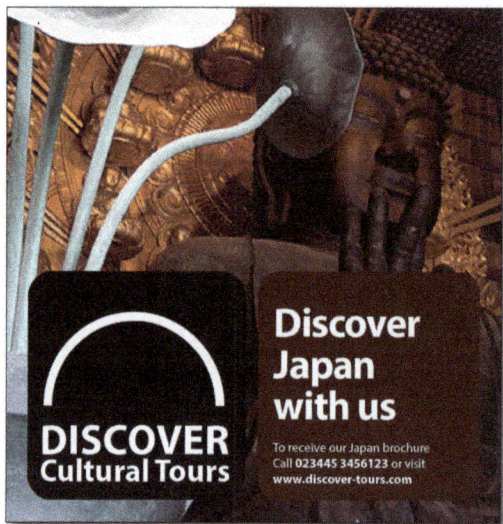

1. From the **File menu** choose **Open** to open the *3-RGB-Images-and-swatches* file. Unlike the previous document it should open without a warning about missing fonts or images*. This is another advert, so bleeds aren't an issue either. Here you'll explore the colours that have been used in the document. To do this, click once on the word *Swatches* on the right of your screen to open the ***Swatches Panel.***

* *If it does, use the skills you learned in the previous exercise to replace missing images or fonts.*

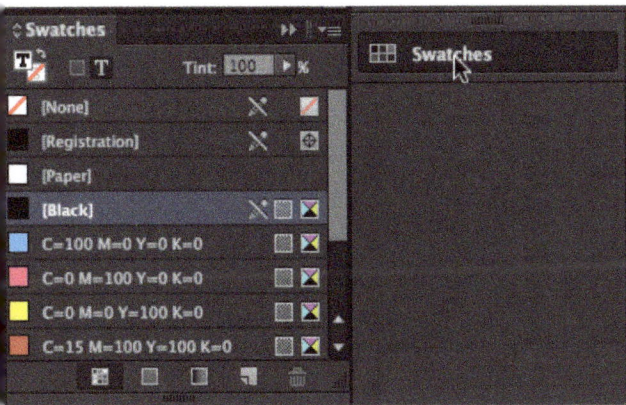

2. In this panel you can see all of the standard swatches that are present by default in every new InDesign document. If you look closely, their names are simply the percentages of the Cyan, Magenta, Yellow and blacK inks that make them up. For example, the *C=0 M=100 Y=100 K=0* (red) swatch uses no cyan or black ink but 100% magenta and yellow. The symbol to the far right of each name also indicates that these are cymk colours and so will print on a commercial printing press.

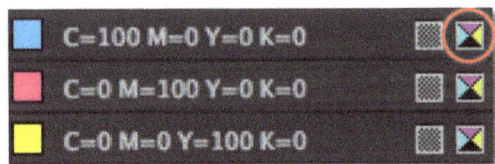

3. When your design incorporates photographs there's a particularly useful feature in InDesign that allows you to sample a colour directly from an image, and that's what's been used to create the brown background to the text in this advert. Unfortunately this colour wasn't saved as a swatch, and that means that you can't check it to see whether or not it's a cmyk colour.

4. To make sure that any colours that have used in a document have been made into swatches, from the **dropdown menu** in the top right of the **Swatches Panel** choose *Add Unnamed Colours.*

. Look again at the **Swatches Panel**. You'll notice that the brown colour has now been created as a swatch, and that it looks a little different from the other swatches. Both its name and its icon indicate that it is an *RGB* swatch, that its colours have been defined by a mixture of red, green and blue light as opposed to cmyk ink. It's RGB because it was sampled from an RGB image as opposed to a CMYK one.

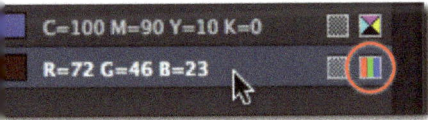

5. To change the swatch into cmyk firstly click on it, then go to the **Swatches Panel dropdown menu** and choose *Swatch Options.*

7. In the dialogue box that appears click on the *Colour Mode dropdown menu,* and scroll up, then click on *CMYK* and press **OK**.

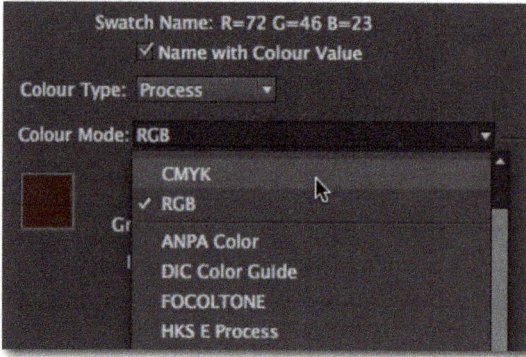

8. Now you've converted the swatch to CMYK, open the **Links Panel** and select the *Discover_japan_nara.jpg* image that the swatch colour was sampled from. From the **Links Panel dropdown menu** use **Edit With** to open the image in Photoshop and convert the image to CMYK as well.*

* *In Photoshop use* Image>Mode>CMYK, *then save the image.*

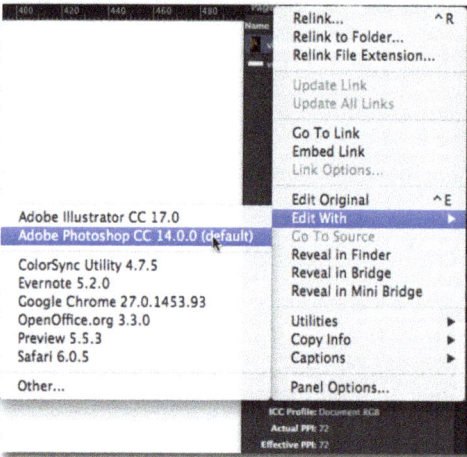

9. To finish, export the advert as a pdf, using the *[PDF/X-1a:2001]* preset from the options at the top of the *Export Adobe PDF* dialogue box.

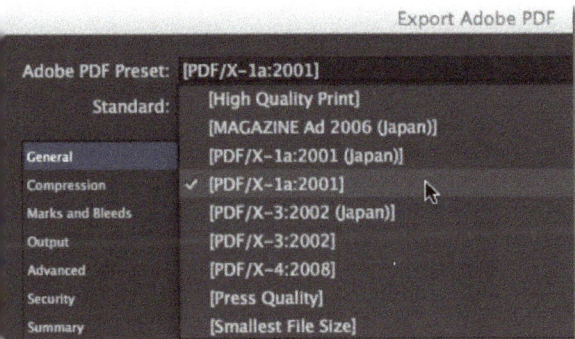

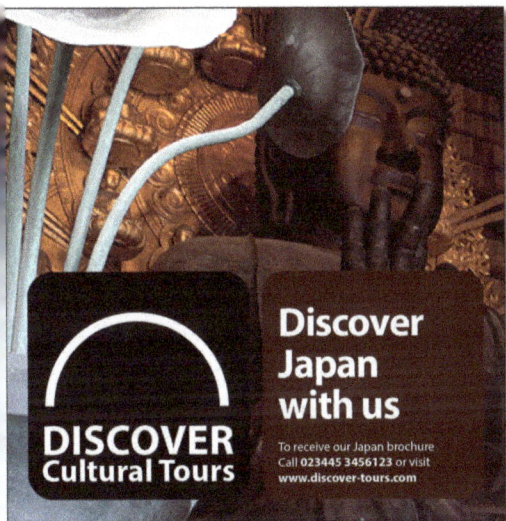

Summary of what you've learned

How to create swatches from colours used in a document

How to identify RGB swatches

How to convert RGB swatches to CMYK

New Commands used

Swatches Panel: Add Unnamed Colours

Swatches Panel: Swatch Options

4) Checking for spot colours

You'll now take a closer look at the Swatches Panel, discover the Separations Preview Panel and learn about spot colours.

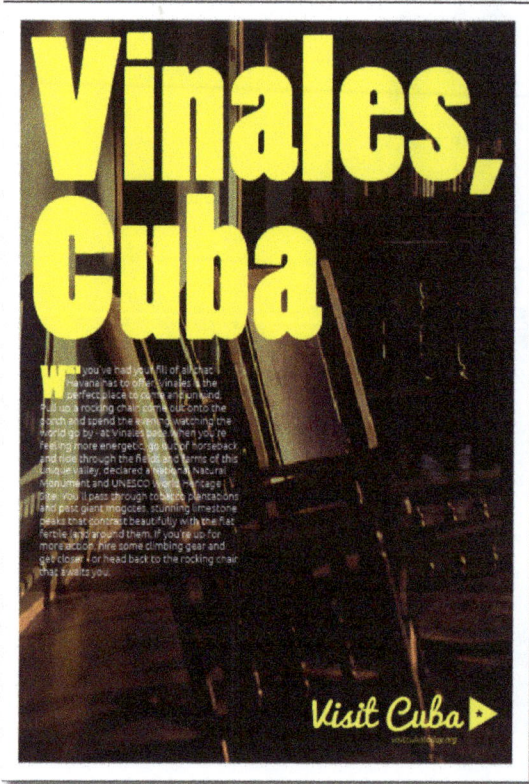

1. From the **File menu** choose **Open** to open the a *4-Spot-colours* document. Unless you've already installed the *Ubuntu Light* font you'll be presented with the *Missing Fonts* dialogue box. If this happens you can either install the font* or press the *Find Font* button to replace the *Ubuntu Light* font with one that you already have on your system**.

* *You can download the **Ubuntu** font family for free from www.fontsquirrel. com. Instructions on how to install them can be found at www.fontsquirrel. com/help You might find this Wiki How tutorial useful for installing on a PC: www.wikihow.com/Install-Fonts-on-Your-PC and Mac users can find a similar tutorial here: www.youtube.com/watch?v=3AIR7_ch9No*

** *Click on the **Ubuntu Light** font at the top of the dialogue box, choose a font from the list at the bottom of the dialogue box, then press the **Change All** button to replace every instance of **Ubuntu Light** with the font of your choice.*

2. The document should have opened without a warning about missing images*. This flyer has a deliberate white border around its edge, so bleeds aren't an issue either.

* If it does, use the skills you learned in the previous exercises to replace missing images.

3. The first thing you'll do is to change the photograph to cmyk, which you can do in two ways. From the **Links Panel** you could either use the **Edit With** command to edit it in Photoshop, or use **Relink** to replace it with the image that you changed when working on the earlier exercise.

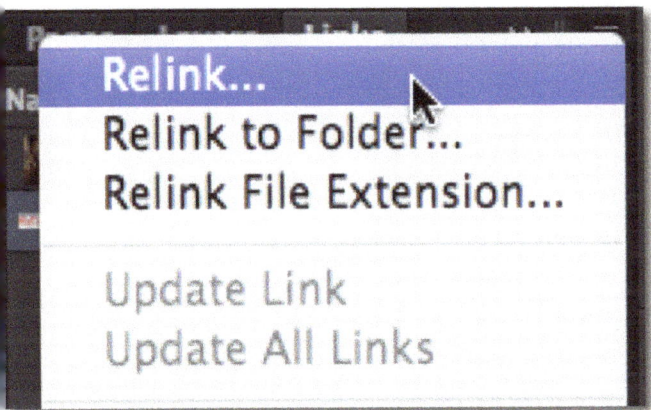

4. Open the **Swatches Panel** and notice that one of the swatches looks different to anything that you've seen previously. This is a *Pantone Spot* colour, and before you go on to do anything with it, you'll learn a little more about what those two words mean.

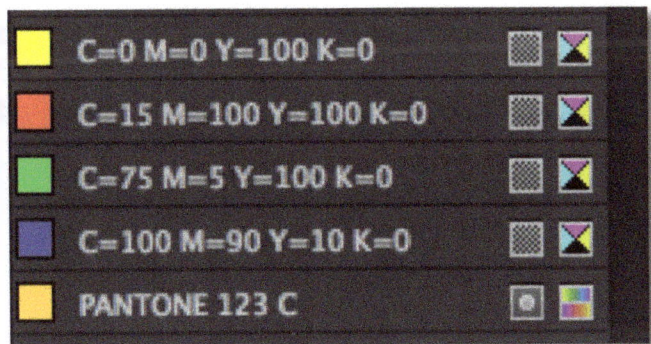

Spot colours

Documents like letterheads and business cards are often printed simply using one, two or three colours only. In these instances the print process is more simple than the four colour process (or cmyk) that you've been learning about so far: rather than mixing up the four process inks on the printing press to produce the required colours, pre-mixed inks of the desired colour are bought in. These are called Spot Colours. These are perfect for jobs such as business cards where only one, two or three colours are required, for two reasons. Firstly, because they can be printed on a smaller printing press (that only needs to apply one, two or three inks rather than four) it typically costs less to print. Secondly, because each colour is made from a pre-mixed ink of that colour rather than being a mixture of the four process inks, they tend to appear more solid.

Pantone colours

The colours you see on screen will not exactly resemble those of your printed document. There are many reasons for this, but the main one is that what you see on a screen is formed by light being "fired" at your eye; whereas what you see in print is formed by light being reflected from your document to your eye. For that reason alone (and there are many other reasons besides), what you see in print will not appear as vibrant as it does on the screen. This can present a real problem when it comes to choosing colours when working on a company's branding, because it's important to know at this early stage what the company's corporate colours will really look like when printed in different ways, as well as on screen. Professional designers use Pantone books when designing the logo and identity for a company, because these books show thousands of *printed* colours, so you can see what they'll look like on paper. There are different books available for different types of print work: inks can be printed as Process or Spot (called *Solid* by Pantone) inks and printed on Coated (glossy) paper or Uncoated paper. So, for example, if they wanted to see how a specific colour would look in a glossy magazine, they'd look at the *Pantone Process Coated* book. Or if they wanted to see how it would look on a letterhead they'd look at the *Pantone Solid Uncoated* book. When creating a logo for a client, a designer would typically create one that uses spot colours (for letterheads, business cards etc.) and one that process colours (for everything else).

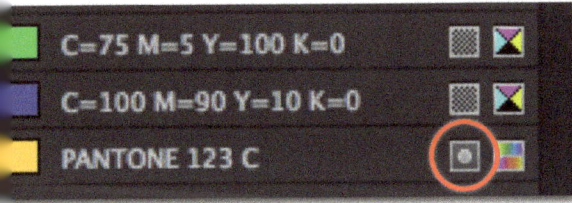

5. The large white dot that you can see highlighted in the swatch shown above indicates that it is a *spot* colour. This has appeared in the document because the spot colour version of the logo has been mistakenly brought in the instead of the process colour version. Using the spot version would indicate to the printer that as well as printing the rest of the document using the cmyk inks, this spot colour would be printed in addition. Whilst this is something that some companies would choose to do, it adds significant expense to the print job, so is not common practice. To have a way of seeing what would happen, from the **Window menu** choose **Output>Separations Preview.** From the *View dropdown menu* choose *Separations.*

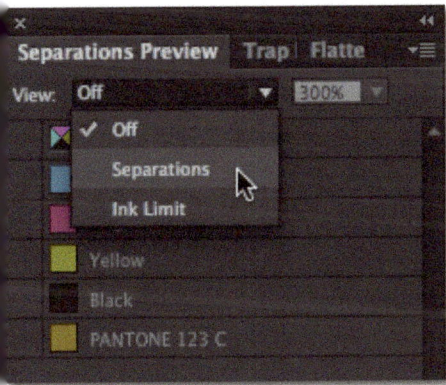

6. This panel shows the actual inks that will be used on the printing press. All of the previous documents you've looked at so far would have just shown the CMYK inks, but this one has the Pantone 123C spot colour as well. To see which areas of the document will print using this ink, hide it by clicking on the eye icon to the left of the Pantone 123C spot colour.

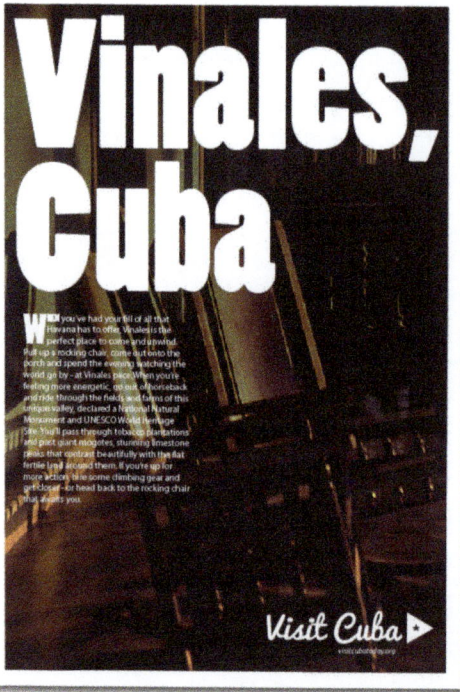

7. The areas now shown in white are those areas that would be printed using that spot ink instead of using a mixture of the cmyk inks. To change the Pantone 123 ink from a spot colour to a process colour, choose **Ink Manager** from the *Separations Preview dropdown menu.*

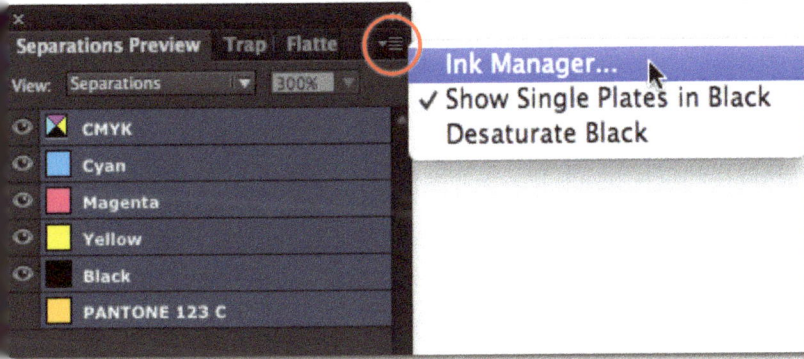

8. Once in the Ink Manager dialogue box, press the *All Spots to Process* checkbox, then press the **OK button.** The Separations Preview checkbox will now show that there only CMYK inks will be used to print the document.

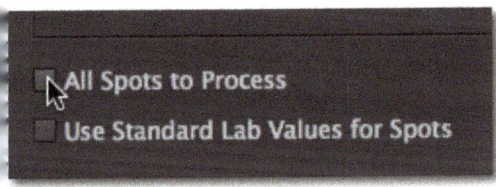

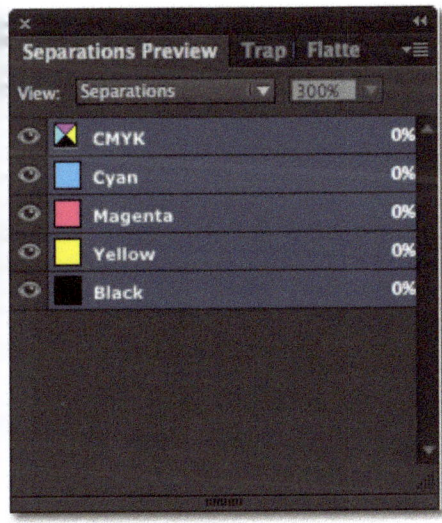

9. To finish the document, export it as a pdf, adding the marks and bleeds.

Summary of what you've learned

How to identify spot colour swatches

How to check which inks will be used when printing

How to convert spot colours to process colours

New Commands used

Window>Output>Separations Preview

Separations Preview Panel>Ink Manager

5) Checking for transparency

This final document flyer uses an image that has been cut out in Photoshop, and gives you the opportunity to look at what can happen when you use transparency.

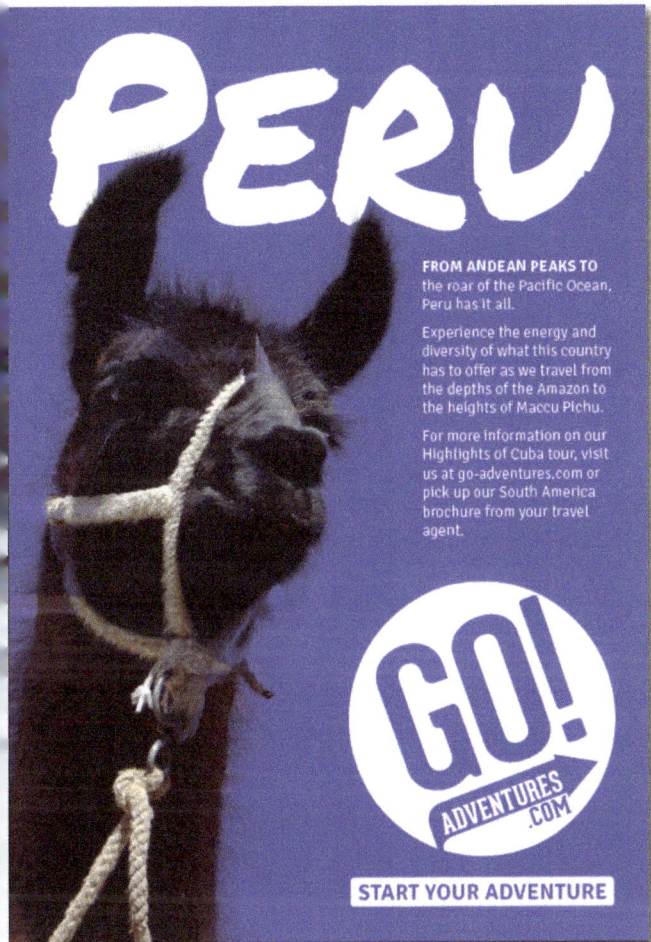

1. From the **File menu** choose **Open** to open the *5-Transparency* document. Unless you've already installed the *Permanent Marker* and *Signika* fonts you'll be presented with the *Missing Fonts* dialogue box. As discussed in the previous exercise, if this happens you can either install the fonts or press the *Find Font* button to replace them with fonts that you already have on your system.

2. Use **File>Document Setup** to add a *3mm* bleed guide to the flyer.

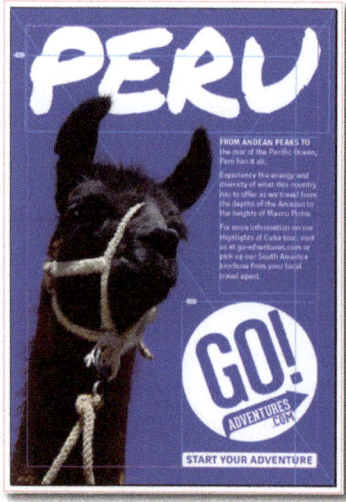

3. Use the **Selection Tool** to extend both the frame that's filled with the blue colour and the one containing the cut out Llama out to meet the bleed guides.

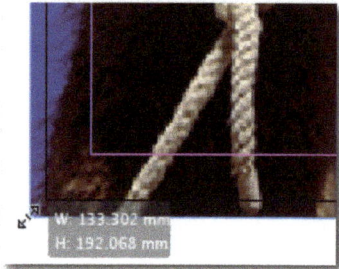

4. Using the **Links Panel,** change the RGB image to CMYK.

About transparency

Some of InDesign's features make use of *transparency,* for example, applying drop shadows, reducing an object's opacity using the *Effects Panel,* or placing an image into InDesign that contains transparent pixels. The image you're working with here has been cut out from its background using a layer mask in Photoshop. If you've not worked with this type of image before, this is what it looks like when opened in Photoshop:

The pattern of grey squares (known as *chequerboard* pixels) indicate pixels that are transparent. In the InDesign document the Llama has been placed on top of a coloured background frame whose colour could be changed easily if desired. One way of telling that a page contains transparency is to display the *transparency icon* in the Pages Panel. To do this, from the **Pages Panel dropdown menu** choose **Panel Options,** then check the *Transparency* checkbox (you can only do this if your page size is set to larger than medium, which you can also change in this dialogue box).

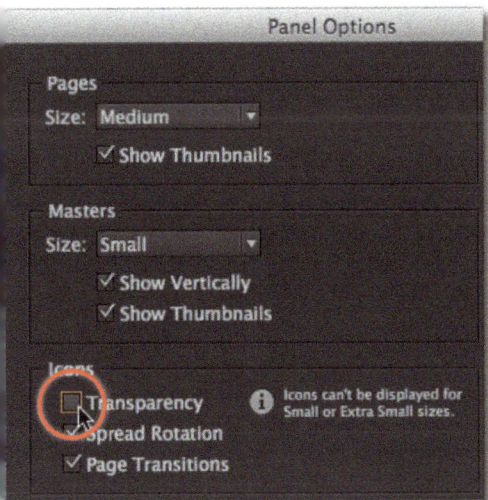

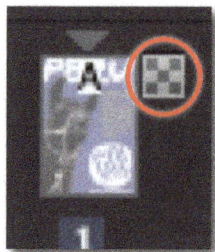

About transparency, printing and flattening

Whilst features that use transparency can make your work look striking, they can also cause problems when the document gets printed. This is because the *Postscript* language, which is used when printing or creating a PDF, doesn't strictly understand transparency*. So InDesign has to interpret these features into a way it can be understood. The way it does this is by a process called *Flattening*.

*As you know there are several presets you can use when creating pdfs. The **PDF/X-1a** preset you've used so far does not support transparency, but the **PDF/X-4**, which is more modern, does. I've suggested already that unless your printer advises you to the contrary you should use the **PDF/X-1a** preset; one of the reasons I've suggested that one is because it makes the fewest assumptions about what equipment your printer will be using. But if you know that your printer can work with a PDF/X-4 file then you can export that from InDesign instead and not worry about flattening.*

Flattening attempts to create the same visual effects but without using transparency. The main problem that people encounter with this is when an image that's been cut out using transparency is placed close to text. This is because the transparent area of the image still contains pixels, and when this area overlaps with text (which is not made of pixels) it combines them by converting the text into outlines*, which can result in text that looks partly bold and partly not.

Outlined text is text that has been converted into a graphic. Its shape that would previously have been defined by the font and other character formatting gets converted to anchor points, the building block of the sort of graphics that Adobe Illustrator creates.

5. To get an understanding of the issues around transparency, from the **Window menu** choose *Output>Flattener Preview.* From the *Highlight dropdown menu* choose *Transparent Objects*.

6. Whilst using the Flattener Preview Panel the document appears in grayscale, with highlighted objects appearing in red. So in this case the Llama image is highlighted in red because it contains transparency.

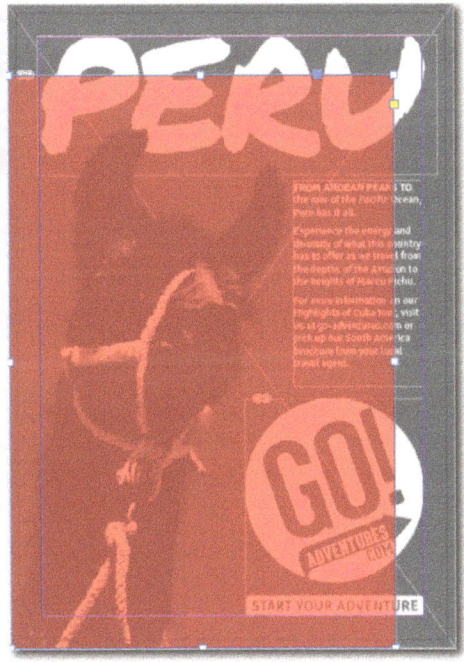

7. The area to be concerned with here is where it overlaps the text, both above it and to the right of it. To give you an idea of what could happen, choose *Outlined Text* from the *highlight dropdown menu.*

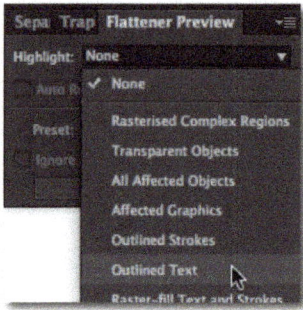

8. As described above, the potential problem here is that the text shown in red would become outlined, whereas the text that isn't highlighted would not be. You'll look at two separate solutions for this. Firstly, use the **Selection Tool** to select the frame on the right containing the descriptive text and choose ***Object>Arrange>Bring to Front.*** This will prevent this text being affected by the flattening process because flattening is applied to the topmost object first (and before the transparent object that's now beneath it).

Object	Table	View	Window	Help	
Transform			▶		
Transform Again			▶		
Arrange			▶	Bring to Front	⇧⌘]
Select			▶	Bring Forward	⌘]
				Send Backward	⌘[
Group			⌘G	Send to Back	⇧⌘[
Ungroup			⇧⌘G		

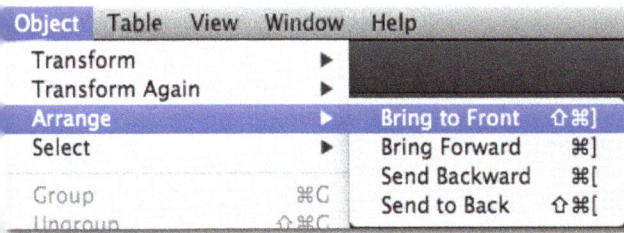

9. To check this has worked, now press the *Refresh* button on the Flattener Preview Panel, and in the preview you should no longer see a red highlight on the text on the right.

✕		**Flattener Preview**	◀◀
Sepa	Trap	**Flattener Preview**	▾≣

Highlight: Outlined Text ▾

☐ Auto Refresh Highlight   **Refresh**

Preset: [High Resolution] ▾

☐ Ignore Spread Overrides

Apply Settings to Print

10. Of course you could also do this to the *Peru* text at the top, but if you want to keep the text behind the image for creative reasons you'll need to use a different approach. Select the frame containing the *Peru* text with the **Selection Tool** and choose ***Create Outlines*** from the **Type menu.**

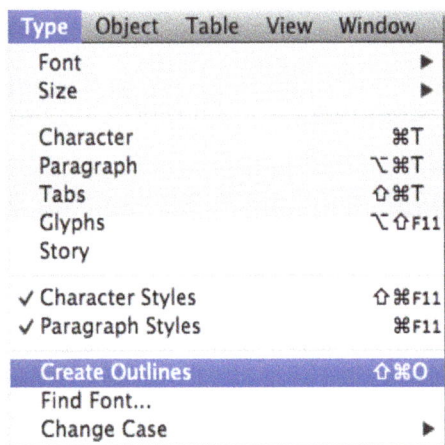

Type	Object	Table	View	Window	
Font					▶
Size					▶
Character					⌘T
Paragraph					⌥⌘T
Tabs					⇧⌘T
Glyphs					⌥⇧F11
Story					
✓ Character Styles					⇧⌘F11
✓ Paragraph Styles					⌘F11
Create Outlines					⇧⌘O
Find Font...					
Change Case					▶

11. This text has now been converted into a vector graphic, so it's no longer strictly text* and won't be affected by the transparency in the image, as you'll see if you press the *Refresh* button again.

* *As it's no longer text, this also means that it'd be very difficult to adjust afterwards – so with your own work you'd be advised to save a copy of the document first.*

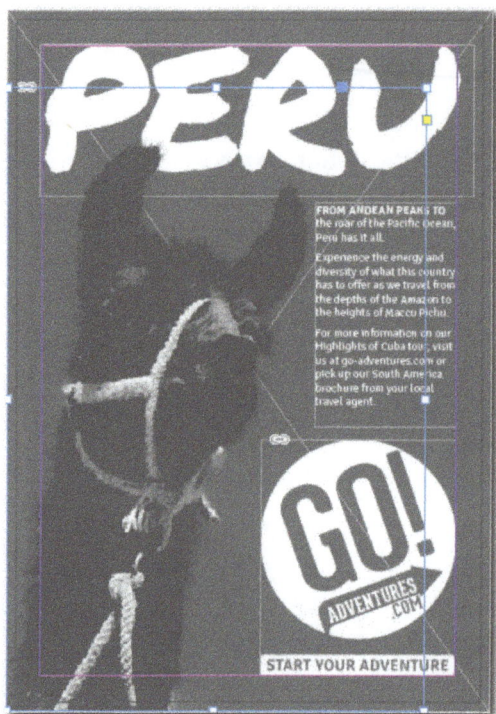

12. To finish, Export a pdf using the *[PDF/X-1a:2001]* preset from the options at the top of the *Export Adobe PDF* dialogue box, making sure you add the Marks and Bleeds on before you save.

Summary of what you've learned

How to tell which pages contain transparency
How to use the Flattener Preview Panel
How to prevent text being affected by the flattening process

New Commands used

Pages>Panel Options
Window>Output>Flattener Preview
Object>Arrange>Bring to Front
Type>Create Outlines

About Packages and Preflight

The usual way for people to send artwork to printers these days is to export an InDesign file as a PDF, as you've been learning about. But there is another approach which can sometimes be more appropriate, know as creating a *Package*. A package is a folder that contains not only the finished InDesign document, but also a copy of any images and fonts used, and some instructions for the printer. In other words, everything the printer would need to reassemble the InDesign document on their computer, and print it from there. It can be a good approach to use if you'd like to give the printer access to your InDesign file, because, for example, last minute changes to the document are anticipated, or if for any other reason you'd like them to be able to make changes to it.

Creating a package

1. To create a package, firstly open any of the documents that you've already checked are suitable for sending to a printer. Then choose **File>Package.**

2. If there are any RGB images or swatches it will show a small yellow warning triangle, in which case you'd be advised to cancel the process, fix any problems before returning later. You are prompted to save the document, after which you are invited to add your own details and specific instructions that will be put into a text file that will be included in the package. By all means add these details in here, but with your own work it would be wise to put important instructions in a separate email as well.

3. Once you've pressed the **Continue** button, the next step is to package everything together in a folder. Specify the folder's name and location, saving it somewhere that you'll be able to find easily later. You'll see that it will include all of the elements mentioned above. Press **Package.**

4. If the document includes fonts a warning will be displayed, reminding you that the manufacturers of the fonts you're planning to send to a printer might not have allowed that in their licence agreement.

5. Once you've finished, leave InDesign and look for the folder it has created for you. Inside it you'll see all of the elements, ready to send to a printer.

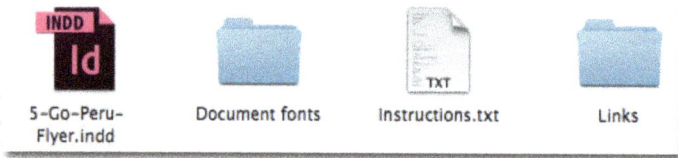

| 5-Go-Peru-Flyer.indd | Document fonts | Instructions.txt | Links |

About Preflight

Throughout these exercises you've learned how to check for the sorts of issues that can come up when sending InDesign documents to a printer, and you've learned how to fix them. This process is often called artworking or preflighting. But preflight also refers to something built into InDesign. Before version CS4 there was a preflight command in the file menu which performed a cursory check, but since CS4 it refers to an automated system which checks in the background whilst you work. If you've worked through the exercises you'll probably have become quicker at making checks and fixing potential problems, so in all likelihood the built in system won't enable you to work any more quickly. The main benefit it offers is that as it's always working in the background it can alert you to a potential problem immediately, for example, that the image you've just placed is too low resolution. Preflight will only check for things like RGB images and spot colours if you set it up to do so.

Setting up preflight

1. From the Window menu choose **Output>Preflight.**

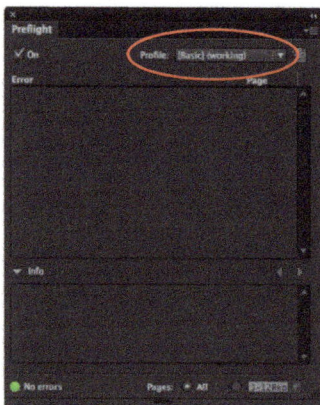

2. The Preflight Panel shows that preflight is on, and that it's using the *[Basic]* profile. To setup preflight to be more useful click on the **Preflight Panel dropdown menu** and choose **Define Profiles.**

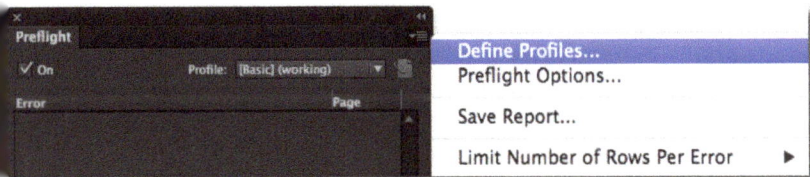

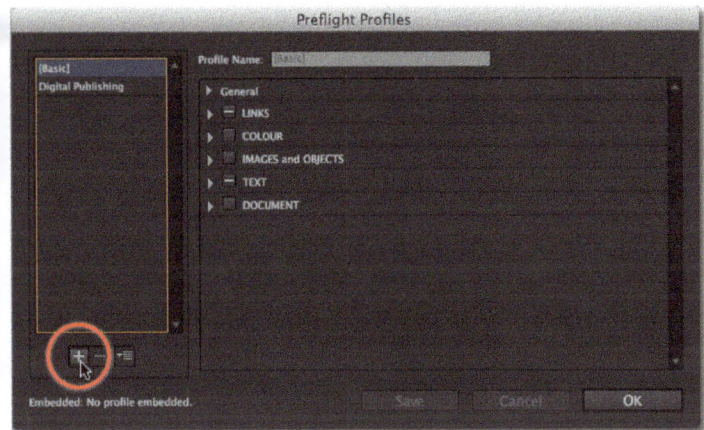

3. Click on the + button in the panel's bottom left to create a new profile. Once you've given it an appropriate name, click on the triangle to the left of the word *Links*. This opens this section up to reveal which checks will be performed using this profile. You can see that checking for missing or modified links is already set up.

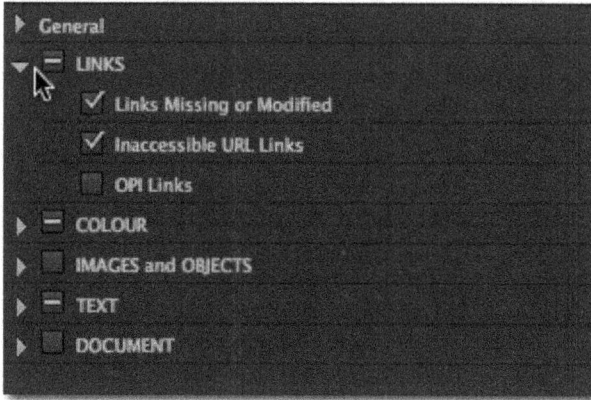

4. Click back on the above triangle to close the *Links* section, then continue working through the different sections to find things you'd want Preflight to automatically check for. For example, in the *Colour* section I've ticked the *Colour Spaces and Modes Not Allowed* checkbox and then specified *RGB* and *Spot Colour.*

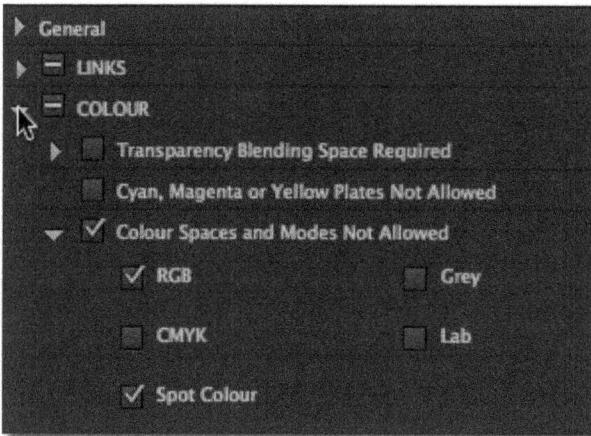

5. Once you've included everything you'd want InDesign to search for, press the **Save button,** followed by the **OK button**.

6. Once you've made the profile you will probably want to make sure that it is used instead of the *[Basic]* one. To do this, from the ***Preflight Panel dropdown menu*** choose ***Preflight Options,*** and change the *Working Profile* to the one you've just created.

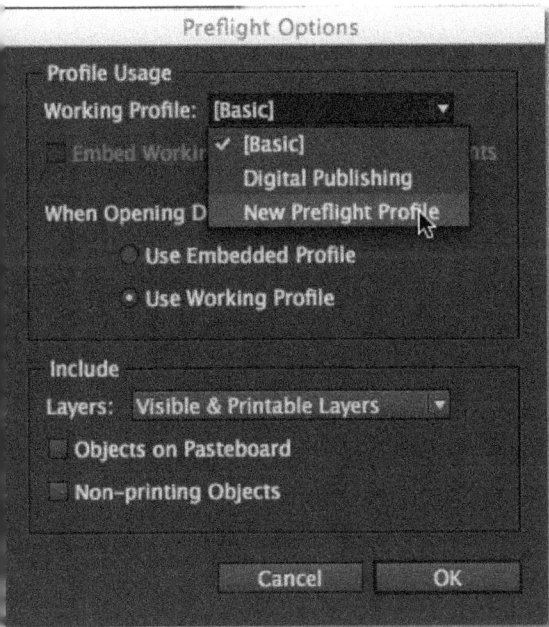

7. Now you've created your own Preflight profile you can use it as well as, or instead of the more manual approach you've learned as you've read through this book.

Summary of checks made

Document
Add a bleed guide **(File>Document Setup)**
Export a pdf with bleeds and trim marks **(File>Export)**
Set up your own Preflight Profile **(Preflight Panel: Define Profiles)**

Images
Notice Missing images **(Links Panel: Status column)**
Relink a missing image **(Links Panel menu: Relink)**
Notice Modified images **(Links Panel: Status column)**
Update a modified image **(Links Panel menu: Update)**
Notice Colour Space of image **(Links Panel: Link Info)**
Notice Resolution of images **(Links Panel: Link Info: Effective ppi)**
Change an RGB image to CMYK **(Links Panel: Edit With...)**

Fonts
Notice / replace a missing font **(Type: Find Font)**

Swatches
Create swatches from colours used in a document
(Swatches panel: Add Unnamed Colours)
Identify RGB swatches
Make RGB swatches CMYK **(Swatches panel: Swatch Options)**
Identify spot colour swatches
Check which inks will be used when printing **(Window>Separations Preview)**
Convert spot colours to process colours **(Separations
Preview panel: Ink Manager)**

Transparency
Identify which pages contain transparency **(Pages panel>Panel Options)**
Use the Flattener Preview Panel
Prevent text being affected by the flattening process
(Object>Arrange>Bring to Front or Send to Back)

Conclusion

Getting something printed commercially is essentially a collaboration between you and a printer. The more you know the terminology and understand process the better, and the more you can establish a rapport with the printer the better. Having worked through this book you'll understand enough of the terminology and process to be able to work better with a printer, and hopefully be able to spot and resolve problems before they arise (and potentially cost money to fix). On that note, despite everything you've learned, and particularly when working with a printer you've not used before, I'd always advise you get them to create a proof for you prior to printing. The cost of that may or may not be already factored into their quote, but it should go without saying that paying for a proof is a lot less expensive than paying to have a job reprinted.

BRIEF NOTES

InDesign in context

It's a fair assumption that anything that you see that's been commercially printed (with a few exceptions, such as product packaging that you might see in a supermarket) has likely been produced in Adobe InDesign. Even though the design will probably incorporate photographs that have come from Adobe Photoshop and logos and illustrations that have come from Adobe Illustrator, InDesign is the place that all those elements come together as a coherent whole.

An overview of InDesign

To create a document with InDesign you start with a page or a number of pages of the desired print size, for example, one A3 page or four A4 pages (you might think of pages as sides). Onto those pages you place *Frames*. Frames contain either text or images. Images will likely come from either Photoshop or Illustrator. Text will likely come from Microsoft Word, another text editing program, from an email or may even be typed in InDesign. If you look at a newspaper, magazine or brochure you'll probably notice there is some repetition of the different elements. For example the text may be in a number of equally sized columns, and pictures may well be the exact width of one or more of the columns. If you can see this, you are starting to get an idea of the underlying structure of the page, and that is one of the keys to using InDesign.

Images from Photoshop and Illustrator

If you look at a photograph, whether on screen or printed out, in reality it is simply a large number of equally sized squares, known as *pixels*. At the moment a digital camera takes a photo or a scanner scans a picture, it converts the image before it into pixels. It is because each of these pixels can have their own unique colour that they can be used to represent anything, so long as the pixels themselves are small enough. Photoshop works with images that are created from pixels, which are generically known as *Bitmap* graphics. The bitmap file formats you'll most likely see are *.jpg* and *.tiff* files. Illustrator works with images that are created from anchor points, known generically as *vector* graphics. These anchor points define paths that can have a fill or a stroke on them or both (like in InDesign). Vector graphics are much more simplistic than bitmap graphics, but are perfect for the sort of things that have clean, clearly defined areas of colour, such as logos, graphs and maps. The vector file formats you'll most likely see are *.eps* and *.ai* files. If you'd like to learn more about creating logos with Illustrator, look at our Intuitive Illustrator series at designtuitive.com

Other options for print and screen

If you want to create a pdf that anyone can download from your website and print out of their own printer you will find two useful options when you export a pdf. There are presets for *Smallest File Size* or *High Quality Print.* The latter is generally recommended unless you're particularly concerned about the file size – in which case use the former option, but be aware that the quality of images is likely to be poor, as they will be low resolution. If you specifically wanted to design something to go on a website, when you first create the document you'd choose *Web* from the *Intent* dropdown menu. This would enable you to specify the document's size in *Pixels* as opposed to Millimetres. Once you'd designed the document you'd use **File>Export** as mentioned previously, but choose either *Png* or *Jpeg* format

Specific guidance for adverts

As mentioned earlier, when you or someone else in your organisation buys some advertising space, you'll be given the size of the finished document, which is what you'll use when initially setting up the document. You may also be given guidance on how they would like you to create a pdf of the advert. In the absence of any such guidance I'd recommend exporting a finished advert as a pdf using the *[PDF/X-1a:2001]* preset mentioned previously. These PDF/X settings were originally developed by people involved with the sending and receiving of adverts to attempt to minimise that problems that had occurred previously. This is one of the reasons that by default, no Marks or Bleeds settings appear on a *[PDF/X-1a:2001]* pdf, because they are not needed when creating an advert (unless it's an advert which will cover a whole page, which you haven't created here) in which case you'd follow the advice under *About bleeds* and *Creating a print-ready pdf.*

.

Thanks

Thanks to all my InDesign students over the years whose questions have helped me shape these books. Thanks to all those who helped me create this series, especially Beki Bateson, David Blatner, Caroline Bone, Hannah Clifford, Zoe Hind, Peter Kent, Vicki Loader, Paolo Pedretti, Peter Michael Rosenberg and Nadia Vistisen. Very special thanks to Julia Ruxton.

About Designtuitive

Designtuitive is a small independent publisher.
We make books and videos to help you get the most out of creating software like InDesign, Illustrator and Photoshop.
Designtuitive.com
@designtuitive

Our books

InDesign Creative Classroom
Intuitive InDesign: Complete Collection
Working from an InDesign Template
Creating Adverts with InDesign
Creating Flyers, Posters & Postcards with InDesign
Creating Leaflets with InDesign
Preparing InDesign files for printing
Creating Logos with Illustrator
Intuitive Illustrator: Complete Collection
Creating Logos from Circles
Creating Logos from Triangles
Creating Logos from Rounded Rectangles
Creating Logos from Type
Creating Icons for Websites & Apps
Improving Images with Photoshop

Our videos

InDesign for Marketers
Illustrator for Marketers

About the Author

Peter Bone has worked in graphic design for over 20 years. During that time he has taught thousands of people to use Quark Xpress, Indesign, Illustrator and Photoshop – at every level from complete beginners through to experts in their field. He has taught designers, marketing people, creative directors, writers, editors, illustrators, fashion designers and photographers for companies as varied as The BBC, The British Museum, Condé Nast, The Designers Guild Disney, Greenpeace, The Guardian, Ralph Lauren, Paul Smith and Price Waterhouse Coopers.
peterbone.com
*@PeterBone_*